'A heart for every fate'

BYRON'S LETTERS AND JOURNALS
VOLUME 10
1822–1823

My boat is on the shore,
  And my bark is on the sea;
But, before I go, Tom Moore,
  Here's a double health to thee!

Here's a sigh to those who love me,
  And a smile to those who hate;
And, whatever sky's above me,
  Here's a heart for every fate.

TO TOM MOORE

BYRON
Drawing by Count Alfred D'Orsay, Genoa, 1823
Reproduced by kind permission of John Murray

'A heart for every fate'

BYRON'S LETTERS AND JOURNALS

Edited by
LESLIE A. MARCHAND

VOLUME 10
1822–1823

*The complete and unexpurgated text of
all the letters available in manuscript and
the full printed version of all others*

THE BELKNAP PRESS OF
HARVARD UNIVERSITY PRESS
CAMBRIDGE, MASSACHUSETTS
1980

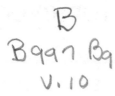

ISBN 0–674–08952–9

Library of Congress Catalog
Card Number 73–81853

Printed in the United States
of America

CONTENTS

EDITORIAL NOTE

Here as in earlier volumes an effort has been made to provide useful information for the reader without reference to other volumes. The statement of editorial principles is repeated, and the appendices give material for ready reference applicable to these letters. The index of proper names is meant to serve the reader until the general index and subject index appear in the last volume.

ACKNOWLEDGMENTS. (Volume 10). With the appearance of this tenth and penultimate volume of *Byron's Letters and Journals* my accumulated debt for the assistance and encouragement of many people has mounted to a sum for which it is difficult to find words to express adequate thanks. The largest of these debts is to my publisher, John Murray, whose attention to details of the publication is a constant source of amazement and pleasure. The personnel of the Harvard University Press have been zealous and energetic in the production and promotion of the American edition. The continued support of the National Endowment for the Humanities has greatly facilitated my editorial labours. Donald H. Reiman, editor of *Shelley and His Circle* for the Carl H. Pforzheimer Library, and members of the Library staff have been constant in their encouragement and assistance. Doris Langley Moore can always be counted on for helpful suggestions and for answers to questions. I am indebted to John Gibbins of the Murray editorial staff for careful reading of copy and proof. And I want to thank again Ricki B. Herzfeld for transcribing and translating Italian letters in this volume: Stewart Perowne for reading the proofs and making corrections and suggestions for notes, and Sir Rupert Hart-Davis for his help in locating some of Byron's obscure references.

For permission to get photocopies of letters in their possession and to use them in this volume I wish to thank the following libraries and individuals: Lord Abinger; Beinecke Rare Book and Manuscript Library, Yale University; Henry E. and Albert A. Berg Collection, New York Public Library; Biblioteca Classense, Ravenna; Biblioteca Labronica, Leghorn; Bibliothèque Nationale, Paris; British Library (department of Manuscripts); Mrs. James E. Fitzgerald; Lord Hindlip; Houghton Library, Harvard University; Henry E. Huntington Library; University of Iowa Library; Keats-Shelley Memorial, Rome;

Commander P.G.A. King; Lord Kinnaird; University of Leeds Library; The Earl of Lytton; John Murray; National Library, Athens; Nottingham Public Libraries; H. F. Oppenheimer; Der Österreichischen Nationalbibliothek, Vienna; Carl H. Pforzheimer Library; Pierpont Morgan Library; Gordon N. Ray; Stark Library, University of Texas; Sudeley Castle; Robert H. Taylor Collection, Princeton University Library; Trinity College Library, Cambridge; Vigo County Library, Terre Haute, Indiana.

For assistance of various kinds I wish to thank the following: Norman Brennan; Cecil Clarabut; John Clubbe; Mario Curreli; Mrs. F. E. Duncan-Jones; Doucet D. Fischer; Paul Fussell; Mihai H. Handrea; Jerome J. McGann; Jo Modert; Andrew Nicholson; Charles E. Robinson; William St. Clair; David H. Stam; George Watson; Maud Wilcox; Carl Woodring.

* * * * * *

EDITORIAL PRINCIPLES. With minor exceptions, herein noted, I have tried to reproduce Byron's letters as they were written. The letters are arranged consecutively in chronological order. The name of the addressee is given at the top left in brackets. The source of the text is indicated in the list of letters in the Appendix. If it is a printed text, it is taken from the first printed form of the letter known or presumed to be copied from the original manuscript, or from a more reliable editor, such as Prothero, when he also had access to the manuscript. In this case, as with handwritten or typed copies, or quotations in sale catalogues, the text of this source is given precisely.

When the text is taken from the autograph letter or a photo copy or facsimile of it, the present whereabouts or ownership is given, whether it is in a library or a private collection. When the manuscript is the source, no attempt is made to indicate previous publication, if any. Here I have been faithful to the manuscript with the following exceptions:

1. The place and date of writing is invariably placed at the top right in one line if possible to save space, and to follow Byron's general practice. Fortunately Byron dated most of his letters in this way, but occasionally he put the date at the end. Byron's usual custom of putting no punctuation after the year is followed throughout.

2. Superior letters such as S^r or 30th have been lowered to Sr. and 30th. The & has been retained, but &^{c} has been printed &c.

3. Byron's spelling has been followed (and generally his spelling is

good, though not always consistent), and *sic* has been avoided except in a few instances when an inadvertent misspelling might change the meaning or be ambiguous, as for instance when he spells *there* t-h-e-i-r.

4. Although, like many of his contemporaries, Byron was inconsistent and eccentric in his capitalization, I have felt it was better to let him have his way, to preserve the flavour of his personality and his times. With him the capital letter sometimes indicates the importance he gives to a word in a particular context; but in the very next line it might not be capitalized. If clarity has seemed to demand a modification, I have used square brackets to indicate any departure from the manuscript.

5. Obvious slips of the pen crossed out by the writer have been silently omitted. But crossed out words of any significance to the meaning or emphasis are enclosed in angled brackets ⟨ ⟩.

6. Letters undated, or dated with the day of the week only, have been dated, when possible, in square brackets. If the date is conjectural, it is given with a question mark in brackets. The same practice is followed for letters from printed sources. The post mark date is given, to indicate an approximate date, only when the letter itself is undated.

7. The salutation is put on the same line as the text, separated from it by a dash. The complimentary closing, often on several lines in the manuscript, is given in one line if possible. The P.S., wherever it may be written in the manuscript, follows the signature.

8. Byron's punctuation follows no rules of his own or others' making. He used dashes and commas freely, but for no apparent reason, other than possibly for natural pause between phrases, or sometimes for emphasis. He is guilty of the "comma splice", and one can seldom be sure where he intended to end a sentence, or whether he recognized the sentence as a unit of expression. He did at certain intervals place a period and a dash, beginning again with a capital letter. These larger divisions sometimes, though not always, represented what in other writers, particularly in writers of today, correspond to paragraphs. He sometimes used semicolons, but often where we would use commas. Byron himself recognized his lack of knowledge of the logic or the rules or punctuation. He wrote to his publisher John Murray on August 26, 1813: "Do you know anybody who can *stop*—I mean point—commas and so forth, for I am I fear a sad hand at your punctuation". It is not without reason then that most editors, including R. E. Prothero, have imposed sentences and paragraphs on him in line with their interpretation of his intended meaning. It is my feeling, however, that this detracts from the impression of Byronic spon-

taneity and the onrush of ideas in his letters, without a compensating gain in clarity. In fact, it may often arbitrarily impose a meaning or an emphasis not intended by the writer. I feel that there is less danger of distortion if the reader may see exactly how he punctuated and then determine whether a phrase between commas or dashes belongs to one sentence or another. Byron's punctuation seldom if ever makes the reading difficult or the meaning unclear. In rare instances I have inserted a period, a comma, or a semicolon, but have enclosed it in square brackets to indicate it was mine and not his.

9. Words missing but obvious from the context, such as those lacunae caused by holes in the manuscript, are supplied within square brackets. If they are wholly conjectural, they are followed by a question mark. The same is true of doubtful readings in the manuscript.

Undated letters have been placed within the chronological sequence when from internal or external evidence there are reasonable grounds for a conjectural date. This has seemed more useful than putting them together at the end of the volumes. Where a more precise date cannot be established from the context, these letters are placed at the beginning of the month or year in which they seem most likely to have been written.

ANNOTATION. I have tried to make the footnotes as brief and informative as possible, eschewing, sometimes with reluctance, the leisurely expansiveness of R. E. Prothero, who in his admirable edition of the *Letters and Journals* often gave pages of supplementary biographical information and whole letters *to* Byron, which was possible at a time when book publishing was less expensive, and when the extant and available Byron letters numbered scarcely more than a third of those in the present edition. Needless to say, I have found Prothero's notes of inestimable assistance in the identification of persons and quotations in the letters which he edited, though where possible I have double checked them. And I must say that while I have found some errors, they are rare. With this general acknowledgment I have left the reader to assume that where a source of information in the notes is not given, it comes from Prothero's edition, where additional details may be found.

The footnotes are numbered for each letter. Where the numbers are repeated on a page, the sequence of the letters will make the reference clear.

In an appendix in each volume I have given brief biographical sketches of Byron's principal correspondents first appearing in that

4

volume. These are necessarily very short, and the stress is always on Byron's relations with the subject of the sketch. Identification of less frequent correspondents and other persons mentioned in the letters is given in footnotes as they appear, and the location of these, as well as the biographical sketches in the appendix, will be indicated by italic numbers in the index. Similarly italic indications will refer the reader to the principal biographical notes on persons mentioned in the text of the letters.

With respect to the annotation of literary allusions and quotations in the letters, I have tried to identify all quotations in the text, but have not always been successful in locating Byron's sources in obscure dramas whose phrases, serious or ridiculous, haunted his memory. When I have failed to identify either a quotation or a name, I have frankly noted it as "Unidentified". When, however, Byron has quoted or adapted some common saying from Shakespeare or elsewhere, I have assumed it is easily recognizable and have passed it by. I have likewise passed by single words or short phrases (quoted or not quoted) which may have had a source in Byron's reading or in conversation with his correspondents, but which it is impossible to trace. And when he repeats a quotation, as he frequently does, I have not repeated the earlier notation, except occasionally when it is far removed from its first occurrence in the letters, hoping that the reader will find it in the general index or the subject index in the last volume. No doubt readers with special knowledge in various fields may be able to enlighten me concerning quotations that have baffled me. If so, I shall try to make amends in the last volume.

Since this work will be read on both sides of the Atlantic, I have explained some things that would be perfectly clear to a British reader but not to an American. I trust that English readers will make allowance for this. As Johnson said in the Preface to his edition of Shakespeare: "It is impossible for an expositor not to write too little for some, and too much for others . . . how long soever he may deliberate, [he] will at last explain many lines which the learned will think impossible to be mistaken, and omit many for which the ignorant will want his help. These are censures merely relative, and must be quietly endured."

I have occasionally given cross references, but in the main have left it to the reader to consult the index for names which have been identified in earlier notes.

SPECIAL NOTES. The letters to Thomas Moore, first published in

Moore's *Letters and Journals of Lord Byron* (1830), were printed with many omissions and the manuscripts have since disappeared. Moore generally indicated omissions by asterisks, here reproduced as in his text.

Beginning with Volume 7 I have divided some of the longer letters into paragraphs, where a pause or a change of subject is indicated. This helps with proof correcting and makes easier reading of the text, without distracting significantly from the impression of Byron's free-flowing and on-rushing style of composition.

BYRON CHRONOLOGY

1822 Oct. 3?—Arrived at Casa Saluzzo, Albaro (Genoa).
Oct. 15—*Vision of Judgment* published in first number of *The Liberal*.
Nov.—Trelawny left on hunting expedition.
Nov.—Visited by Wedderburn Webster and Lady Hardy.
Nov. 23—Murray published *Werner*.
Dec. 14—Sent 12th Canto of *Don Juan* to Kinnaird—seven new ones ready for publication.

1823 Jan. 1—*Heaven and Earth* published in second number of *The Liberal*.
Jan. 10—Finished *The Age of Bronze*.
Feb.—Finished *The Island*.
March 31—Visited by Henry Fox, Lord Holland's son.
—Blessington party arrived in Genoa.
April 1—Blessingtons called on Byron.
April–May—Visits and conversations with Blessingtons.
April 5—Blaquiere and Luriottis called on Byron.
May 6—Finished Canto 16 of *Don Juan*.
May 12—Received word that he had been elected a member of the London Greek Committee.
May—Sold the *Bolivar* to Lord Blessington.
June 1—Paid farewell visit to the Blessingtons who left the next day.
June—Engaged the brig *Hercules* to take him to Greece.
—Dr. Bruno recommended by Dr. Alexander to be Byron's personal physician.
—Trelawny returned to Genoa to join Byron's Greek expedition.
—Quarrels with Hunt and Mary Shelley.
July 13—Went on board the *Hercules* with Pietro Gamba and Trelawny.
July 14—Teresa left with her father for the Romagna.
—Ship becalmed—on shore again.
July 15—Started but sent back by storm.

7

July 16—Finally on way.
July 21—Arrived at Leghorn.
July 22—Replied to letter from Goethe.
July 24—Left Leghorn for Greece.
Aug. 3—Landed at Argostoli, Cephalonia.

BYRON'S LETTERS AND JOURNALS

The Sopha which I request is *not* of your furniture—it was purchased by me at Pisa since you left it.——It is convenient for my room though of little value (about 12 pauls) and I offered to send another (now sent) in it's stead.—I preferred retaining the purchased furniture—but always intended that you should have as good or better in it's place.—I have a particular dislike to any thing of S[helley]'s being within the same walls with Mr. Hunt's children.—They are dirtier and more mischievous than Yahoos[;] what they can['t] destroy with their filth they will with their fingers.—I presume that you received ninety and odd crowns from the wreck of the D[on] J[uan] and also the price of the boat purchased by Capt. R[oberts].—if not you will have *both*—Hunt has these in hand.——With regard to any difficulties about money I can only repeat that I will be your banker till this state of things is cleared up—and you can see what is to be done—so—there is little to trouble you on that score.——I was confined four days to my bed at Lerici.——Poor Hunt with his six little blackguards—are coming slowly up—as usual—he turned back⟨twice⟩ once—was there ever such a *kraal* out of the Hottentot Country before?——

                                                               [scrawl]

Sir,—I have received the enclosed paper for which I am extremely obliged to you—but there is one part which I must request the police to alter.—I am qualified in it as "proprietario Inglese"—I will trouble them to change it to "Pari d'Inghilterra" which is my proper title as they will perceive in my passport.——I care as little about such things as anybody—but there being courtesies of modes and forms as I know by experience—it is as well to require from them—what they exact from others.—I have the honour to be

                 your much obliged & very faithful humble Sert.
                                                           NOEL BYRON

Dear T.—I can only say that by Dunn's account the men and expenses were paid *up* to Octr.—and in this month we are only advanced

---

[1] British Consul-General at Genoa.

a week.—I suppose that you make Frost[1]—(who is a *rogue* as you say yourself) keep some sort of an account otherwise there will be no end to this kind of thing.—I shall take care to punish the Coachman's impudence—I presume that the farrier is really *up* to his business—otherwise I can't risk experiments—but if you will assure me that he knows it—he shall do the work.—We have so much occasion for Gaetano[2]—that he must be sent up—for this plain simple reason—that the horse is more immediately wanted than the Schooner.—I shall see you to-day & we will talk over these matters

yrs. ever & truly
N B

[TO JOHN MURRAY]   *Genoa. Octr. 9th. 1822*

Dear Murray,—I have received your letter—and as you explain it —I have no objection on *your* account to omit those passages in the new Mystery—(which were marked in the half sheet sent the other day to Pisa) or the passage in *Cain*—but why not be open and say so at *first*—you should be more strait-forward on every account.—Mr. K[innair]d has four cantos of D[on] J[uan] sent by the post—(or should have)—I have a fifth (the 10th.) finished but not transcribed yet—and the *eleventh*—begun.——With regard to Werner and H[eaven] & E[arth] why are they not published? I should have thought the latitude I gave about terms—might have set you at ease on their account.—— I have carried D[on] J[uan] through a siege—to St. Petersburgh—&c. &c. thence to *England*—how do you like that?—I have no wish to break off our connection—but if you are to be blown about with every wind—what can I do?—You are wrong—for there will be a *re-action*— you will see that by & bye—and whether there is or not—I cannot allow my opinions—though I am ready to make any allowance in a *trade* point of view—which unpalatable speculations may render necessary to *your* advantage.——

I have been very unwell—four days confined to my bed in "the worst inn's worst room"[1] at Lerici—with a violent rheumatic and bilious attack—constipation—and the devil knows what—no physician —except a young fellow who however was kind and cautious & that's enough.—Amongst other operations—a *Glyster* [sic] was ordered—and

---

[1] One of the boatmen employed on board the *Bolivar*.

[2] A groom. Apparently Trelawny brought some of the servants up to Genoa in Byron's schooner.

[1] Pope, *Moral Essays*, Epistle III, line 299.

administered in such a manner by the performer—that I have ever since been wondering *why* the legislature should punish Bishop Jocelyn and his Soldado?[2]—since if the episcopal instrument at all resembled the damned squirt of the Ligurian apothecary—the crime will have carried it's own chastisement along with it.———At last I seized Thompson's book of prescriptions—(a donation of yours) and physicked myself with the first dose I found in it—and after undergoing the ravages of all kinds of decoctions—sallied from bed on the fifth day to cross the Gulph to Sestri.—The Sea revived me instantly— and I ate the Sailors cold fish—and drank a Gallon of Country wine— and got to Genoa the same night after landing at Sestri—and have ever since been keeping well—but thinner—and with an occasional cough towards evening.——

With regard to Mr. J. Hunt how could I tell that he insulted you? of course if he did—show him the door—or the window—he had no warrant from me but the letter you received—and I think that was civil enough.——I am afraid the Journal *is* a *bad* business[3]—and won't do—but in it I am sacrificing *myself* for others—*I* can have no advantage in it.—I believe the *brothers* H[unt] to be honest men—I am sure that they are poor ones.—They have not a rap—they pressed me to engage in this work—and in an evil hour I consented—still I shall not repent if I can do them the least service.—I have done all I can for Leigh Hunt—since he came here—but it is almost useless—his wife is ill—his six children not very tractable and In the affairs of this world he himself is a child.—The death of Shelley left them totally aground— and I could not see them in such a state without using the common feelings of humanity—& what means were in my power to set them afloat again.——So D[ouglas] K[innair]d is out of the way? he was so the last time I sent him a parcel—and he gives no previous notice— when is he expected again?

yrs.

N B

P.S.—Will you say at once—do you publish Werner & the mystery or not?—You never once allude to them.——That d————d advertisement of Mr. J. Hunt[4] is out of the limits I did not lend him my name to be hawked about in this way.——

[2] See Vol. 9, p. 191 n.

[3] The first number of *The Liberal*, which appeared on Oct. 15, 1822, was violently attacked, particularly because it contained Byron's *Vision of Judgment* satirizing the Poet Laureate's (Southey's) apotheosis of George III.

[4] In order to increase its sales, Hunt had advertised that Byron was a contributor to *The Liberal*.

My dearest Augusta,—My date will inform you that I am an hundred miles or better nearer to you than I was.—Address to Genoa where we all are for the present—i.e. The family of Count Gamba— who left Romagna in 1821 with me on account of the political troubles —together with myself &c. &c. &c.——Lady B[yron] has done a very acceptable thing to me—and I presume to you—in sending you the game,—it is the first thing of the kind too for these seven years—for what with trustees—lawyers—bankers—and arbitrators—both sides have hitherto proceeded as they did in the feudal times—where people used to shake hands with iron *gauntlets* or through a hole in a door— after being searched for concealed arms—by way of ascertaining the sincerity of their politeness.——You cannot conceive how such things harass me—and provoke me into expressions which I momentarily feel; it appears to me that persons who are in our peculiar situation— and can never see each other as long as they live again—should at least be courteous in their distance——*because* they never can come in contact.——

She has lately had a chance of having the estate to herself—for I was for four days confined to my bed—in "the worst inn's worst room" at Lerici—on my way here—with a very painful attack of bile and rheumatism and I know not what besides—no physician—but a young Italian in no great practice—however I got over it—and on my journey further got well again.—the English Physician here—says I am bilious—and must take the "blue pill" &c.—I have no objection to take all the colours of the rainbow—if they can make them into a prescription.——I saw Mr. Hobhouse at Pisa before I left it—he is gone to Rome I believe.——He told me that the Revd. Thomas Noel[1] (who married us) had requested him to ask me for the promise (in case of the incumbent's demise) of some living or other at Kirkby Mallory.— I wish you would ask Lady B[yron] about it—for in the first place I know nothing of any living—and in the next place—to *this hour*—I do not know whether the estate is in *her*—or in *me*—or in the *trustees*—or whether this living is in her gift—or mine—or anybody's—or nobody's ——I greatly fear by what I hear on these subjects that we shall have all to go into *Chancery*—which—Heaven knows—is but a prospect of no pleasing augury.——About the living you may tell her—that *I* (if I have a voice in the matter) can have no views or preferences—that as T. Noel is the Son of Ld. W[entworth] and—poor fellow—in the

---

[1] Illegitimate son of Lord Wentworth, Lady Byron's uncle.

awkward situation of seeing what should have been his own in the possession of others—had his father observed the rights of the Church—it is but fair that the Church should give him some portions of what would have been his rights.——If therefore he can obtain Lady B[yron]'s promise—I will not withhold mine—but in any case (supposing that the whole right was vested in me) I should not put myself in opposition to her—if she had any other views upon the subject.—But I know little or nothing of the matter.——Address to Genoa—

yrs. ever & truly
N B

[TO AUGUSTA LEIGH]   *Genoa. Octr. 20th. 1822*

My dearest Augusta/—I answered your letter the other day.—I have a proposition to make to you & your husband which I think would be for your advantage.—You must find it sad work living in that expensive England with so large a family.—If you would like to come to *Nice* (a hundred miles from hence) I will furnish you for the journey of the *whole* family—free of any expence—and have a home provided for you there &c.—You can have no idea of the *saving* and the extreme difference of expences for a family—and every species of masters &c. for the children are so much better, & cheaper—you know the [area?] of Nice is a french pro[vince].—You would also be *near* me if that would be any allurement.—I assure you that with your income—you might live not only comfortably but almost splendidly—with carriage &c.——I would remove from Genoa to Nice to be near you—if you would like that—(but I should occupy a separate house) or just as you like.—I advise you & George to think seriously of what I say—as I assure you it is worth your consideration.—I would guarantee the expence of the journey (by *land* too) and it is not so very far.—The gain in point of economy—would be something of which you have little idea.—Pensez.

yrs. ever
N B

P.S.—If you think of it—you should do so *now*—or—if not now—come over when the winter is waning.——
Novr. 7th.—I send this as written—though I suppose that it is only to produce a civil answer—you may however think it over by *Spring*— the time of touring.

[TO JOHN MURRAY]   *Genoa. Octr. 22d. 1822*

Sir,—You have delivered to Mr. Hunt the Vision of Judgement— without the *preface* with which I had taken particular pains—& particularly desired you to forward to him—is this fair—is it honest?—is it proper to be thus remiss with papers committed to your charge— and in which you knew that I was interested?—You have also delivered to him some prose tracts incomplete—which you sent to me *complete* at the beginning of the year.—I have no wish to repeat what I have so often been obliged to say—and I leave you to your own reflection on the manner in which you have conducted yourself towards me in this matter.—I am yr. obedt. Servt.

NOEL BYRON

P.S. If you have (as seems apparently to be the case) purposely kept back the preface to the Vision—I can only say that I know no words strong enough to express my sense of such conduct—⟨and that you will be⟩

[TO JOHN HANSON (*a*)]   *Genoa. Octr. 23d. 1822*

Dear Sir,—Mr. Godwin has waited on you by my desire on the subject of the affairs of the late Mr. Shelley Son of Sir T. Shelley to whose will I am appointed one of the executors.—I wish you to apply in behalf of the widow to Mr. Whitton—Sir T's solicitor—to ascertain if any provision is intended to be made for Mrs. Shelley and the surviving infant son of Mr. S.—it is presumed that at any rate the *last* quarter due on Septr. 21st. will be paid into the hands of the usual receiver.—I should also be glad of your own opinion of the will—& what you think best to be done in the extraordinary circumstances in which the relict is placed.—A Mr. Peacock is joint executor—he is of the India house.—Mr. Godwin probably can obtain for you a sight of the will or a copy thereof. I remain very truly

yrs. ever
NOEL BYRON

P.S.—Address to *Genoa.*—If there is anything to be said on my own private concerns you will add it to your answer.—

[TO JOHN HANSON? (*b*)]   *Genoa. October 23, [1822?]*
[Part of letter quoted in catalogue]

I by no means recognize any claims of Mrs. Bellamy or Miss M[assingberd] as either legal or equitable. Any idea of my ever allow-

16

ing their usurious pretensions is out of the question, nor will I enter into any discussion of the kind whatever, till *all other* debts of mine whatsoever are previously settled. I have transmitted the Rochdale title deeds duly signed to Mr. Kinnaird . . . . I am extremely anxious to liquidate the remaining debt . . . as soon as practicable. It will then be time enough to discuss these . . . claimants who start up after an interval of years . . . with their pretended demands which have no foundation either in law or equity . . . .

[TO JOHN MURRAY]   *Genoa Octr. 24th. 1822*

Dear Sir,—After I had thought the subject at an end—I have been obliged by yesterday's post to address a letter to you (through the care of Mr. J. Hunt) which will be unpleasant to you and is far from agreeable to me.—But contrary to my repeated & earnest request you have not forwarded to him the *preface* to Quevedo redivivus—on which I laid great stress—and now it has appeared without!——Many of the other things sent are also incomplete—you forget that a publisher is as responsible for the M.S.S. of a writer—as a lawyer for his Client's title deeds.—If you hold them back on purpose—it is a breach of trust & confidence—if you lose them by negligence—it is *culpable* negligence— and not to be excused on the plea of carelessness—who permits you thus to play with the feelings & reputation of a man who placed confidence in you?—I must add that if the preface and other things are not forthcoming I shall be under the necessity of making your treatment of me in this respect public.——You have also withheld the publication of Werner &c. *why?*—you can make no plea about *terms*—since none are settled—on that subject.——If you are offended with—or affronted by Mr. J. Hunt—that is not a reason to juggle with *me*—and I will show you that I am not disposed to permit you to take advantage of my absence—in a manner—which whatever may be your motive—can do little credit to you—& less to your instigators—for I firmly believe that there is some one behind the curtain playing you off upon this occasion.—I know enough of the baseness of Mr. Southey—and his employers to believe them capable of any thing——and as for yourself —though I am very unwilling to believe you acting *wilfully* & *wittingly* —as their tool—you leave me no other supposition but that either by menaces or persuasions they are rendering you an instrument—of their purposes personal and political,—"on *fair* ground I could beat forty of them"[1] but not if my Armourer proves treacherous—and spoils my

[1] *Coriolanus*, Act. III, scene 1.

weapons.——I am truly sorry to be obliged to address you in such a manner—but you have forced me to do so.—

your obedt. St.
N B

P.S.—I have since the above was written—received yrs. of the 11th. —and as I am "a pitiful-hearted negro" and can't keep resentment—it hath melted my flint.—It is *you* who force yourself into contact with Mr. J[ohn] H[unt]—if you deliver to him the M.S.S. mentioned—in their complete state you will have no more trouble on that score.—— You must not separate Werner from the Oratorio H[eaven] & E[arth].[2] I have agreed to your omitting the *one passage* you objected to in the ultimate or penultimate chorus.——You had better not send me the Quarterly on Cain—as it can only be in the preaching style—& may make me answer or say something disagreeable.—I have completed and had copied the 10th. and 11th. Cantos of D[on] J[uan] making in all 6 new ones—4 already sent to Mr. Kinnaird which I hope have arrived safely—pray enquire and tell me if *he* is returned or no. I shall not assail Rogers if he lets me alone—but it is a sad old fellow.—I have lost the original copy—which made me send for this one—of which I shall not make any use.—Put me down twenty five pounds for Godwin. —You shall have the busts—also the picture of the Countess G[uic-ciioli]—I hear that both are very like her & much admired—but West's picture of me for the New York Academy[3] is preferred to Bartolini's bust of me done at the same time at the *request* of *both* artists—for I had resolved to sit no more for such vanities.——

[TO JAMES WEDDERBURN WEBSTER]   *Albaro. Octr. 26th. 1822*

Dear W.—Any time from two till three, and if you like to ride, I can have you mounted on one of my horses. I called at three precisely, and asked *thrice* distinctly for the Cavalier Webster, in much *better Italian* than is spoken at *Genoa*; but the *name* seemed incomprehensible, tho' not ye. title. The answer was—Do you mean the "nobile Inglese" who came here two days ago? I replied—I mean the Gentleman who called on me yesterday. "He is gone out and returns at 5—to Dinner" was the reply. I left no card, as it was not impossible that they w'd have

---

[2] Murray published *Werner* on November 23, 1822, in a volume by itself, avoiding the inclusion with it of *Heaven and Earth* as Byron had wished. The latter, with its dangerous theme of the love of angels and human beings, was finally published by John Hunt in the second number of *The Liberal* on Jan. 1, 1823.

[3] The portrait is now in the National Portrait Gallery of Scotland in Edinburgh.

left it with a Stranger. It is provoking enough that you should have been detained by their stupidity, for such it was as Count Gamba, who was with me, not only heard my inquiries, but repeated the *name* himself—as well as an Italian can repeat a name with four consonants in it.

Believe me, yours ever and very truly,

N B

[TO DOUGLAS KINNAIRD]   *Genoa. Octr. 27th. 1822*

My dear Douglas/—I have to acknowledge your packet with many thanks—much of it is very satisfactory.—Did I overstate the funds fee?—is it not *2525*—from the original investment—and also 190 pounds a year from Sir Jacob's 4000 (now paid) and is not that 2715? —With regard to my savings of this year—you will see that the surplus will be 3000 as I stated——that is including 630 pounds sterling invested with messrs Webb of Leghorn for the present—in *gold*— which I had about me for some time—& did not like to take on in our Journey.——I enclose you the 10th. & 11th. Cantos of D[on] J[uan] making (with those you have received) *six* in all—now—what ought M. to advance?—you will please to recollect that if I had kept back these *two* till a third was completed they would have formed another volume—and I should have charged accordingly—whereas by printing them in one—he will naturally have an advantage in terms.—He once of his *own free motion*—offered me a *thousand pounds* (*Guineas* that is) per Canto—for as many Cantos as I chose to send him.—*That* of course I would *not* receive—on *his* account—and is out of the question —but it is no reason that he should treat me as he did about the *three* former—(the 3—4—5th.) in 1821[;] if he has lost as he says by a *brother in law-£16000*—that is not a reason that he should levy it by lowering on his publishees.——I think you will perceive that the enclosed as well as the former are of very salable qualities—and against piracy—let him provide by selling *cheap editions*—reserving his octavos for the purchasers of the former volumes.——

I have been very unwell—four days in bed at Lerici with a violent attack of bile and rheumatism & constipation &c. &c. &c. &c. but recovered—all but a cough—which has somewhat thinned me.—I shall submit to your judgement on all the Noel questions—because I see you have taken the right line.—The moment I know the *exact* amount of outstanding demands—& also of probable *Assetts*—(M's included) I will tell you what to pay & what I wish done with the remainder—for I am economizing—have sold three horses and pay all bills in person—

keeping a sharp look out—on the candle's ends.———Firstly—I pray thee to increase the insurance on Lady B's life to 15000—or even eighteen or twenty—if you think it *affordable*.———Secondly—*if* there should be any surplus—either from my own saving at the end of the year—or otherwise—could you not put me in the way of investing them—however small—so as to receive a *moderate* but secure interest for the money——if *you* state rightly—there are hardly *two* thousand pounds of outstanding debt—and if *I* state rightly—(supposing Lady B. to live) the *whole* of the year's income for 1823—might be saved.— I repeat to you that I have at this moment—*3500*—in bank of the present year—and if I were to spend the odd 500 before J[anuar]y—it would still leave a surplus of 3000—which would suffice for my year's expenditure. Now if you can obtain anything like a proper price from M[urray]—*that ought* to *more* than cover any outstanding debts—and thus at least a considerable portion of the income could accrue—and might be invested in exchequer bills—or some other security—from which I might *reconvert* it (if necessary) into cash.—I suppose that you will laugh at all my pecuniary plans—but after having known the miseries of embarrassments—it is natural to try to provide against their recurrence.—Let me know your notions to which I attach great weight as you know.

yrs. ever
N B

There are some stanzas in the D[on] J[uan]'s which I can alter or omit if requisite or proper.

[CONTE LEOPOLDO CICOGNARA]   *Genova 28 8bre [1822]*

Stimo Signore—La proposizione ch'Ella mi fa colla di Lei Pregia- tissima mi onora; e sarà per me un vero piacere d'unire il mio nome a quello degl'Italiani associati ad un Opera si degna, come quella che dee [deve] rendere Omaggio alla memoria di Canova.—Senza determi- nare pertanto il numero delle voci da tenenti per mio conto—il quale dipenderà dalle circostanze dell'Associazione ella mi ponga fuore nel Catalogo degli Associati.—E nel protestarle il mio obbligo—e la mia più distinta considerazione—ho l'Onore di dirmi——Di lei Stimo Signore

Devot[issi]mo U[milissi]mo Serv[en]te
NOEL BYRON

Genoa October 28. [*1822*]

Esteemed Signore,—The proposition that you make me in your highly esteemed [letter] honours me; and it will be a true pleasure for me to unite my name with those of the Italians subscribing to such a worthy work as that one, which will pay homage to the memory of Canova. Without determining therefore for my information the number of supporters—which will depend on the circumstances of the subscription—you could show it to me in the list of the subscribers. And in declaring to you my gratitude—and my most distinguished consideration—I have the honour of calling myself—your esteemed Signore's

Most devoted and humble servant
NOEL BYRON[1]

[TO LEIGH HUNT] *Albaro 8bre. 29th. 1822*

My dear Leigh,—It is as I conjectured. Mr. Murray has given the *wrong copy* to your brother—with all the errors—and without the preface.—I am apt to think and hope that it is a mere piece of negligence though not a very pardonable one—after my repeated letters on the subject.—Had he done it on purpose—it would betray an equal ignorance of the honesty of a tradesman and the honour of a Gentleman.—All that can now be done is to obtain the corrected copy with the preface without delay.—If he pretends that it is not to be found—that is at his own peril—and may lead to a not very pleasing exposure of his conduct upon this occasion.—As he refuses to see your brother; —Mr. J. Hunt had better depute some friend with a copy of this note to Mr. Murray—and require from him on my part the delivery of the corrected copy (i.e. the proof which I went over myself) with the prefatory remarks——both were furnished a year ago, and redelivered to him by the Honourable Douglas Kinnaird at my request.—

Yours ever
NOEL BYRON

[TO JOHN MURRAY (*a*)] *Genoa—Octr. 31st. 1822*

Sir,—I have received a note addressed by you to Mr. Kinnaird—in which you complain of some letter of mine and talk of a "condition" what condition? I invoked none nor does Mr. Kinnaird.—If there is

---

[1] Translated by Ricki B. Herzfeld.

anything unjust in the letter it will be now easy to answer it—if on the other hand it is a new excuse—I regret that you should have recourse to such expedients—which were unnecessary—The best way to settle the matter at once will be to deliver into Mr. K[innaird]'s hands all compositions of mine now in your possession—and not referring to the Memoirs which you purchased of Mr. Moore——I write also to ask you to replace them in an unmutilated state and not to send the uncorrected copies—like that of the [Vision] which you dispatched in an incorrect state to Mr. L. [J?] Hunt without the preface—I should hope through negligence only. I remain

> Your obedt. Servt.
> NOEL BYRON

[TO JOHN MURRAY (*b*)]   *Genoa. 8bre. 31st. 1822*

I have received and answered through Mr. Kinnaird your enigma of a note to him—which riddle as expounded by Œdipus—means nothing more than an evasion to get out of what you thought perhaps a bad business—either for fear of the Parsondom—or your Admiralty patrons—or your Quarter*lyers*—or some other exquisite reason—but why not be sincere & manly for once—and say so?—recollect—when I wished to put an end to the connection this year—it was at your own especial request to Messrs Moore and Hobhouse—that I agreed to renew it—since that period—what your conduct has been you *know*—and so do *I*; —the truth is that you never know your own mind—and what between this opinion and that—and sundry high & mighty notions of your own extreme importance in the planetary system— you act like the philosopher in Rasselas who took the direction of the Winds under his auspices—take care—that one of them don't blow you down some morning.—

However I believe—at least—hope that after all you may be a good fellow at bottom—and it is on this presumption that I now write to you on the subject of a poor Woman of the name of *Yossy*[1] who is or was an author of yours—as she says—and published a book on Switzerland in 1816—patronized by the "Court and Col. Macmahon"—but it seems that neither the Court nor the Colonel could get over the portentous price of "three pounds thirteen and sixpence" which alarmed the too susceptible Public—and in short "the book died away"

---

[1] Madame A. de Yosy published in 1815 in 2 vols. *Switzerland, as now divided into Nineteen Cantons . . . with Picturesque Representations of the Dress and Manners of the Swiss.*

and what is worse—the poor Soul's husband has died too—and She writes with the man a corpse before her—but instead of addressing the Bishop or Mr. Wilberforce—she hath recourse to that proscribed—Atheistical—syllogistical—phlogistical person—*mysen*—as they say in Notts.—It is strange enough—but the rascaille English who calumniate me in every direction—and on every score;—whenever they are in great distress—recur to me for assistance—if I have had one example of this—I have had letters from a thousand—and as far as in my power—have tried to repay good for evil—and purchase a shilling's worth of Salvation—as long as my pocket can hold out.——Now—I am willing to do what I can for this unfortunate person—but her situation and her wishes (not unreasonable however) require more than can be advanced by an individual like myself—for I have many claims of the same kind just at present, and also some remnants of *debt* to pay in England—God he knows—the latter how reluctantly! Can the "Literary fund" do nothing for her? by your interest—which is great among the pious—I dare say that something might be collected—can you get any of her books published? suppose—you take her as *author* in my place now vacant amongst your ragamuffins.—She is a moral & pious person—and will shine upon your shelves.—But seriously—do what you can for her.

[TO JOHN HUNT]   *Genoa. 8bre 31st. 1822*

Sir,—I have this morning received a letter from the Hon[oura]ble Douglas Kinnaird—enclosing a note from Mr. Murray which will probably put an end to any further connection with the latter.—Mr. Kinnaird is my particular friend—and trustee in all matters of business—and I have therefore in my answer to him—referred him to *you* on the subject of some probable future publications.—If you will send him this letter—I have no doubt you will be able to discuss during an interview several points which would be tedious upon paper.——Mr. Kinnaird has in his possession—six Cantos (new) of Don Juan,[1] and he will obtain from Mr. Murray all papers of mine now in his hands—amongst these are "Werner" a drama—and another dramatic poem called "Heaven and Earth" either or both of which would answer for "the Liberal".—But I particularly request that they may be obtained *complete* and *unmutilated*—& not in the state—in which Mr. Murray

1 It was some time yet before Byron consigned the publication of *Don Juan* to John Hunt. He was still hoping that Kinnaird could get some publisher to buy the copyright, which Hunt was unable to do. In the end he gave that and all his subsequent publications to Hunt on a profit sharing arrangement.

has either ignorantly—or unfairly sent you "the Vision &c." and some other papers of mine.—The 6 Cantos of D[on] J[uan] must of course form a separate publication—and the question is how to make such an arrangement as may best oppose the piracies.—You will perhaps confer with Mr. K[innair]d on this subject—his address is—Pall Mall at Messrs Ransom & Co. Bankers—he being a principal partner in that house.—I am Sir

very truly yrs.
NOEL BYRON

P.S.—You must be very particular in recovering the papers from Mr. M[urray] and pray—press this upon Mr. K[innaird]'s attention.

[TO DOUGLAS KINNAIRD]   *Genoa. Octr. 31st. 1822*

My dear Douglas,—By last post—I sent you *two more* Cantos of D[on] J[uan]—I now forward to you a note for Mr. Murray—with whom it is concluded.—You will I suppose try to arrange with some other bookseller for the publication (the 6 Cantos I mean)—as well as for that of "Werner" and the Oratorio—called "Heaven and Earth". —This will however probably be difficult—and in that case—perhaps you had better see *John* Hunt—(Leigh Hunt's brother) with whom it will be easier to settle some arrangement—I don't mean as to Copyright—for he has no capital—but as to publication—and my receiving a certain portion of such profit as may arise therefrom.—I will however be guided by your opinion—Murray's is obviously a mere evasion;— he says that he has lost 16000 by a brother in law—and as I take it is out of cash.—He has behaved ill too—in giving incorrect copies of the Vision &c. to John Hunt—perhaps with the view of getting him into a scrape,—Mr. M[urray] has perhaps another object in view—he knows that they will be *pirated*—and that he can then re-publish them too with impunity.——Some day or other—he will regret his present behaviour.

yrs. ever & truly
N B

[TO HENRY HUNT]   [*Nov. 1822*] *p.m. Nov. 21, 1822*

[Interpolations in letter of Leigh Hunt to Henry Hunt][1]
[Concerning the original and the translation from Pulci] . . . the original may however be printed in a smaller character . . . .

[1] The son of John Hunt.

In one of the stanzas of the Vision—the rhyme is printed *"war"* instead of "roar" ("amidst the *roar*["]) which is not only false rhyme but nonsense—It is in the Stanza about the witnesses—the 6th. line. Instead of amidst the War The Voice of Jonathan &c.—read "amidst the roar"—this however is the fault of honest Mr. Murray . . . . . ["of the *Hints from Horace* Lord B"] thinks a proof had better be sent . . . . [Concerning material for the second number of *The Liberal*] [The 1st Canto of Pulci] with the Original however—because as it is a *close* translation I wish it to be judged by the Original . . . .[2]

[TO EDWARD JOHN TRELAWNY]   *Genoa. 9bre.* [1822]

My dear Trelawny—I do not see how the Chain Cable can enter into the account *here*—seeing that I paid Dunn's whole account before I left Pisa—as far as regards the Bolivar[1]—and I should be glad to know also what Capt. R[oberts] has paid <u>us</u> <u>for</u> I recollect nothing but the ballast.—Will you let me know how this stands—no news of any *kind* from Eng[lan]d which *don't* look *well*

yrs. ever & truly
N B

P.S.—When shall I see you to settle the acc[oun]t?—

[TO LEIGH HUNT]   [*Nov. 1822?*]

The letter to which the pious & trustworthy Mr. Murray [refers?] . . . was written in full confidence,[1] and before the publication of "the Liberal" so that I was totally unaware of Mr. Murray's conduct in furnishing your brother with an incorrect copy of some compositions of mine . . . In a subsequent part of my letter, I said . . . "what would you have me do? The death of Mr. Shelley had thrown Hunt on landing

---

[2] The whole letter with Byron's interpolations was published by Payson G. Gates in the *Keats-Shelley Journal*, Vol. II, pp. 13–17 (Jan. 1953).

[1] After Trelawny brought the *Bolivar* to Genoa Byron laid it up to save money, since he could not use it.

[1] Hunt wrote to his sister-in-law Elizabeth Kent on Nov. 22, 1822: "Lord B. in some idle moment of spleen, had been saying something about us in a letter to Murray; and Murray, it seems, has been exaggerating,—for so Lord B. says he must have done. He is sorry for it, and says (as, indeed, I know) that he has spoken in the handsomest manner of us to many persons, and in a MS., to which Murray himself might have referred; but he ought to have cut the matter short by saying as much now in public. This, however, he is not bold enough to do. He has the best natural disposition I have no doubt in the world; but a variety of circumstances have brought upon him the most deplorable weaknesses, as Shelley had reason to find out, and so have I . . . ." (*Correspondence of Leigh Hunt*, I, 200.)

into unavoidable difficulties; would you have had me abandon him without resource . . . . ['']

[TO DOUGLAS KINNAIRD]   *Genoa Novr. 2d. 1822.*

My dear Douglas,—I have forwarded to you the 10th. & 11th Cantos—(making six in all) with an answer to your *business* epistle.— Also a letter enclosing a reply to Mr. Murray's note—which I consider with you—as a mere evasion, & pretext.—That worthy person is a curious riddle, and I have chiefly to regret having at the beginning of the year—at *his own especial* request to Hobhouse & Moore—recalled my resolution to have nothing more to do with him.— —To dispose of the new Cantos elsewhere—you will find difficult from the same reasons that operated with regard to the Vision &c. which by the way —the *loyal* bookseller—despite of all instances to the contrary—put into Mr. John Hunt's hands in it's most republican and uncorrected state—& without the preface—which you will recollect was the best part of it perhaps.—Now—was this a trap of the indignant M[urray]'s for Hunt? to give him another chance of an indictment? Be it negligence —he is still culpable—for a publisher ought to take as much care of his author's M.S.S. as a lawyer of his Client's title deeds.—He must be trounced for this—and so tell him—and get all my papers out of his hands—except those sold to him by Moore.—

I do not know what to suggest about the new Cantos—and suppose one must give up the notion of turning them to advantage—but you will turn this in your mind.—I am however not at all sorry to be rid of him—for he was a sad shuffler.—So you see one part of the *Budget* has evaporated—let us hope better of the remainder—which rests but on a frail tenure however.—It will be better to carry the insurance to fifteen at *least*—or—I should say—twenty thousand pounds.—I have very much retrenched my expences—and will justify to you my assertion that I shall have three thousand pounds of this year's proceeds—still in hand at the beginning of the other—I have *now two thousand nine* hundred in your *notes* (not counting your letter of credit which is superfluous) and 630 pounds in Messrs Webbs—bank of Leghorn— this makes three thousand five hundred & odd don't it?—now I shall hardly (I trust) spend five hundred before the close of the year.—If it had not been for this Contre-temps about the Cantos—I should have had a sum sufficient from them only to liquidate my remaining debts— as *you* state them—which has really surprized me—for I had no notion so much had been paid,—& can't make out—even *yet*—how it has been done.—Who is *Maddison*? Baxter I recollect of course—but thought that he was *ought* [owed] 2000—& not *one* thousand only—Mealey's bill must be taxen [*sic*]—he is and was always a rogue.——Do you really mean to say that those three and the impudent Attorno are the only outstanding claims?——

If you can settle anything (I don't mean with Murray) about the M.S.S. now in your hands with some publisher—or with John Hunt— (I leave all this to your wisdom however—in pecuniars you are a cut above most people) so as to render them productive—let me know— something they may possibly produce—though greatly [smaller?] than a regular price from an established Publisher—and perhaps much longer in realizing.—I suspect that our fantastical friend M[urray] is either out of pocket—or afraid of the parsons—or of his Quarter*lyers*— or of the politics—or of losing—or some other exquisite reason.— But his conduct is equally strange about "Werner" & the other poem —which he has not published—although terms were left to time—and the chances of success.—I do not understand the fellow—but enclose two of his letters—from which you can judge for yourself.

ever yrs.

N B

[TO DOUGLAS KINNAIRD]   *Genoa. Novr. 6th. 1822*

My dear Douglas—Will you have the goodness to deliver this yourself?—Mr. Murray has no right to be at once insolent & dishonest.——I have written to you three times lately—(with two Cantos additional of D[on] J[uan]) about the six of which I crave your opinion—and how they may be least disadvantageously published & by *whom*.—You can judge from circumstances—though profit is of course (like Honour) agreeable when it comes reasonably—yet it is not the sole object of

yrs. ever & truly

N B

P.S.—You will let Mr. J. Hunt have such pieces as are mentioned in my letters to him as "Werner" & "Heaven & Earth" &c.

P.S.—You will *recollect* that you yourself delivered into Murray's hands the *preface* and carefully corrected copy of the "Vision &c." which I transmitted to you—I have your letter stating that you had done so—and another of yours approving the preface and the corrections.—If Murray plays these tricks purposely—he is a villain—& shall be exposed accordingly.

P.S.—If Murray has delivered up the papers in their perfect state the enclosed is unnecessary; if *not* he deserves it.—

[TO JOHN MURRAY]   *Genoa. Novr. 6th. 1822*

Sir—I have been again informed by Mr. Hunt that you have not paid the smallest attention to my repeated letters.—Of this you will one day find the consequences.—You will be pleased to deliver into the hands of the Hon[oura]ble Douglas Kinnaird—(who takes charge of this note—)all M.S.S. or printers' proofs of mine whatsoever—and in their corrected state—not omitting Werner—& the other piece which was to have been published with it.——As a publisher I bid you a final farewell.—It would have been my wish to have remained on terms of acquaintance with you—but your recent—& repeatedly rude neglect of my earnest directions to you in matters of business—render that also impracticable.—I had believed you infirm in your purposes occasionally—and not very open in explaining your intentions—but I did *not* believe you capable of the conduct you are now holding—or at least have held up to my latest advices from England.—What *that* is— you may yet be told—by me—as well as by others.—You seem to forget that whether as a tradesman or as a gentleman you are [ever?] bound to be decent and courteous in your intercourse with all classes— and I had hoped that the race of Curl and Osborne was extinct.[1]— Perhaps you wish that of Pope to revive also[2]—

yr. obedt. St.
N B

[TO AUGUSTA LEIGH]   *Albaro. Genoa. Novr. 7th. 1822*

My dearest A.—I have yrs. of the 25th.—My Illness is quite gone— it was only at Lerici—on the fourth night, I had got a little sleep and was so wearied that though there were three slight shocks of an Earthquake that frightened the whole town into the Streets——neither they nor the tumult awakened me.—We have had a deluge here—which has carried away half the country between this and Genoa—(about two miles or less distant) but being on a hill we were only nearly knocked down by the lightning and battered by columns of rain—and our lower

[1] Unscrupulous publishers castigated by Pope.
[2] The implication is that Byron would write another *Dunciad* aimed at Murray. This somewhat paranoiac letter was not delivered to Murray. It remained among Kinnaird's papers.

floor afloat——with the comfortable view of the whole landscape under water—and people screaming out of their garret windows— *two bridges* swept down—and our next door neighbours—a Cobbler a Wigmaker—and a Gingerbread baker delivering up their whole stock to the elements—which marched away with a quantity of shoes— several perukes—and Gingerbread in all it's branches.—The whole came on so suddenly that there was no time to prepare—think only at the top of a hill—of the road being an impassable cascade—and a child being drowned a few yards from it's own door (as we heard say) in a place where Water is in general a rare commodity.——Well—after this comes a preaching Friar—and says that the day of Judgement will take place positively on the *4th*—with all kinds of tempest and what not—in consequence of which the whole City—(except some impious Scoffers) sent him presents to avert the wrath of Heaven by his prayers—and even the *public authorities*—had warned the Captains of Ships—who to mend the matter—almost all bought *new Cables* and anchors—by way of weathering the Gale.—But the fourth turned out a very fine day.—All those who had paid their money—are exceptionally angry—and insist either upon having the day of Judgement—or their cash again.—But the Friar's device seems to be "no money to be returned"—and he says that he merely made a mistake in the time— for the day of Judgement will certainly come for all that either here or in some other part of Italy.—This has a little pacified the expectants— you will think this a fiction—enquire further then—the populace actually used to kiss the fellow's feet in the Streets. His Sermon how- ever had small effect upon some—for they gave a ball on the 3d.—and a tradesman brought me an *over*charge on the same day—upon which I threatened him with the friar—but he said that that was a reason for being paid on the 3d.—as he had a sum to make up for his last account. —There seem to have been all kinds of tempests all over the Globe— and for my part it would not surprize me—if the earth should get a little tired of the tyrants and slaves who disturb her surface.——

I have also had a love letter from *Pimlico* from a lady whom I never saw in my life—but who hath fallen in love with me for having written *Don Juan!*—I suppose that she is either mad or *nau*[ghty].—do you remember *Constantia* and *Echo*—and *la Swissesse*[1]—and all my other inamorate—when I was "gentle and juvenile—curly and gay"[2]—and

---

[1] See June 8, 1814, to Henrietta D'Ussières (Vol. 4, p. 122).

[2] Thomas Moore, *Epistles, Odes, and Other Poems* (1806). This quotation is from the last lines of Moore's translation of Horace's *Ode* XI, Lib. ii. Moore pre- tends that it is by G. R., speaking of the Marchioness of Hertford, the King's favourite, who was not "juvenile". The irony is obvious.

was myself in love with a certain silly person—[line crossed out]?——
But I am grown very good now—and think all such things vanities
which is a very proper opinion at thirty four.—I always *say four*—till
the five is out.—Since I last wrote—I had written the enclosed letter—
which I did not send—thinking it useless³—You will please to recollect that you would not be required to know any Italian acquaintance
of mine—the Countess G[uiccioli] has a distinct quarter and generally
[in a] house with her father and brother—who were exiled on account
of politics—and she [was] obliged to go with them or be shut up in a
Convent. The Pope gave her a regular separation from her husband
like Lady B[yron]'s—three years ago.—We are all in the same house
just *now*—only because *our* Ambassador recommended it as safer for
them in these suspicious times.—As to our *liaison*—you know that *all*
foreign ladies & most English have an amitié of the same kind—or not
so good perhaps, as *ours* has lasted nearly four years.

[TO LADY HARDY (*a*)]¹   *Albaro. 9bre. 7th. 1822*

My dear Cousin—For I believe we are cousins are we not?——I am
very glad indeed to hear from you—and should be no less so to see you
—if you can make it convenient.—My "general rule" applied only to
Welbeck Street and Devonshire Place² broke loose—with the inhabitants of which Italy has recently been inundated.—It was not quite
without cause—for besides other inconveniences—I found out that an
unknown gentleman for want of a better had taken my not very orna-
mental name upon him—and had actually ran *here* and elsewhere before
me—in a character which I hope was of more use to him than ever it
has been to me.—I do not like to think of old times—as many changes
have taken place—death—and marriage—and other things which are
neither death nor marriage—but make a great change nevertheless.—
There are for instance—our friends the Rancliffe's—Lord Clare told
me not long ago—that they were disunited—and in short one is afraid

³ The letter of Oct. 20, 1822, in which he had invited Augusta and her family to
come abroad at his expense.
    ¹ Anne Louisa Emily, daughter of Admiral Sir George Berkeley, married in 1807
Admiral Sir Thomas Masterman Hardy, who was in the *Victory* with Nelson when
the latter died in 1805. Hardy was sent on an expedition to South America in 1819
and did not return until 1824. Lady Hardy was in her early thirties when she
stopped in Genoa on her travels in Italy and saw Byron briefly. Through the
Berkeley family she was distantly related to Byron, whose great-grandmother, wife
of the fourth Lord Byron, was a daughter of Lord Berkeley of Stratton. Lady Hardy
had met Byron in London in 1814.
    ² Fashionable residential streets in early nineteenth-century London.

to enquire after any body.—I heard of Lady Jersey the other day
through my Sister.——I am sorry that you are going to Leghorn—
because I left it not very long ago.—When do you go? if you don't
start tomorrow I would take the chance of finding you at home at any
hour you please—but if otherwise I can only wish you a good journey
—and beg you to believe me

ever and affect[ionate]ly yrs.
NOEL BYRON

P.S.—You talk of your "eldest Girl" this has a very domestic
sound;—I have just got the picture of mine—I have never seen the
original since she was a month old.—

[TO LADY HARDY (*b*)]   *Albaro. 9bre. 7th. 1822*

My dear ------. —I don't know whether to say *"Cousin"* or no—
but the relationship is your own fault for you told me at some Masquerade or party in 1814 (you see I have a *long* memory if not an
accurate one) that there was some connection between the *Berkeleys*
and *Byrons*—and *that* is enough for one who is also half a Scotchman to
found a pedigree upon.——But to continue—I will ride down at half
past *two* tomorrow to take another leave of you—for such it seems to
be ordained rather than a renewal of "auld lang syne".——I said half
past two—that I might not by naming an earlier hour deprive you of
the benefit of divine service—where it is not impossible that you may
hear the English Chaplain preach against *me*—at least the one at Pisa
did me that honour some time ago.—I had heard that Lady Jersey was
very glad of her female acquisition after the number of little honourable
Misters with which she had presented Jersey.—The *picture* of mine—
is alas still detained by the unfilial duties of the [five or six lines cut
out of letter] and somewhat [short?] but of course a prodigy—like all
only Children.——You talk of your *three*,——I envy you their company—which is one advantage which women have over men—and they
ought to have many more—to compensate for our tyranny.—Believe
me my dear ------ (fill up the blank with Cousin if you like it)
with equal sincerity—and—I suspect [end of letter missing].

[TO HENRY DUNN]   *Albaro. Genoa. 9bre. 9th. 1822*

Sir—This will be sent to you by Lady Hardy—wife of Admiral Sir
Thomas Hardy—she is now about to stay some time at Leghorn for the

benefit of the Sea-Baths for her Children.—If you can be of any use to her at Leghorn I shall feel obliged to you—and as she is a stranger it may be serviceable to her—and not unuseful to you in your business. ——On the receipt of this you may draw on me at sight for one hundred Francesconi—or the value thereof—in part of the remaining account, we will talk of the Hock when I get your answer.—

yrs. very truly
NOEL BYRON

[TO LEIGH HUNT] *Genoa. 9bre. 11th. 1822*

My dear H—I have no wish whatever to see yr. letter to yr. nephew —nor do I see any advantage in it.—I have shown you such letters as referred to the M.S.S. to be reclaimed from Murray—because they regarded "the Liberal".——There was no reason why I was not to write to him in a friendly manner *"at that* time" because the Liberal was yet unpublished and I was not aware of the actual conduct which he had held till it's arrival—further than that he had a repugnance to see yr. brother which I thought ridiculous—but not deserving of any severe reprehension.——I repeat, as aforesaid—that I do *not* believe that I used those expressions quoted in the paragraph of H[enry] H[unt]'s letter—but it is not impossible that I may—and if it were so—*that* does not justify Murray's circulation and garbled publication of a private Correspondence.——That I said that Mrs. H[unt] is sick and the children are "not very tractable"—is very true—and I wish that I could unsay either with any justice.—You will also recollect that I had no particular reason to be pleased with the published Circular with both our names in capitals making the tour of Booksellers' back-parlours.—As to Murray's knavery—"the knave was mine honest friend"[1] at least in most of his dealings till now—though always wavering and rather mysterious—I never detected him in any *great* piece of malice till in the late business.——The whole of the letter to him as far as I remember—contains merely what I have said to yourself over and over on the subject of the *Journal* (the *personal* part I will continue to doubt till I see it—always excepting the sickness of Mrs. H[unt] and the conduct of the children—who I really must say—what you may hear from any one—are likely in their present state to become any thing but a comfort to you) the success of which I always doubted —and yet was willing to make the experiment (rather than see you dis-

[1] Probably adapted from *Othello*, Act III, scene 1: "Dost thou hear, mine honest friend?"

appointed)—against the remonstrances of all parties—for like Legion you know they were many.——Indeed at the time M[urray]'s letter arrived—we were not decided on attempting it[.] [End of letter missing.]

[TO DOUGLAS KINNAIRD]   *Genoa. 9bre. 13th. 1822*

My dear Douglas—The papers say that you have met with a serious accident.[1] I hope that they lie—or at least exaggerate as usual.—But pray let me know—I shall not be easy till I hear that you are well.—— I had written to you lately on business two or three letters and sent a packet—but it is no time to be bothering you now with such matters.— Only let me know how you are—or tell some one else to write to say how you are going on.

yrs. ever very aff[ectionate]ly
N B

[TO MARY SHELLEY]   *9bre. 14th. 1822*

Dear M.—The letter is all very well—but I wish that he would press upon his brother (what is of more importance at least to the *quantity* of the publication) the expediency of seeing Mr. K[innair]d the moment he is well enough to receive visitors—else he may never get the M.S.S. at all from Murray—who seems to stick at nothing in all that relates to Hunt's family. As to any expressions in private letters about Hunt or others—I am not a cautious letter-writer and generally say what comes uppermost at the moment, but I remember in my more deliberate Memoirs (which Murray bought of Moore) having done his character justice—why didn't M. allude to them?—it were less a breach of confidence than the other?——The whole thing has been a piece of officious Malice on the part of M. & not very discreet zeal on the part of Hunt's friends.—

yrs. ever
N B

P.S.—I send you the completion of the *first* part—of the drama[1]— as I think it may be as well to divide it—although *intended* to be *irregular* in all it's branches.

1 Kinnaird was injured by a fall from his horse. See Nov. 28, 1822, to Kinnaird.
1 Byron had since Shelley's death been sending Mary his first drafts of poems for her to make fair copies. This was a service to both, for Byron hated to copy a poem after he had written it and it gave Mary occupation and increased her income when she needed it. The drama mentioned here was *The Deformed Transformed*.

* * * * * * * * * * * * * * *

I presume that you, at least, know enough of me to be sure that I could have no intention to insult Hunt's poverty. On the contrary, I honour him for it; for, I know what it is, having been as much embarrassed as ever he was, without perceiving aught in it to diminish an honourable man's self-respect. If you mean to say that, had he been a wealthy man, I would have joined in this Journal, I answer in the negative. * * * I engaged in the Journal from good-will towards him, added to respect for his character, literary and personal; and no less for his political courage, as well as regret for his present circumstances: I did this in the hope that he might, with the same aid from literary friends of literary contributions (which is requisite for all journals of a mixed nature), render himself independent.

* * * * * * * * * * * * * * *

I have always treated him, in our personal intercourse, with such scrupulous delicacy, that I have forborne intruding advice, which I thought might be disagreeable, lest he should impute it to what is called "taking advantage of a man's situation".

As to friendship, it is a propensity in which my genius is very limited. I do not know the *male* human being, except Lord Clare, the friend of my infancy, for whom I feel any thing that deserves the name. All my others are men-of-the-world friendships. I did not even feel it for Shelley, however much I admired and esteemed him; so that you see not even vanity could bribe me into it, for, of all men, Shelley thought highest of my talents,—and, perhaps of my disposition.

I will do my duty by my intimates, upon the principle of doing as you would be done by. I have done so, I trust, in most instances. I may be pleased with their conversation—rejoice in their success—be glad to do them service, or to receive their counsel and assistance in return. But as for friends and friendship, I have (as I already said) named the only remaining male for whom I feel any thing of the kind, excepting, perhaps, Thomas Moore. I have had, and may have still, a thousand friends, as they are called, in *life*, who are like one's partners in the waltz of this world—not much remembered when the ball is over, though very pleasant for the time. Habit, business, and companionship in pleasure or in pain, are links of a similar kind, and the same faith in politics is another. * * *

Genoa. 9bre. 18th. 1822

My dear Douglas—As I hear no further of yr. accident—I trust that all is well, and you also.—I enclose an open letter for Mr. Deardon of Rochdale[1]—which I request you to forward—and after perusing it to do all you can to forward an accommodation—I want the lawsuit concluded or off my mind.—I will be guided by any thing you think fair on the subject.—Pray—weigh this well—you can easily get the requisite information. I enclose also a letter from Murray—who does not even allude to yr. accident—which confirms me in the notion that it is not dangerous.—Both the epistles will explain themselves.—

yrs. ever
N B

[TO DOUGLAS KINNAIRD (*b*)] *9bre. 18th. 1822*

My Dear Douglas—Since I wrote the enclosed I have received another letter from Murray—which he had directed to Pisa.—Of the truth of both you can judge as well as any one.—To me publication is a matter of no great importance—and no outcry or diminution of popularity—or extinction of it—will alter my way of thinking.—The Juans shall either be published or not as you think proper.—I sent you *six* Cantos in all—*four* first—and two since—between M. & the Hunts— I am in a dilemma—as a Man always is—who wishes to do a good action.—You see that M. is frightened or pretends to be so—so—the truth comes out at length[1]——With regard to the letter to Deardon— I will act according to your advice.

yrs. ever
N B

P.S.—I hope that you will carry the insurance of Ly. B[yron]'s life up to 15—or 20000 £ S. D.

---

1 James Dearden (Byron regularly spells the name "Deardon") was the lessee of the Rochdale coal-pits. Byron had been in litigation to recover the lease for many years without success, but Hanson encouraged him to continue the appeals, though Byron was more inclined to seek an accommodation, or settle the matter by arbitration. Just before Byron died at Missolonghi Dearden bought the Rochdale estate.

1 See Murray's letter on his reaction to *Don Juan*, Marchand, *Byron: A Biography*, III, 1040. Byron referred to this letter in writing to Murray on Nov. 23, 1822: "your pretended regard for my fame".

I have—since I received yr. letter of the 5th received yrs. of the 29— which you had directed to Pisa.—It puts the affair in a different aspect —and at this distance I cannot take upon me to decide—though prima facie—your showing my letter—without permission—was to say the least of it indiscreet enough,—though I should wish repelled the attribution of a mercenary motive. With regard to the rest of your letter— I dare say that it is true—and that you mean well.—I never courted popularity—and cared little or nothing for the decrease or extinction thereof.—As to any other motives—they will of course attribute motives of all kinds—but I shall not abandon a man like H[unt] because he is unfortunate—why I could have *no pecuniary* motives & least of all in connection with H[unt]—and at any rate at *present*—for I have more money than is requisite—at least in this Country—and I should conceive that the terms—or rather *no* terms on which—Werner &c. were left with you—must laugh to scorn such a supposition.——I care but little for the opinions of the English—as I have long had Europe and America for a Public and were it otherwise I could bear it.——My letters to you were written under the impression that you had acted unfairly by Hunt—and *when* that is cleared up—of course I have no complaint against you.——I shall withdraw from you as a publisher— on every account even on your own—and I wish you good luck elsewhere—but if you can make out that you treated H. fairly—you may reckon me in other respects—as

yrs. very truly
N B

P.S.—I send you my letter written previously to the receipt of yours from Pisa (direct to *Genoa* if you write again) if you do not deserve it —it is harsh—& would have been written more mildly had I got yrs. of the 29th. before that of the 5th.——

Dear T.—Mr. Bees has made the expected reply—that Capt. Roberts said—"that *he* was to have the cloathes" or to that effect.—If Capt. Roberts said anything to this effect it was *without previously acquainting* me—or indeed *subsequently* for I never heard him say so— nor *would* have consented—he might as well have said that he was to have the rigging of the Schooner when he went ashore.—I have allowed the expences of the Bolivar's building to pass without a cavil—or a question—I have tripled the original estimate; I have never opposed her being lent to the pleasures of any acquaintance or even of [a] respectable stranger—but I do not see that I am at all to be expected to allow Messrs Bees and *Frost* (the latter by your own account—a notorious and convicted *thief*) to carry away that to which they have no right—because they have lounged about for an 100 miles along the Coast—on high pay—and with little work.———I hate bothering you with these things—but I could not take steps at the police against them —(which I shall perhaps be obliged to do) without apprizing you— previously—and on account of the bad character of Frost—in whose case I shall perhaps have occasion for your testimony.—Believe me

yrs. very truly
N B

P.S.—You must take care to separate any articles of yr. own from those on the Schooner to prevent confusion.———

[TO DOUGLAS KINNAIRD] *Genoa. 9bre. 20th. 1822*

Dear Douglas,—The enclosed draft will be forwarded to you with this note of advice—by Miss Kent[1] a young Lady who sent a draft for twenty five pounds to some of her relations in this Country. As they had not occasion to use it—they wished to return it—but having some apprehensions of the post—requested me to receive it and give a draft on your house for the amount which I have accordingly done.—I yesterday received the value in cash from my banker here—so that it is money strictly due to Miss K[ent]—and I request that you will have the goodness to reimburse that lady—and place it to my account with Messrs. Ransom.———I have written to you lately on various subjects —some important—and one on the Rochdale business particularly so. —As neither the papers nor the letters I have received speak further of yr. accident—I trust that [it] is as trifling as I hoped it would be.—

believe me yrs. ever
N B

P.S.—Pray let me know how you are as soon as possible.———

[1] Elizabeth (Bessy) Kent was Mrs. Leigh Hunt's sister.

Genoa. 9bre. 20th. 1822

Dear Sir—As I perceive that the funds are falling—and that war appears imminent by all accounts—I wish to inform you that if Stocks fall below the price at which I bought in—I will not consent to sell out —even to complete the loan to Ld. Le Despenser. You have had ample time to complete a hundred investigations of title-deeds and I need not add that I cannot permit your delays to put me at length thousands out of pocket—I have written to Mr. Kinnaird to the same effect—and as I said before—upon whomever the blame may be laid—if the affair is *not* concluded and the Stock now sold out—I will not accept a rate below the price at which I bought it—I pray that you all apprize the trustees of this my determination.—If [the] funds continue at about their present price—it is very well—but if otherwise—I trust that you will not neglect my present directions.— —Believe me

yrs. very truly
NOEL BYRON

[TO DOUGLAS KINNAIRD] *Genoa. Novr. 21st. 1822*

Dear Douglas—I trust that you are up again & well.—You will find loads of letters from me to amuse your convalescence.—I see that the funds are falling (I always told you that it would be so) and war impending.—Recollect that if they fall below the *point* [at] which I bought in—I won't sell out for all that is come and gone yet with Lord Le Despenser;—I can't afford to throw away thousands to please anybody.—Pray write—I have written to Hanson to-day—to repeat what I here say.

yrs. ever & truly
N B

P.S.—I hope you won't deem this unreasonable—recollect—that I am selling out to obtain perhaps no higher interest—and of course cannot afford to lose thousands for such a paltry compensation.—I have written to you on various subjects—but all my affairs—literary— personal—or pecuniary—appear to be out of luck—though I do all I can—by economy on one hand—and urgency on the other (as far as the distance will permit) to reestablish them—and in the mean time *you* (my sheet anchor) contrive to get laid up!—This would not have happened to any other man's trustee—Remember to carry the L[ady] B[yron] insurance to 20000.

Dear H.—I return you your dogs—which I would recommend you to think twice upon before you publish them at the present moment[1]— but that is for yr. own consideration.—Would you mention to yr. brother—that if he obtains "Werner" &c. he must not omit the preface—or the dedication—Murray has the former—Mr. Kinnaird the latter.—He must also obtain the *revised* proofs—or it will be full of errors like the "Vision".—I suppose that there is no particular hurry for the second number—as it will be better to have a good than a hasty one—(and as far as *I* am concerned) if Murray should have published Werner &c.[2]—I have nothing worth the publication—"the Vision" was the best—the rest were mere translations from Pulci,—or imitations of Horace—and prose tracts of personal controversy.——In a literary point of view—I shall only suggest two things to yr. judgement—in the *Dogs*—the first is to alter the motto—which is neither very good—nor true—for it is not a common phrase—at least to my knowledge—and I have heard the objurgations of many different communities—from the Dandy's to the Dragoman's. In ye. 2d. place— there are a few of the rhymes especially in the latter part which ought to be altered. (Calendar
(Purveyor for example
The intended prosecution by yr. brother of the poachers—will I hope be let alone.—

yrs. ever
N B

Dear T[relawn]y—Thank you—I was just going to send you down some books of yrs. and the Compass of the D[on] J[uan] which belongs to Capt. Roberts—if there is any thing else of yours let me know that I may send it or keep it for you.———Beese's wages will be paid the moment he delivers up the things—I do not know how our own account stands—the twenty louis made about 88 dollars more or less—and the balance stated was 70—but there may probably have accrued other

---

[1] A rather heavy-handed satire called "The Dogs", on the feeding of Wellington's hounds by hungry soldiers. It appeared in the second number of *The Liberal.* Byron thought it unwise for Hunt to print it while his brother was being prosecuted for the lèse majesté of publishing *The Vision of Judgment.*
[2] Murray published *Werner,* but Byron gave *Heaven and Earth* to Hunt for the second number of *The Liberal.*

expences since then—but you will let me know if there is any balance due to you that I may settle it.——I am willing to make an agreement with a proper person in the Arsenal to look after her—and also to have the rigging &c. deposited in a safe place—can you recommend any place or person—or shall I apply to the Consul!——I have given the boy his cloathes—and if Mr. Beese had been civil—and Mr. Frost honest—I should not have been obliged to go so near the wind with them.[1]——I agree with you in your parting sentence—but hope that we shall have better luck another time—there is one satisfaction how-ever—which is that the displeasures have been rather occasioned by untoward circumstances—and not by the disposition of any party con-cerned.—But such are human things even in little—we could hardly have had more plague with a first rate.—

yrs. ever & truly
N B

[TO JOHN MURRAY]   *Genoa. 9bre. 23d. 1822*

I have to thank you for a parcel of books, which are very welcome, especially Sir Walter's gift of *Halidon Hill*.[1] You have sent me a copy of *Werner*, but *without* the preface: if you have published it *without*, you will have plunged me into a very disagreeable dilemma, because I shall be accused of plagiarism from Miss Lee's German's tale[2], whereas I have fully and freely acknowledged that the drama is entirely taken from the story.

I return you the *Quarterly Review*, uncut and unopened, not from disrespect or disregard or pique; but it is a kind of reading which I have some time disused, as I think the periodical style of writing hurt-ful to the habits of the mind, by presenting the superficies of too many things at once. I do not know that it contains any thing disagreeable to me—it may or it may not; nor do I return it on account that there *may* be an article which you hinted at in one of your late letters; but because I have left off reading these kind of works, and should equally have returned you any other Number.

I am obliged to take in one or two abroad, because solicited to do so; but do not read them. The *Edinburgh* came before me by mere chance in Galignani's pic-nic sort of Gazette, where he had inserted a part of it.

---

[1] Byron had objected to giving their uniforms to these men when they were dismissed from the *Bolivar* because of their insolence and dishonesty.
[1] *Halidon Hill, a Dramatic Sketch from Scottish History* was published in 1822.
[2] *Kruitzner, or The German's Tale*, by Harriet Lee.

You will have received various letters from me lately, in a style which I used with reluctance; but you left me no other choice, by your obstinate refusal to communicate with a man you did not like, upon the mere simple matter of transfer of a few papers of little consequence (except to their author), and which could be of no moment to yourself.

I hope that Mr. K[innair]d is better: it is strange that you never alluded to his accident, if it be true, as stated in the papers.

I am yours, etc.,

N B

I have sent the parcel by the Diligence, to save you post, which would be heavy.

You have put the concluding speech of Werner in the mouth of Josephine, instead of that of Siegendorf, though I particularly recollect correcting it: is this repeated and doubly repeated negligence in printing my writings (recollect the *Juans* too), a sign of your pretended regard for my fame? They are so full of gross misprints, that a publisher might be ashamed of himself who allowed them to go forth in such a state. It is no *fault* of mine, for I most carefully corrected them: I shall be obliged to state this to the *reader* if you go on so.

[TO DOUGLAS KINNAIRD]   *Genoa 9bre. 28 o¹ 1822*

My dear Douglas—Yrs. of ye. 15th. arrived yesterday.—It is the *first* I have heard of yr. accident from *yourself* though you seem to refer to a prior letter. Will you please to recollect that I have few friends and only one potestas of Attorneo—and that I cannot afford to lose you in either capacity.—Why will you ride impracticable cattle? you are, or used to be, an excelling horseman—and therefore must have sought out the brute for his bad qualities—unless indeed he *fell* with you—which may happen to any horse or man.—Now to your Yepistle.
——Of Mr. Maddison—I know nothing—my subscriptions at Watier's were paid up to my departure from Englonde—and I thought —that being abroad—neutralized further disbursements during absence.—What is the amount—or what is the excuse for it?—a large demand is impossible—I never dined at the Club—but once with Hobhouse to meet G[enera]l Sebastiani & Flahau[l]t—and I paid my conscription regularly.—It is a mystery to me—except that nothing in the impudence of mankind ought to surprize a philosopher.——

¹ The "*o*" here and in subsequent letters is an abbreviation of the Italian ordinal numbers: primo, secondo, etc.

It is my intention when assetts are at a certain height—to liquidate the remaining debt but it is best to have double funds in hand first.— — About June—if you have three thousand pounds of mine in hand—you can pay five or six hundred—and so on—in proportion—till the whole two thousand—or thereabouts (you seem to think that it is the remaining debt not more) are liquidated.—The three thousand *four* hundred—(which with yr. circulars and six hundred at Messrs. Webb's Leghorn I have at present disposal) I reserve for the expence of living &c.—and hope to make it last me a year—and perhaps two—and peradventure three.—How far the Noel and the funded property are likely to render an addition to be depended upon—you who know what the funds are—and land is—can tell better than I.—In the mean time till the landed part at least produces something more substantial than it hath hitherto exhibited— —the few remaining claimants must wait for some months, methinks they might and may.—

With regard to any literary products—they are so fluctuating and uncertain—that I can make no near calculation.— —I shall trust the management of those as of other affairs of more importance to your discretion—only requesting that you won't settle them on horseback. — —I leave it to you to decide between Messrs Ridgeway and J. Hunt; —what Ridgeway is disposed to advance you do not say—but as I doubt not—you will do what is best—I am not very anxious to enquire. — —The publisher must send me proofs (by a Canto at a time) of the whole.— —Does R[idgway] publish the four or the six—if the four only I can add a (12th) new Canto to the remaining two—which would form another volume—i.e. two in the whole of the new publication— of about the same size as the two former.— —I have no objection to re-consider any passages—and to alter several—though I cannot promise very largely—being obstinate on such points.—About Werner—you are to decide also—I mean as to letting Murray publish— for as to any profit from it—our friend of Albemarle Street would sacrifice even his *own*—(far more mine) to gratify his unintelligible spite against the Hunts—and me for having assisted—or endeavoured to assist them.— —The Copy of the thing—which is to go into Hunt's new Journal—ought to be the corrected *proof*—with Murray's—or Gifford's *pencil marks* around one passage—near the close—which G. thought had better be omitted—and I am of his opinion—as a point of expediency for the publisher to avoid piracy;—I am not aware of anything unorthodox in the rest.—You need not send me any Circulars from fee at Xmas—(the funds I mean) but merely let me know from time to time—as any thing drops in from whatever quarter.—I have carried my own economy into effect hitherto—even better than I expected—I have laid up my Schooner in the Arsenal—(which stops that expence of wages &c.) reduced my establishment—sold some horses—and mean to sell another—thereby keeping five—instead of ten——and I wish if possible—to live as simply as need be—for some years—though not sordidly.———Now I wish to know—when I have got a few thousands together say two or three even—how I could invest it in exchequer bills or otherwise—at a low but secure interest—so as to be convertible to immediate use if wanted—and so on with my further monies that might accrue;———You see that the whole of the year 1823 incomings—ought to be disposable product—since I have reserved the three thousand and odd hundreds surplus of 1822 for my maintenance &c.———The debt remaining can be liquidated in proportion to our receipts———if you receive on my acct in the course of the current year —£6000—or above—pay off one thousand of debt—if £8000—fifteen hundred of debt may be liquidated—then recollect—that the expence of insurance is to be deducted and is heavy—(20000 as we agreed) and pray however keep it—*regular*—without the loss of a day —and do not let any of the insurances (as they are at different offices) expire without immediate renewal.—You will smile at all this tirade upon business—but it is time to mind it—at least for me to mind it—for without some method in it where or what is independence? the power of doing good to others or yourself.

yrs. ever & truly
N B

[TO CAPTAIN DANIEL ROBERTS]   *Genoa. 9bre. 28 o 1822*

Dear Sir,—As you had never mentioned the condition to me—I necessarily was unaware of it—and I cannot draw upon you for the amount—as I had already given the boy and Gaetano their clothes without reserve—and perhaps should have been disposed to do the same by the other two—but Frost as Trelawny can tell you—turned out a thief —and robbed Trelawny—and Bees conducted himself to me with great insolence—neither of which circumstances I conceive entitled them to much regard on my part, I understood that Bees was about to enter into your service—and I presume in that case—that it will be the same to you—whether you cloathe him yourself or I draw upon you for the amount—which besides would not be fair on my part—because I should come upon you for the *original* price—whereas the dress at present cannot be stated at the same value—and I believe I need hardly say—that it cannot be their value—which can be an object either to you or to myself.—

Both Frost and Bees conducted themselves as I have told you—for the behaviour of the former I can refer you to Trelawny—and for that of the latter I presume that my own word will be sufficient—even if the man should deny it—which I rather suspect that he will not.—I regret very much that we had no previous conversation on the subject which would have prevented any misunderstanding ⟨on the subject⟩—but as the matter stands—I do not see how I was bound to terms which you had not mentioned to me—because I understood that the full power which I readily granted with regard to the building of the vessel &c. extended only to the period of my liquidating all demands—and not after she was ⟨arrived at⟩ afloat;—suppose for instance one of the men had misbehaved himself the first week—would you have set him ashore with his *spolia opima*[1]—at that rate we must have new-rigged them once a month.——You must excuse me from drawing upon you for such a purpose—if you think that these fellows deserve any compensation—you can make it up to *them*—which I dare say they would like better—but I hope that you will not—for *two have* their cloathes—and the other two have not behaved well—as before stated.——I am sorry that in addition to the trouble I have already given you—you should have that of this correspondence—how goes on the D[on] J[uan]?[2] I gave Trelawny her Compass (which I believe is yr. property) for you—Believe me

> ever & very truly yrs.
> NB

[TO EDWARD JOHN TRELAWNY (*a*)]   *Genoa. 9bre. 29 o 1822*

Dear T.—I enclose you a letter from Capt. R[oberts] [and one *to* him?] which may be more to your taste—but at any rate it contains—all that I have to say upon the subject.——You will I presume write tomorrow—and enclose it—or not—according to your own opinion.——I repeat that I have no wish for a quarrel—but if it comes unlooked for—it must be received accordingly; I recognize no right in any man to interfere between me and the men in my pay—of whose conduct I have the best right to judge.—

> yrs. ever & affectly.
> NB

[1] The choicest spoils.
[2] Roberts had brought Shelley's boat ashore and was trying to repair it.

Dear T.—I have consulted gov[ernmen]t authority—and I find that *I have* a right to recall the Cloathes which I furnished to the Crew.—I shall enforce that right if necessary by the police—but I trust that there will be no occasion.—It would be hard indeed—if after the expences— with which this Goletta [Schooner] has encumbered me—I should be obliged to let these fellows off with their Spoils.—The new Master of Bees should cloathe him—this is but fair on both sides.—I am sorry to give you the trouble of this note—but as I stated to you my opinion on the subject yesterday—I thought it but right to tell you that I had that opinion confirmed by those in the Consular office.—It never was—nor ever could be my intention—that they should carry away their best cloathes—and as I paid for them I beg leave to dispose of them.——
Believe me

yrs. ever & truly
N B

Dear Sir,—As to the best of my knowledge—you never mentioned the Condition to me, I could not be supposed to act upon it—I cannot draw upon you for the amount—as I have no claim upon you whatever. —Frost behaved *dishonestly* to Mr. Trelawny and Bees *insolently* to myself;—I therefore did not consider either of those persons entitled to any regard on my part.—The boy—and Gaetano had their dress given to them by me without question.—I regret that you should have felt surprized upon the subject—or annoyed; as it has always been my wish to give you as little trouble as possible.—With regard to what you have heard upon the subject—you will be aware that you had only heard one side of the question—and it could hardly be the *value* of the articles which could induce me to be strict with those two persons.— For Frost's behaviour I can refer you to Mr. Trelawny—for that of Bees—I should conceive that my own explanation may be sufficient. ——If Bees has been mischief-making—it is only of a piece with the rest of his behaviour to me—which indeed deserved a much severer chastisement—than it is my propensity to inflict upon any one.——I merely reclaimed that to which I conceived he had no title.—The most painful part to me is—that after the trouble you have had in building the Schooner &c.—anything should have occurred to annoy yourself or your friends—but under the circumstances I could not act otherwise than I have done.——I have the honour to be

your obliged & very sincere obedt. humble Servt.

N B[1]

[TO CHARLES HANSON] *Genoa. 9bre. 30 o 1822*

My dear Charles—The papers for the right of water have only just arrived—and I will sign and send them by the first opportunity.—The Scotch release I could not understand—or have mislaid—the instructions were so obscure—if you send me another copy—tell me exactly what to do.—Your parchments require so much precision—that in a foreign country—it is difficult to go through with them correctly.—— With regard to the advance of the 500 pounds—I must refer you to Mr. Kinnaird on that topic—I have no objection whenever your *accounts* are presented.—For years after years have I been urging for these accounts—though I should think that there can be no great balance *now*.—Besides the two thousand seven hundred pounds paid in 1813;—since the sale of Newstead in 1818—many thousands have been paid to you—and all on an unpresented account.——I presume too (though *that* of course cannot enter into any statement between us nor ought) that you did not make a very bad thing of my bond to Claughton—which you purchased at a discount.——With all this before us— I do not quite see the reason of much impatience—but as I said—I am willing—and indeed desirous to settle accounts between us—if you will but present them to Mr. D. Kinnaird to be looked over as is usual I am told in all such transactions.——It is true there is the appeal before the House of L[or]ds—but I am told that appeals are not very expensive—nor ought they to be so—before the present Chancellor;— for I greatly doubt his hearing fairly any cause of mine.—Will you make my remembrances to your father and believe me.

ever and truly yrs.

NOEL BYRON[1]

[TO DOUGLAS KINNAIRD] *Genoa. 9bre. 30 o 1822*

My dear Douglas,—Enclosed are two letters from young Hanson— with my answer—will you read the reply—wafer—and forward it.—

---

[1] This seems to be the revised letter to Roberts mentioned in Byron's letter of Nov. 29(*a*) to Trelawny.

[1] The complimentary close and signature cut off from the manuscript, are in the Pforzheimer Library.

I think that you will not disapprove of the Contents.——I desired him to take Bell's opinion on the Noel Business—but will not act upon it without the maturest reflection—and in my case—not without hearing you fully on the subject.—What you wrote to me has altered my opinion considerably on that topic.—I have lately written to you reams upon business.—

yrs. ever & truly
N B

P.S.—How much has Hanson *had* in all? and how much *ought* he to have? can't he give in the accompt?—

[TO JOHN HUNT]   [*December, 1822?*]

. . . I offered to your brother to stand the trial instead and to go over to England for that purpose but he told me that this could be of no use to you nor would probably be permitted by the Gang.[1] With regard to the arrangements for the publication of D[on] J[uan] Mr. Kinnaird is my trustee in all matters of business. I am not very sanguine on the subject, and would not have you to be so, for you cannot be aware how violent public opinion is at this moment against myself . . . .

[TO DOUGLAS KINNAIRD]   *Genoa. Decr. 1 0 1822*

My dear Douglas—The best way to settle Mealey's account[1]—will be to pay Mrs. M. a hundred pounds per quarter till the whole is liquidated.—Till I know what my actual receipts are to be (and I can not till you have transferred from the funds—and we have something more palpable from the Kirkby property) I cannot approve the paying away of considerable sums at once—which might leave me out of cash —and consequently liable to incur new debts.—As they are *sure* in any event of being paid (the Creditors—that is) there can be no objection to the gradual extinction of the remaining claims—which are not or ought not to be very large.—I enclosed you young Hanson's letters with my answer—if his father has had—(or both between them) "nearly eight thousand pounds of my money" (your own phrase in a recent letter) I should be glad to know what he *would have* further—or

---

[1] John Hunt was prosecuted by the Constitutional Association for publishing Byron's *Vision of Judgment* in the first number of *The Liberal* (Oct. 15, 1822). The trial was delayed and did not take place until 1824, when Hunt was convicted and fined £100.

[1] Owen Mealey was the steward at Newstead Abbey. Apparently his widow was making a claim for an unpaid balance of his wages, which had been paid irregularly during Byron's impecunious youth.

what he is really entitled to have? otherwise there seems to be no end to his demands.—Had he not Claughton's balance?—I do not object to his having the 500 from the Market tolls—but I must & will have a regular account of the *whole* of his bill *audited* by a professional man of your choosing.—It may not be my interest—and it is not my wish to quarrel with him—but better do anything than have thousands asked for yearly—without a bill or account to show for it.—Master Charles too is a purchaser of bonds at a discount—and made a pretty thing probably of mine to Claughton since paid by me some years ago.——

I have just seen the illustrious James Wedderburne Webster—who came to visit*ate* me here.—I had not seen him these ten years.—He had a black wig on—and has been made a knight for writing against the Queen.—He wants a diplomatic situation—and seems likely to want it.——He found me thinner even than in 1813, for since my late illness—(at Lerici on my way here) I have subsided into my former more meagre outline—and am obliged to be very abstinent by medical advice—on account of liver & what not.—I found him increased rather —but not much;—looking redder—but tolerably fresh—and no wiser than heretofore.—He talked a deal of skimble skamble stuff—and is gone to Florence.—But to the point—or at least my point in mentioning this new Chevalier our old acquaintance.—Ten years ago I lent him a thousand pounds on bond, on condition that he would not go to the *Jews.*—He took the money and went to the Jews.—Hanson has this bond—and there is ten years interest due upon it.——I have never dunned him—but I think that he might at least have paid some of the interest.—The Bond (though a good bond) is—I presume—valuable according to the possibility or probability of recovering said monies.— Now a Mr. C. Hanson is a purchaser of bonds—(it hath a judgement probably to it) will he purchase this of me? or will any body else at a discount—somewhat considerable?—What effects the Grantor of said bond may now have I know not—but I presume—*some* still—though he has parted with his wife who was the best of them.—He had (besides her) a considerable property at one time.—He might have repaid me out of Wellington's money[2]—or Petersham's.[3] Now what shall I

[2] In 1816 Webster had won a libel suit (Webster v. Baldwin) for £2,000 as damages. Baldwin had charged Lady Frances Webster and the Duke of Wellington with being guilty of adultery.

[3] Charles Stanhope, later Earl of Harrington (1828), styled Viscount Petersham, had been a guest at Webster's when Byron was having an abortive affair with Lady Frances Webster in 1813. Petersham had also flirted with Lady Frances and must have been obliged to pay damages. He was the older brother of the Hon. Leicester Stanhope, with whom Byron was associated during his last months in Greece.

take for said bond? or rather what is to be got?—Perpend—pronounce.
—Hanson will perhaps want it as *"part* of his account"—but he shan't
have it—nor shall he have any more *"parts"* till we know the Whole.
——I have never pressed Webster—but to say truth—he has behaved
shabbily about it—and had the impudence to ask me the other day—
whether "my *heirs* could act upon it".—I feel disposed to save them the
trouble—but should I not—I trust they will require their due—I am
sure that all my creditors have been a good deal less patient.

You will have had quantities of letters from me lately—which is
natural in the uncertainty of every thing at this time—and indeed at all
times.—I sent you also a conciliatory proposition for Deardon—in a
letter to that personage—to be forwarded by you—and the business to
be treated *of* with you—I give you full powers on my part to open a
negociation to end that lawsuit—if lawsuits ever do really end.—
Better sacrifice—any remote contingent or possible advantage—to
close at once the jargon of the Courts.——In that case—we might
dispose of the unlitigated part of the Manor[4] also—for what it would
fetch—and then we should know more exactly what to trust to.—
Ensure and assure Ly. B's life for £20000.—

> yrs. ever & truly
> N B

[TO LADY HARDY]   *Albaro. 1Obre. 1 o 1822*

My dear "Cousin (*not*) of *Buckingham* and sage grave Woman"[1] it
was my intention to have answered yr. letter sooner—but in the
interim yr. Chevalier arrived[2]—and calling upon me had not been two
minutes in the room (though I had not seen him for these nine years)
before he began a long story about you—which I cut short as well as I
could by telling him that I *knew* you—and was a *relative* and was not
desirous of his confidence on the subject.—He—however—persisted in
declaring himself an illused Gentleman—and describing you—as a
kind of cold Calypso—who lead astray people of an amatory disposition
—without giving them any sort of compensation—contenting yourself
it seems—with only making *one* fool—instead of *two*—which is the
more approved method of proceeding on such occasions.—For my part
—I think you quite right—and be assured from me that a woman who
—(as Society is constituted in England—) gives any advantage to a

---

4 Rochdale.
1 *Richard III*, Act III, scene 7: "Cousin of Buckingham, and sage, grave men."
2 James Wedderburn Webster.

49

man—may expect a lover—but will sooner or later find a tyrant.—
And this may not perhaps be the Man's fault neither—but is the
necessary and natural result of the Circumstances of Society which in
fact tyrannize over the Man equally with the woman—that is to say—
if either of *them* have any feeling or honour.—He (the Chevalier)
bored me so upon the subject that I greatly fear (Heaven forgive me
for you won't) that I said something about the "transmutation of hair"
but I was surprized into it—by his wanting to [swear?] me out that his
black wig—was the shock (or shocking) flaxen poodle furniture with
which Nature had decorated his head ten years ago.——

He is gone post to Leghorn in pursuit of you—having (I presume in
consequence of your disappearance) actually—(*no* jest I assure you)
advertised "for an agreeable companion in a post-chaise["] in the
Genoa Gazette.—I enclose you the paragraph.—Have you found any
benefit for your girl from the L[eghorn] Baths? or are you gone to
Florence.—You can write to me at yr. own leisure and inclination.—I
have always laid it down as a maxim—and found it justified by experience—that a man and a woman—make far better friendships than
can exist between two of the same sex—but *then* with the condition—
that they never have made—or are to make love with each other.[3]—
Lovers may [be]—and indeed generally are—enemies—but they never
can be friends—because there must always be a spice of jealousy—and a
somethi g of Self in all their speculations.—Indeed I rather look upon
Love altogether as a sort of hostile transaction—very necessary to
make—or to break—matches and keep the world a-going—but by no
means a sinecure to the parties concerned.——Now—as *my* Love perils
are—I believe pretty well over—and yours by all accounts are never
to begin;—we shall be the best friends imaginable—as far as both are
concerned—and with this advantage—that we may both fall to loving
right and left through all our acquaintance—without either sullenness
or sorrow from that amiable passion—which are it's [unnoble?] attributes.——I address this at hazard to Leghorn—believe me my dear
Coz

ever & affectly yrs.
N B

---

[3] Byron carried this thought into *Don Juan*:

> "No friend like to a woman Earth discovers,
> So that you have not been nor will be lovers."
> (Canto XIV, stanza 93).

[Note added to Italian letter of Lega Zambelli]
  D[ea]r S[i]r—I did not order the firearms—but will take them rather than plague you by returning them.—I want some *Russia* oil and the real good Arquebusade in *long* bottles—such as you sent me at first—and not this d————d trash—which I return.—I told you long ago that I wished the *former* quality or none.—You may draw on me for a hundred crowns at *Xmas*.—and for the remainder in J[anuar]y 1823, but not for more than 100 crowns at a time—as it makes *broken* money —& deranges my accounts—being no great Arithme[ti]cian.—Please to forward ye. enclosed letter to Lady H[ardy].

yrs. &c.
N B

[TO DOUGLAS KINNAIRD] *Genoa. 10bre. 9 o 1822*

  My dear Douglas,—I address to you a line of advice that I have received—signed—& will forward to *you* the deed for the Rochdale Tolls' purchase.——*You* can, if it seems fitting pay the money to Messrs. Hanson—when *their account* is duly examined and audited by the proper persons chosen for the purpose.—In the mean time— methinks the amount (i.e. the five hundred pounds) are quite as well in your hands as theirs.—I shall send the deeds by the diligence—or some of the E[ngli]sh Minister's Messengers—to avoid postage which is heavy upon parchments.——I have also to tell you that I have completed the 12th. Canto of D[on] J[uan] & will forward it when copied over fairly.—With the three first (6th. 7th. 8th. i.e.) in one volume— (as being the longest—) and the 9th. 10th. 11th. 12th.—in another— the whole may form two volumes—of about the same size as the two former.—But—I will correct the proofs of the whole when you send them to me.—Perhaps you had better publish one with one publisher and the other with another—it would be [a] new experiment—or *one* in one month—& the other in the next—or *both* at once?—what thinkest thou?—There are some good things in them, as perhaps may be allowed.——Are you not quite well yet?—I hope so.—I am selling two more horses—and dismissing two superfluous servants.—My horses now amount to *four* instead of *nine*—& I have arranged my establishment on the same footing.—So you perceive that I am in earnest in my frugalities.—

yrs. ever & affectly.
N B

[Fragment of a letter]

... very willing to lighten any losses—"Go to" (thou art "a fellow that hath had losses" like Dogberry[1]—is it not so) which you may experience from my becoming obnoxious to the Blue people.——I hope that you have a milder winter than we have here—we have had inundations worthy of the Trent or Po—and the Conductor (Franklin's) of my house was struck (or supposed to be stricken) by a thunderbolt.—I was so near the window—that I was dazzled—& my eyes hurt for several minutes—and every body in the house felt an electric shock at the moment.—Madame Guiccioli was frightened—as you may suppose.——I have thought since—that your bigots would have "saddled me with a Judgement" as Thwackum did Square[2] when he bit his tongue in talking Metaphysics—if anything had happened of consequence.—These fellows always forget Christ in their Christianity—and what he said when "the tower of Siloam fell".[3] Today is the 9th.—and the 10th. is my surviving daughter's birthday—I have ordered as a regale a mutton chop and a bottle of Ale—she is seven years old I believe.—Did I ever tell you that the day I came of age—I dined on eggs and bacon and a bottle of ale;—for once in a way—they are my favourite dish & drinkable but as neither of them agree with me—I never use them but on great Jubilees once in four or five years or so. I see some booby represents the Hunts and Mrs. S[helley] as living in my house—it is a falsehood—they reside at some distance—and I do not see them twice in a Month. I have not met Mr. H. a dozen times—since I came to Genoa—or near it.

yrs. ever

N B

[TO DOUGLAS KINNAIRD]   *Genoa. 10bre. 11 o 1822*

My dear D.—Yrs. of ye. 29 o to be acknowledged.—I am more glad to see your handwriting again—and to hear that you are doing well—than sorry for any hitch about the D[on] J[uan]s—of which by the way—there is a 12th. Canto ready—and to be forwarded when copied out fairly.—The *three* first in one vol. and the *four* next in another would form two vols of about the preceding size of M[urray]'s post Octavo's or foolscap Octavos—I forget the exact technicals.—

---

[1] *Much Ado About Nothing*, Act. IV, scene 2.
[2] In Fielding's *Tom Jones*.
[3] *St. Luke*, XIII, 4.

You ask "what is to be done"?—I really do not know.—Hunt has no capital and can't purchase a copyright—and as a matter of business it is always better to sell the Copyright.—Besides I would *not* come upon *him*—in case of his failing and therefore it is at a disadvantage that we should negociate with him.—As to division of profit, and reserving the Copyright—I never yet heard of this answering—at least to a writer. —The publishers generally contrive the Contrary.——

You can perhaps at leisure try amongst one or more publishers— for the purchase—and if we do not have an adequate & secure proposal —we will *not publish at all.*—In the latter case—keep the M.S.S. carefully—Murray has sickened me of *mislayments*—& bickerings about M.S.S. carelessly thrown by.—Three years ago—a certain Fairman[1] of Bond Street proposed of himself—to publish (on a misunderstanding with M[urray] being supposed) the D[on] J[uan]s—who or what he is I know not—except that he is of the profession yclept the trade.—I suppose that he is obscure. You can perpend—& look about—and if ever anyone is finally agreed with—the proofs must be carefully sent for correction to me wherever I may happen to be—supposing me in life, that is to say.—I have written to you on a good many subjects of business lately—and am anxious as ever to hear of ye. conclusion of ye. Mortgage—and ye. extrication from ye. funds.—Also what you think of my pacific legal proposition on the Rochdale law-suit enclosed to you some time ago.—I can not make a lawyer's defence for H[unt]—he must get that done by the technical people—there is ample scope for it.—

yrs. ever & affectly.
N B

P.S.—If a *fair proportionate* price for the 7 Cantos (in two vols.) is not to be obtained—they can be kept back—that is all—after a fair trial, you will be able to judge—I have ceased to be sanguine on the subject—but do not on that account choose to throw things away altogether.——As to "Werner" there is no hurry—and M[urray] will doubtless still less be in any—you can see by and bye how it succeeds (or not sells) and settle accordingly—if he loses I am willing to bear my part.——

---

[1] See March 9, 1821, to Murray (Vol. 8, p. 90). The name there was spelled "Fearman".

My dearest A.—Whatever mistake there may [be] about the Revd.
T. Noel's application[1]—arises from the less Revd. Member for Westminster[2]—his statement was such as I have represented it.—It is not
very likely that the collation—or translation or whatever the thing is
called of ye. Revd. T. N's living to his son on ye. decease of ye. parent
incumbent should occur in my time—(which I have no reason to
believe very long—since last Summer having never been quite right,—
but since *very temperate now* as once in my youth therefore not quite
wrong) and if it should—I do not know whether the voice potential
rest with Lady B[yron] or with me—I merely expressed a simple
opinion—for in my foolish notion of right and wrong I have always
thought Tom Noel unhappy—or unhappiest in being situated as dependent where by dint of a few words from infallible Church said over
his parental congress—he needed not have recurred to her for tithes—
instead of the nine remaining parts of ye. property.——In a word—to
make the Man's mind easy is the great point—(and it is much to make
any man's so—even for a moment) if an assurance on my part that in
the event of such opportunity falling into my way—& the son being an
eligible Clerical Character (easy enough in these times) I will give my
consent—or nomination & so forth—will please the R[evd.] T. N.—
Let him be gratified.—Always subject however to Lady B's approbation—what her power may be—I know not—being totally ignorant
of my own—but she is a better judge of persons than I am and I had
much rather that She made their livings than me.—But I like Tom—
though he *did* marry me—and I have often looked upon myself as an
usurper of his *natural* rights.—This—or as much as you think communi-
cable to Lady B—communicate—I really have no motive but to gratify
Tom The Clergyman—and *not* to oppose her—if she opposes I withdraw.——

There has been tell her a stupid story in the papers about the burial
of my poor little natural baby—which I directed to be as private as
possible; they say that she was to be buried and epitaphed opposite
Lady B's pew——now—firstly—God help me! I did not know Lady B
had ever been in Harrow Church and should have thought it the very
last place she would have chosen—and 2dly. my *real* instructions are in
a letter to Murray of last Summer[3]—and the simplest possible as well

[1] Thomas Noel, illegitimate son of Lord Wentworth, uncle of Lady Byron. See
letter of Oct. 12, 1822 to Augusta.
[2] Hobhouse.
[3] See May 26, 1822, to Murray note 2. (Vol. 9, p. 164).

as the inscription.—But it has been my lot through life to be *never pardoned and almost always misunderstood*—however I will go on & fight it out, at least till I survive (if it should be so) the few who would be sorry that they had outlived me.—The story of this Child's burial is the epitome or miniature of the Story of my life.—My regard for her—& my attachment for the spot where she is buried—made me wish that she should be buried *where*—though I never was *happy*—I was once less miserable as a boy—in thinking that I should be buried—and you see how they have distorted this as they do every thing into some story about Lady B.—of whom Heaven knows—I have thought much less than perhaps I should have done in these last four or five years.—

I have not read the book you mention nor indeed heard of it—but the out-cry against it seems to be one proof more of the hypocrisy of your people.——I am glad that *you* like "Werner" and care very little who may or may not like it—I know nothing yet of opinions about it—except your own.—The Story "the German's tale" from which I took it [ha]d a strange effect upon me when I read it as a boy—and it has haunted me ever since—from some singular conformity between it & my ideas.——You will have time to think of the project by Spring—& can then decide as you please—you must not believe the nonsense about the Hunts &c. residing with me—I do not see them three times in a month and they reside at some distance—and if you came to Nice and I went there—they would be probably in Tuscany—at any rate not near me.—The political circumstances of Count Gamba's family—I already explained to you—and that it is by the English minister's desire that *they* are now near me—as a protection to them for the present.—You would see nothing of them.—I must tell you an anecdote of *her*—the Sister and daughter of the Counts G[amba]—When Allegra died—as she—(the Countess Guiccioli) had left everything and was persecuted by her husband before the Pope—&c.—I wish[ed] to *bequeath* to *her* the same sum (5000 £) which I had left in my will to Allegra—but She refused in the most positive terms—not only—as she said—as a degradation to her—but injustice to Lady B[yron]'s daughter—& to your children.

yrs. ever,
N B

[TO JOHN CAM HOBHOUSE]   *Genoa. 10bre. 14 o 1822*

My dear H[obhous]e—Yrs. of Turin arrived yesterday. If Lady M[organ] arrives safely she will be received—but I suspect that the

Dogana will detain her.[1]—We are all in great surprize and displeasure at the Marchesa's[2] mancanza—which is the more extraordinary—as She is a particular friend of the Count G [amba](the father who gave the letter) who It is supposed went still further than Pius 6th. with her in their Gioventu—and as at this very time—as all along—she has been a staunch supporter of Me. Guiccioli's suit against her Sposo—still pending in appeal before his Papal Majesty.—Be this as it may—Count G[amba] writes to enquire and remonstrate.—She must have known you—as being herself a friend and what's more a witness of the late Queen's and must have heard your name—or even seen you in the course of that conflict of testimonies.——But we have had a complaint from Florence from Madame Regnier that you either did not—or would not avail yourself of your letter to Madame Regnier[3]—who says she would have been glad to see you.—By my own experience and that of all I ever heard of—I know what Italian introductions [are?];—the Stranger pays the visit—and invites to dinner—and perhaps the *visit* is repaid.—This is generally the case—unless you settle in a place—and then you may have enough of mummery and maccaroni —opera boxes—and conversazioni—(criminal ditto included) but a flying Stranger must take "Folly as it flies".[4]——

You ask after my health—it has been worse since I saw you—is better now—and may be better still—without being what Scrope used to call "rude Health".—I never quite recovered that stupid long swim in the broiling Sun and saline Sea of August.—At Lerici I was in my bed for four days—and it is not the best place for beds and physicians. —The Doctor made his debut by talking of Hippocratè—in consequence of which I sent him away—but the women being clamorous as usual—and myself as Fribble says in "exquisite torter"[5]—he was recalled and after several formidable administrations of medicines which would not remain in the stomach, and of glysters which could not be persuaded to quit it again,—Nature I presume did the business —and saved me from a threatened inflamation of the bowels—during which (by way of rocking my cradle) we had a slight shock of an

[1] Lady Morgan's *Italy* was published in 1821. Since then all her books had been proscribed in Italy.

[2] The Marchesa Sagrati. See Jan. 9, 1823, to Hobhouse.

[3] Probably the Madame Regny, who was a friend of John Taaffe. Artemesia Castellini, daughter of an Italian but born in Spain, married a Frenchman who later became financial adviser to Otto of Bavaria when he took the throne of Greece. She was an artist and a woman of culture and charm who had a wide acquaintance among painters and intellectuals of Pisa, Lucca and Florence. (See Cline, pp. 19–21).

[4] Pope, *Essay on Man*, Epistle 1, line 13.

[5] David Garrick's farce, *A Miss in Her Teens*, Act II, scene 1.

earthquake—such as we felt at Athens; probably an echo of that of Aleppo.—Well—I scuttled out of bed—the moment I was convalescent—got to Sestri by dint of rowing in twelve hours—and came on per terra—to Genoa the same night—verily believing that the journey did me more good than the physic or the physician.——All went on very well till about a month ago—when I had and have a cutaneous and very uncomfortable eruption—for which by the advice of an *English* Physician—I am taking what he calls *"a decoction of Woods"* (and of *Forests* too I should think by its variety of tastes) and I am so pleased with the name that I swallow a pint daily with more faith than effect hitherto.—

Since I have been here—I have seen Dick Fitzgibbon (Lord Clare's brother and your brother M.P.) Lady Hardy—and various of your Country people—and lastly that little and insane James Wedderburne Webster—now conceited into a knight (but of no order—a regular Address and City knight) yclept Sir James Wedderburn.——I saw little change in him except that his countenance rather more resembled his *back*side (do you remember Mr. Frank of the coffee-house's accentuation of that injured word) than heretofore——and that he had gotten a new wig—and says he means to marry—having a wife living from whom he cannot get divorced.——You will have heard before this reaches you that our friend D[ouglas] K[innair]d has had *another* fall from *another* horse—and thereby broke his collar-bone besides being grievously contused—but he is getting well—and I wish that he would choose his stud better.—I shall look in vain for such another Potestas of Attorneo—and still more vainly for a similar friend—that is to say—who could unite the power and the will to undergo the drudgery he has done for "P. P. Clerk of this Parish"——I trust that this will find you flourishing in speech as in health. I doubt if the Congressors will be so pacific as you anticipate.—Henry Hunt is out of prison[6]—and John Hunt is in a fair way of going into it—by what I hear—all you predicted has come to pass.—I have gotten myself into a scrape with the very best intentions (—i.e. to do good to these Sunday paper patriots) Murray hath behaved scandalously to them—too long to relate—Doug. will narrate as much as you care to listen to.—Leigh Hunt is discomposed because said Murray showed (and be d — — — d to him) a letter in which I qualified that illustrious Editor as "a bore" ——and I have offended everybody like the old man and his Ass—

[6] Henry ("Orator") Hunt (1772–1835) was a radical politician. He presided at the Manchester meeting in 1819 which ended in the "Peterloo Massacre" and was arrested and served a two-year prison sentence in connection with his part in the "rabble rousing".

what is to be done with mine?—Pray excuse this long epistle.—All here salute you with meridian cordiality,—remember me to Burdett and the Dougal—and &c. &c. believing me

ever yrs. & faithly.

N B

My dear Douglas/—Enclosed is the *12*th Canto of D[on] J[uan]— the 6. 7. 8th. will make one volume—the 9th. 10th. 11th. 12th.— another—*both* of about the same size with the two former published by Murray.—"What is to be done?" you say—I do not know—at the worst we are but where we are as far as regards these things—and luckily are in no violent hurry.——Murray long after the *"piracies"* offered me a thousand pounds (guineas) a canto for as many as I chose to write—you know how he has since shuffled out (*not* of *that proposal* —for it was too much—and I would not take advantage of it) and this *not* from fears about the sale—but bullied by the priests and the Government.—He is a dirty fellow as you will one day find out.—You recollect how he kept back the 4. 5. 6th. [3, 4, 5] and published them at last in a slovenly manner.—And yet they succeeded and are as good as the former—and as for these latter—I am clear that they are in no respect inferior.—Take care in showing them about that *copies* are not taken before publication—or we shall have some underhanded doings of the kind.—With regard to Hunt—he has no Capital—and what are his bills worth without a guarantee?—As to *accounting*—it never yet answered that ever I heard of.—There is a mystery in the craft of which these publishers only know the key.—You can try and obtain a fair proposal from some of the trade—if none is offered—it is but *not* publishing—or publishing on the half and half account at last.—— That Murray will intrigue and do all the mischief he can from hatred to the Hunts—and pique at me—is certain—& has been already seen—but I'll weave him a web before I have done with him.—You can keep the M.S.S. by you and be careful not to *lose* or mislay any part of them.—If anything is agreed upon I must revise and correct the proofs myself— they can be sent by the post as usual.—I am confident that you will like this as well as the others.

yrs. ever

N B

P.S.—I should be glad to know how H[unt] proposes to counteract the effect of the piracies—and as to accounting—the difficulty is that *no one* can understand a bookseller's accounts—when *Crabbe* published with *M[urray]*—M showed Moore an *account proving* that he had *lost* two thousand pounds by Crabbe—*now*—I fancy it is pretty well understood that in *fact* he *cleared* a good deal by Crabbe.——You can use yr. own Judgement and let me know what you think—presuming always (what may be but a presumption) that the 7 new Cantos are on the whole equal to the 5 former.——Suppose he (H[unt] or somebody else) was to publish *one Canto* a week—of the same size and paper to correspond with the various former editions; but this is merely a vision—and may be foolish enough for aught that I know.——Please to wafer and forward my letter to Mr. Hanson.——By the way *fifty* pounds is a large sum for *two* seals! you have seen the size by the impression—they are handsome to be sure—but let us have the *items*.

[TO DOUGLAS KINNAIRD]   *Genoa. Decr. 16 o 1822*

My dear Douglas,—Yours of ye. 5th. 10bre.——I am glad that you approve of the letter to Deardon—and think that it can do no harm.—If he is not indisposed—I am willing to refer the matter either to Arbitration—or to settle it (on your Judgement) between ourselves—that is by his in person or by a confidential friend treating with you as my representative.——I greatly regret the hitch about Lord Le Despenser's mortgage—are we never to get out of these tremulous funds?——I sent you answers at length upon the D[on] J[uan]s—also another Canto—the 12th. Canto—it would be preferable to have them published—if practicable—on many accounts—but how far you will meet with a favourable proposition is another and a doubtful question apparently—you can try—I do not think it would be advisable to publish with *H[unt]*—because firstly he has no capital—and 2dly. I *would not* come upon him if he failed.—As to "the Vision" never mind—they will find out it's merits by & bye——at present they are "tired of hearing Aristides called the just"—and besides the English are no great Athenians. You will perhaps—(when it is generally known amongst the *trade* as they call them that *you* have the seven new Cantos to dispose of—) have a proposition of some kind or other—and may choose which you think best—if we have not—why—we are but where we were.——

Of the ensuing half year in J[anuar]y—(from the funds) I do not require any notes (besides I have a superfluous letter of Credit of yrs. which I have no occasion to use) but merely let me know that you have this sum in bank—or any other from the Kirkby Estate (of which by the way you say nothing further i.e. upon Crabtree's report) and I will tell you what to reserve and what to pay—of course carry the insurance to £20000 without waiting to hear from me.———I have saved as I told you—this year three thousand three hundred pounds—that is to say—there is that surplus from what I received in the course of it—and there would have been much more—if I had not been a fool—and thrown away a thousand on a Schooner—and five hundred (whereof more than three on Mr. L[eigh] H[un]t) on needless expences.—I sent you last week the deeds (signed) for the Rochdale tolls—which please to forward & receive the am[oun]t—or rather *on* receiving the amount [convened?] for the purchase of said purchasers.—When Hanson gives in anything like an account you can let him have it—but I wish to know at least what he has had so many thousands *for*.—Also as I said before —on ye. 14th. inst. I sent you the 12th. C[ant]o of D[on] J[uan] which perhaps is equal to the former. Even M[urray] in the letter which I sent to you—allows that "in talent they have not been heretofore exceeded by me" that is something.—Of "Werner" I hear nothing except that you say that M[urray] has sold six thousand copies.—I have no wish to press him—nor is there any hurry—the price of the book and the extent of it's circulation will be yr. proper Guide when-ever you come to an arrangement on that topic.—I hope that he did not omit the preface and dedication to Goethe—the preface was essential— as explaining the story from which my work is taken.—

I am living very economically—have sold five horses—retain four have laid up my Schooner in the Arsenal and—dismissed some super-fluous servants.—I had calculated—that with the surplus of this year (now in Coffers) the 6000 and upwards (your computation) of the Kirkby and funds productions—that could you have sold the D[on] J[uan]s tolerably and "Werner" bore a decent value—I should not have had less on the whole then twelve or even fourteen thousand pounds—as it is there are 9000—aye nearly ten—i.e. 6465 (your own account of the year 1823 and quarter of 1822 from Kirkby *added* of *course* to my own from the funds) also five hundred pounds from the Rochdale tolls—and my saving of three thousand three hundred pounds.—From this of course must be deducted first the insurances— the remaining debt—and Hanson's remaining account—but I cannot decide what or how much I shall pay—till I know what we have to receive.—I will do my best to live on a thousand or twelve hundred pounds per annum till I have realized.—My present ordinary expences do not in fact amount to *half* that sum.—

Can't you sell—Webster's bond—(Hanson has it) with ten years interest due—(an excellent recommendation!) principal a thousand, interest five hundred pounds.—It hath a judgement—or a "Vision of Judgement" to it.—I would take almost anything for it.—After all— the D[on] J[uan]s *must* bring *something* even if less than expected— rating them by the former ones,—and "Werner" (in a few months) be not altogether unproductive—as it will be added by former purchasers to the former works.——Much of all this must be casual—& may be chimerical—but it is worth attending to—*Mind* the *insurances*—if it is a good year—I would carry them to 25000 even.——I shall be very willing to settle with Deardon—if he is at all practicable—but in all cases the will of the Gods must be obeyed.—Send me a *good Cocker*[1]— or the best Simplifier of Arithmetic—I cast up my household accounts —& settle them daily myself—and you cannot imagine the difference. —Enclosed is a slip of a note which please to present to Hobhouse— tell him also that I have written to Whitton. He thought proper to send Lady M[organ?]'s [book?][2] to me *here* from Turin—& has nearly gotten me into a scrape—although I positively desired him not.—I pray you to accelerate—or rather facilitate these subjects which I sub- mit to your experience—and it is not impossible (if they are adjusted) that we may meet in England some years sooner than we think.

ever yrs. & truly
N B

[TO DOUGLAS KINNAIRD]   1Obre. 19 o 1822

My dear Douglas—As you are convalescent—that is to say not quite well—but not ill enough to find yourself *not* ennuyè—I have less hesitation in writing frequently—because after having yawned suffi- ciently over present friends—you can fairly go to sleep over an epistle from the absent.—When you are once abroad again—haranguing— galloping—banking—and prospering—I shall have less chance of attention—but nevertheless I pray you—to "ride gently over the testicles" as Mrs. Matlock of Cambridge memory was wont in her improvement of language—to direct her Coachman in driving over the Stones.—One would think you had been breaking in my Pegasus—by the falls you have undergone.—Prithee—be careful—after a Man is turned of thirty—why should he ride a mad horse—except in case of

1 Edward Cocker (1631-1675) published his arithmetic in 1664. It went into more than a hundred editions and was still in the 19th century the most popular calculator for people who kept their own accounts. Hence the phrase "According to Cocker".

2 Perhaps *The Mohawks: A Satirical Poem* published in 1822. Lady Morgan was anathema to the Italian authorities because of her book *Italy* (1821).

war or woman? in all other respects a hackney—or other Coach—is more becoming his age and station.—I have been pondering over the late vicissitudes of our D[on] J[uan]s—I am not quite clear that if we had a proper security for the *accompts* being as correct as Cocker—it would not be the best plan of the two.—As for M[urray]'s intrigues—and R[idgway]'s demons—they are not worth a thought;—I tell you that the two most successful things that ever were written by me—i.e. the E[nglish] B[ards] and the C[hilde] H[arold]—were refused by one half *"the trade"* and reluctantly received by the other.

There are two or three ways to proceed.——1stly.—You can cast about and see if any proposition is made by these *tanners* of Authors—the Calf-skin and Morocco—and Muscovite publishers.—If eligible—you can decide;—when it is known you will probably have proposals. 2dly.—If not—we have always the option of stamping (an Italic phrase) upon the "touch and go" own account score——which is only objectionable in as much as it never yet succeeded—but it *may*—as Steam has—and balloons will.——3dly. If so concluded—we must have securities that said publisher or Author & Self's account—shall have his Arithmetic summed up and checked by the skilful in such affairs.—4thly. Are the D[on] J[uan]s subject to any laws? that is *your* laws?—which are somewhat of the queerest—and *is* my compact respecting them *binding* to the contracting party?——5thly.—If Mr. J[ohn] H[unt] publishes them eventually—his Son (if of age) ought to be comprized in the stipulation to render a fair account of "meum et tuum" quarterly to persons appointed by the Author for such purposes. —6thly. Some other ought to be bound—*not* for the assetts—but merely in case of nonfulfilment—to see and guarantee that the account (be it good—bad, or indifferent) is a fair and true one—for it is a difficult piece of Antiquarianism to decypher the Hieroglyphic of a publisher's balance—pro—con—or otherwise—or anywise.—I venture to throw out these hints to yr. Honour's Convalescence—but how far they may merit attention in yr. sickness or your health is left to your consideration——"and your petition shall ever &c. &c. &c.["]——

I am not very well—I suspect worse than you are—at least I hope so.—Ever since the Summer—when I was fool enough to swim some four miles under a boiling Sun at Via Reggio—I have been more or less ailing.——First my Skin peeled off—Well—it came again.—Then I had a fever and a portentious Constipation and inflammation which confined me to my bed in a bad Inn on a worse road.—Well—I thought I was well quit for the winter at least—but lo!—I have within this last month had eruptions and the devil knows what besides—so that I have

called in an English Physician—who hath decocted and concocted me—
"secundum artem" so that I am turned inside out but the malady still
continues—and is very troublesome.—I should think that it was the
itch—but that it don't infect anybody—and I might think that it was
something else—were it not for the same reason.———I am as temperate as an Anchorite—but I suspect that temperance is a more
effective medicine at twenty than at thirty and—almost five—Oh
Parish Register!—Oh Peerage why?—

>   Record those years that I would fain deny?[1]

I shall not trouble you further—and I merely do it now—as a
sleeping draught to your Collar-bone.——

You will have seen Hobhouse by this time—with his relations—
who I hope returned safely.—I had a letter from his brother dated 1821
introducing an Overland Gentleman from India—whom I wished back
again.—However I mounted on "tit-back for to ride" paid him a visit
up four hundred pair of stairs at a Genoese Inn—and came back again
half-frozen from politeness to an Equinoctial new acquaintance. Pray—
make this a merit to the Demag[og]ue,—it is all out of deference to the
M.P. who I hope gets on and neither suffers from Oligarchy—nor that
more severe Aristocracy—*Polly*-garchy—I don't mean from "πολλοι"
—to recur to the tondapemoibomenosity[2] [?] of our Alma [M]ater
(with her sour milk) but the regular petticoat regency of all wearers
of that magic garment.———I do believe that if women did *not* wear it
—their sway would be less—for few C – – – s come up to the previous
preconception—or pre-deception—while the Drapery is floating about
them like an Admiral's flag.——Here is a long letter—but you make
the reading as short as you like.——

>   yrs. ever & truly
>   N B

P.S. *Insure*! hast thou? at the Pelican? the Phoenix?—and all life
assurances whatsoever?

[TO JOHN MURRAY]   *Genoa. 10bre. 21st. 1822*

It is my hope that our concluding transaction should be an amicable
one—and I wish that it may be so still.—But I perceive by some ex-
tracts in a paper that you appear to have omitted contrary to my
repeatedly urged requests—both the *conclusion* to the preface (written

---

[1] Probably adapted from Crabbe's "Parish Register".
[2] A jocular compression of a phrase in Homer—"to him in answer spake".

last Summer—and carefully sent to you) referring to the E[dinburgh] R[eview] and also the inscription to Goëthe.[1]—If Mr. K[innair]d had it—you knew where to find it—you also knew my desire—particularly as you had already omitted it from before Sardanapalus—for which I reproved you—and yet you seem to have repeated the same omission. —Is this courteous—is it even *polite?*—I repeat to you that *no publisher* has a right to be negligent upon such subjects.—Here was *no parson* to bully you—nor Society to threaten you—that I know of.—And why omit the concluding part of the preface which was of great importance to *me* as giving a contradiction to a false statement of the *labour* employed on the composition of the preceding dramas.—I wrote to you lately also on another subject—that of the calumnies you have allowed to circulate in the papers on the subject of the funeral of Allegra.— You *knew* and *know* how desirous I was that the funeral might be private—and you also knew or might have known—that I had not the most distant idea that Lady B[yron] was a frequenter of Harrow Church—and to say the truth—though I have no reason to believe her a woman of much feeling—I should have thought it the last place—she should have frequented as every part of Harrow must have reminded her of one whom it had been better she should forget.—However had I known it—the infant would not have been buried there, nor would *I* myself (though it is the spot where I once and long wished to have had my ashes laid) now rest in my grave—if I thought this woman was to trample on it.—It is enough that she has partly dug it.——

I wrote to you some time ago on the subject of a poor woman (one of your writers) a Madame de Yossy—requesting you to apply to the literary fund for her—as she is in great distress.—I sent you her letter and address.—I have sent her three hundred francs—and I should expect that amongst your acquaintance of the literary fund—something might be done for her;—I know nothing of her personally except from her letter.—I remain

yr. obedt. & very humble St.

N B

P.S.—If you see Mr. Moore I would request you to tell him that I wrote *twice* to Passy—about the time of his departure—if the letters seem worth it—he can have them forwarded from Paris.——Replace at your best speed—the inscription to Goethe—and the addition to the preface—I also wish for my own satisfaction—for the *correct* and *complete* copy of the letter to the B[lackwood's] M[agazine].—I sent it back

---

[1] The dedication "To the Illustrious Goethe" appeared in *Werner* when Murray published it on November 23, 1822.

this year early in the winter—it was sent by *you* to me—and returned.—Do not force me to do disagreeable things—but in case of your non-attention I must not only write to Goëthe—but publish a statement of what has past between us on such subjects.——Why not tell me what were or are the objections to the inscription over poor little Allegra?[2] Was there anything wrong in it? Cunningham is known for a notorious hypocrite—I remember Lady B[yron] telling me that she had heard of (from a Lady Olivia Sparrow) or seen him—and that *her Lady B's* belief—was that he made his devotion subservient to his views of worldly advancement.—He is the same Coward who wrote to me that he did *not* intend some poem or other called De Rancy for a description of my character.—I never cared whether he did or not—but some review had frightened him—by hinting that he might as well have let me alone.—I merely answered his letter—(as I recollect at least) by a civil verbal message through Henry Drury.—The best answer to all these liars and slaves will be my letter to you on the subject of the interment—which contains also the Epitaph.—You can add—what is also true—from yourself—that I never was aware of Lady B[yron]'s residing at Harrow or frequenting the church.——

[TO DOUGLAS KINNAIRD (*a*)]   *Genoa. 10bre. 23d. 1822*

My dear Douglas—I enclose to you as my "adviser behind the throne" the enclosed letters from Messrs. Hanson & Mr. J[ohn] H[un]t.—I also acknowledge yours of the 10th.—And firstly of the first.—With regard to the minority annuities I must observe that Mr. Bellamy was *never security* on *my* account—the whole was a gross extortionate transaction—the principal has been more than paid by the interest for several years—and the fact is that the fellow was *the lender* (behind hand it is supposed) and not the Security—he never was servant to my mother—and I never saw him ten times that I know of. —Miss M[assingber]d's claim is in the same predicament—they had share and share—(she and her Mother that is) and I paid & paid till I had no longer the wherewithal to feed the Usurers—but "did thou not'st share? had'st thou not eighteen pence?"[1] as Mr. Shakespeare says,—what do they mean by starting up of a sudden at the end of ten years with a Cock and a Bull story?—You know well what all Minors'

[2] See Vol. 9, p. 164.
[1] *Merry Wives of Windsor*, Act II, scene 2: "Didst thou not share? hadst thou not fifteen pence?"

transactions of that sort must be and the hands into which they fall.—*Legal* claim—they have none nor any indeed in point of equity;—to settle with them on their own rascally terms—I will never agree—and to settle with them at all for some time to come is also not to be acceded to—till all other claims whatsoever are liquidated.—*Then*—perhaps—I may consent to some advance—but not till I have had a fair and equal statement—and balanced it with my own knowledge of the transaction.——

With regard to Mr. J[ohn] H[unt] you may by all means retain Scarlet or other able Counsel.—With regard to *how* far I am called upon for the expences—I propose to you the following considerations. —I advanced to Mr. L[eigh] H[unt] two hundred and fifty pounds in January or February 1822—& *since* about one hundred & fifty—nay nearly *three* hundred more—if I include furniture which I bought for him—the expence of his Journey (which *he would* take against my wish) to Genoa—& a bill I paid for him at Leghorn.—The day after his landing He came to me & Shelley on his brother's account—I could not furnish further cash at the moment.—He then asked for an M.S.— and I reluctantly acceded—particularly cautioning them *to omit* any *actionable* passages from "the Vision &c."—I even proposed to them to give up the notion of the Journal—L[eigh] H[unt] agreed—but J[ohn] H[unt] *would* publish it.—For my *own* share of "the Liberal" I have declined taking anything whatever for the present—and I have furnished them with "the Pulci" and "the new Mystery"—However I will be guided by what you please—and will even come to England— if *that* will remove the prosecution from *his* shoulders—and have desired his brother to *say* so.—The prosecution will at least help his Sale.——

As to the D[on] J[uan]s—he seems to hint—that *you* do not like them—you said to me that you *did*—& I remember you did not like the three 3—4—5—but you see that they succeeded as well as the first and second. I sent you the 12th Canto the 14th. inst.—You have now *seven* cantos—which will make two volumes.—If you think it can be done with Mr. J[ohn] H[unt] (the publication I mean) you can come to an agreement with him—he giving securities—that he and his *Son* Henry (if of age) will submit their accounts of the profits to proper referees of our choosing.—As to my writing a defence—that is lawyer's work— and I desired him to consult one before he published the vision &c.— —As to the D[on] J[uan]s they ought to be published immediately— that is—(after *I* have revised the proofs which should be sent accordingly) we must not allow ourselves to be bullied by gangs—whether of

Admiralty or Bridge-Street—"Arcades Ambo" "Murrays both".[2]—
—With regard to me—I am reducing my establishment—have sent
away for sale two more horses—and am about to dispose of a superfluous carriage or two—and various other useless books and furniture
—such as Snuff-boxes—trinkets &c. &c.—I repeat to you that no
proposition on the *Jew* annuities can be listened to till all others are
discussed—

yrs. ever & affectly.
N B

[TO DOUGLAS KINNAIRD (*b*)]   *Genoa. 10bre. 23d. 1822*

Dear Douglas—As the packet would have been too large I divide it
into two—i.e. two letters in each.—Remember to increase the insurance and assurance to *twenty* thousand forthwith.—

yrs. ever & truly
N B

P.S.—The Seven Cantos will make *two* vols—never mind M[urray]
& R[idgway?]—we *know* the one's motives—and the other is no
great things.——I tell you that E[nglish] B[ards] and the 1—& 2d. of
C[hilde] H[arold]e were refused by half the Craft and even *Crafty* in
London—although *no* demand was made.—Decide for yourself from
such premises—they *know nothing*.

[TO JOHN MURRAY]   *Genoa. 10bre. 25 o 1822*

I had sent you back "the Quarterly" without perusal—having
resolved to read no more reviews good bad or indifferent—but "who
can control his fate?"[1] "Galignani to whom my English studies are confined" has forwarded a copy of at least one half of it—in his indefatigable Catch-penny weekly compilation—and as "like Honour it came
unlooked for[2]"—I have looked through it.——I must say that upon the
whole—that is the whole of the *half* which I have read (for the other
half is to be the Segment of Gal[ignani]'s next week's Circular) it is

---

[2] See *Don Juan*, IV, 93: "Arcades Ambo . . . blackguards both", adapted from
Virgil's phrase. Charles Murray was an attorney for the Constitutional Association
of Bridge Street, which was active in bringing charges against John Hunt for
publishing Byron's *Vision of Judgment*. John Murray was publisher to the Admiralty.
[1] *Othello*, Act V, scene 2.
[2] *Henry IV*, Part I, Act 5, scene 2.

extremely handsome & any thing but unkind or unfair.[3]—As I take the good in good part—I must not nor will not quarrel with the bad— what the Writer says of D[on] J[uan] is harsh—but it is inevitable— He must follow—or at least not directly oppose the opinion of a prevailing & yet not very firmly seated party—a review may and will direct or "turn away" the Currents of opinion—but it must not directly oppose them.—D[on] Juan will be known by and bye for what it is intended a *satire* on *abuses* of the present *states* of Society—and not an eulogy of vice;—it may be now and then voluptuous—I can't help that —Ariosto is worse—Smollett (see Lord Strutwell in vol 2d. of R[oderick] R[andom]) ten times worse[4]—and Fielding no better.—— No Girl will ever be seduced by reading D[on] J[uan]—no—no—she will go to Little's poems—& Rousseau's romans—for that—or even to the immaculate De Stael——they will encourage her—& not the Don—who laughs at that—and—and—most other things.—But never mind—"Ca ira!"—And now to a less agreeable topic, of which "pars magna es"—you Murray of Albemarle St.—and the other Murray of Bridge Street—"Arcades Ambo" (*"Murrays both"*) et *cant*-are pares[5] —ye I say—between you are the Causes of the prosecution of John Hunt Esqre, on account of the Vision;—you by sending him an incorrect copy—and the other by his function.——Egad—but H[unt]'s Counsel will lay it on you with a trowel—for your tergiversifying as to the M.S.S. &c. whereby poor H[unt] (& for anything I know—myself —I am willing enough) is likely to be impounded.——

Now—do you see what you and your friends do by your injudicious rudeness?—actually cement a sort of connection which you strove to prevent—and which had the H[unt]s *prospered*—would not in all probability have continued.—As it is—I will not quit them in their adversity—though it should cost me—character—fame—money—and the usual et cetera.—My original motives—I already explained (in the letter which you thought proper to show—) they are the *true* ones and I abide by them—as I tell you—and I told L[eig]h H[un]t when he questioned me on the subject of that letter.———He was violently hurt —& never will forgive me at bottom—but I can't help that, —— I never meant to make a parade of it—but if he chose to question me—I could

<hr>

[3] Reginald Heber, preacher at Lincoln's Inn, later bishop of Calcutta, and author of some famous hymns including "From Greenland's icy mountains", reviewed *Sardanapalus, The Two Foscari, and Cain* in the *Quarterly Review* of July, 1822 (which appeared in October) with a mingling of high praise for Byron's genius and regret for his "degradation".

[4] See Feb. 12, 1823, to Kinnaird, note 1.

[5] Virgil, *Eclogue* VII, 4.

only answer the plain truth—and I confess I did not see anything in that letter to hurt him—unless I said he was "a *bore*" which I don't remember.—Had their Journal gone on well—and I could have aided to make it better for them—I should then have left them after my safe pilotage off a lee shore—to make a prosperous voyage by themselves. —As it is—I can't & would not if I could—leave them amidst the breakers.—

As to any community of feeling—thought—or opinion between L[eigh] H[unt] & me—there is little or none—we meet rarely—hardly ever—but I think him a good principled & able man—& must do as I would be done by.—I do not know what world he has lived in—but I have lived in three or four—and none of them like his Keats and Kangaroo terra incognita—Alas! poor Shelley!—how he would have laughed—had he lived, and how we used to laugh now & then—at various things—which are grave in the Suburbs.—You are all mistaken about Shelley——you do not know—how mild—how tolerant—how good he was in Society—and as perfect a Gentleman as ever crossed a drawing room;—when he liked—& where he liked.——I have some thoughts of taking a run down to Naples—(solus—or at most—*cum sola*) this Spring—and writing (when I have studied the Country) a fifth & sixth Canto of Ch[ild]e Harolde—but this is merely an idea for the present—and I have other excursions—& voyages in my mind.— —The busts are finished—are you worthy of them?—

yrs. &c.
N B

P.S.—Mrs. Sh[elle]y is residing with the Hunts at some distance from me—I see them very seldom——and generally on account of their business.—Mrs. S[helley] I believe will go to England in the Spring.——Count Gamba's family—the father—& Son—and daughter are residing with me—by Mr. Hill (the minister's) recommendation as a safer asylum from the political persecutions than they could have in another residence—but they occupy one part of a large house—and I the other—and our establishments are quite separate.——Since I have read the Q[uarterl]y—I shall erase two or three passages in the latter 6 or 7 Cantos in which I had lightly stroked over two or three of your authors—but I will not return evil for good.—I like what I read of the article much.—Mr. J[ohn] Hunt is most likely the publisher of the new Cantos——with what prospects of success I know not—nor does it very much matter—as far as I am concerned—but I hope that it may be of use to him—for he is a stiff sturdy conscientious man—and I like him—he is such a one—as Prynne—or Pym might be. I bear you no ill will for declining the D[on] J[uan]s—but I cannot commend yr. conduct to the H[unt]s.—Have you aided Madame de Yossy, as I requested?—I sent her 300 francs—recommend her will you—to the literary F[und] or to some benevolence within your Circles.—

[TO DOUGLAS KINNAIRD]   *[Post mark, Dec. 25, 1822]*[1]

P.S.—Since I wrote ye. enclosed I have seen Leigh H[unt] who knows no more what to think than I do—best for his brother about the D[on] J[uan]s——I enclose you a letter from Mr. J[ohn] H[unt] at the risk of double postage—which of course (as on all business) will be right to be charged to my banking account.——You may "try back the deep lane" of Pater Noster—and other rows—and—at any rate—we can but *not* publish.—and *not* publish as well without a fair prospect.—If there were any Guarantee for H[unt] or any other Man's keeping a true account of in the mysteries of publication I would say well—and good—but there is no instance in their annals—& without precedent we may distrust the future of those regular "on account of the Author".—J[ohn] H[unt]'s Copyright offer—we cannot accept—because he has no capital, and *if* he could *not* pay—nevertheless I would not persecute a poor man to make him poorer.—As to Murray's intrigues—and Ridgeway's paltriness—they may surprize you—but not me.——Murray will exert his whole chicane to ruin all publications of mine in which he is not concerned—but I'll fix him before we have done.—As to the rest—when I tell you that two or three booksellers refused the 1st. & 2d. Childe Harold—and no less than *ten* or *twelve* E[nglish] *Bards*—it will show you what their Judgement is worth.—When it is *generally* known that you have seven Cantos of the Continuation of a popular work to print in hand—mark—that this "will raise the waters".—At the worst it is but publishing on "own account" or not publishing at all, at least for the present. Is the prior part of the work read and re-read or no?—*You* can ascertain that — if it is—let it be merely understood that the remaining Cantos (supposing these as good in composition) will be for the fairest and you will have offers.—If not—I will set up a printing office of my own—and publish them in my own way.—Do not be discouraged—you see what a juggle the whole thing is—Murray selling 6000 &c. of Werner[2] and struggling

---

[1] This postscript probably belongs to the letter of December 11.

[2] According to the Murray Register of Nov. 1822 (Ledger B289), 5000 copies of *Werner* were printed and 4900 sold in the first year. The press received 18 copies and 82 were still on hand. The gross revenue was £940. 16. 0. The pro-

to prevent all other sales.—But I am sick of the subject and you will be more so—and rightly.——

I pray you do not neglect my various requests on the subject of business—especially as I only require my own—& not another's. If we can dispose of these M.S.S.—well—if not—patience—but all's well still.——I have as I said—a balance of three thousand three [hundred] pounds clear still of my own—at the end of the year i.e. two thousand seven hundred in your bank—and six hundred & thirty pounds in that of Messrs. Webb of Leghorn.—Of my own you will have something to receive in J[anuar]y—and of Lady B's I know not—when—but something something—some time or other.——Of this or these I want only the account—and that the surplus (*however small*) may be laid out at *low interest*—but *safe security*.——The remaining debt (but small by yr. statement) may be liquidated by degrees—according to the proportion received.——I can make my present surplus of three thousand three hundred last *two* years—perhaps *three*—so that the whole of this year—(i.e. 1823) may be allotted to liquidation of debt—or saving of income.——I have reformed my establishment—reduced my horses from nine to four—and will go still further if necessary.—Servants & Sundries have been reduced in proportion—it is my wish to keep floating in bank about a thousand or two for any emergency—and to devote the rest to the acquisition of a dependence.—I will discharge the remaining bet [debt?] only at the rate of two hundred paid per thousand received; this year 1823 if all had gone properly—I should have had between twelve and fourteen thousand—(the three thousand & odd surplus of this year included—) This would have discharged all debt and left a surplus of several thousands—as it is I will retrench—and may starve—perish—but—as far as human means can go in retrenchment—I *will* have—the proper over-plus—and enough to put out at interest as it should be; low but *safe*—so as not to look to paltry contingencies.—To this I entreat yr. attention—but *first get well*—I would rather be out of cash than out of the few friends I retain; the former may be replaced—but I have no funds which can re-instate the latter.—So Get thee weell—and look to your concerns—also when at ease don't forget those of yrs.

ever & truly
N B

---

duction cost was listed as £329. 15. 0 and £64. 18. 2 was spent on advertising. "Lord B. ⅔ profit", is given as £364. 15. 3 and "Mr. M ⅓ Profit", £182 7. 7. But Byron complained in numerous letters to Kinnaird that Murray had made no accounting, and he repeated many times that Murray had sold 6000 copies, apparently basing his figure on what Kinnaird had told him.

My dear Douglas—Since I wrote to you on ye. 23d. I have thought further over the matter—and *am* of opinion that Counsel should be retained (at *my* expence) in behalf of Mr. Jno. Hunt. Choose whom you & he think best—Scarlet—or Denman (*my* personal friend the latter is or was) or any other fit Advocate.——This will be delivered to you by Mr. John Hunt—I am further of opinion that the *seven* new Cantos of D[on] J[uan] ought to be published *immediately*—(*the proofs* however to be sent first to & corrected by *me*) but *who* the publisher is to be or on what conditions—I must leave to you to decide—as it may perhaps be already settled before this arrives. If it should not—pray—decide in some way——Mr. H[unt] and his *Son* (if of age) ought to give guarantees that the accounts shall be subject to all pro[per] investigation previously [to] their being past,—the [Copy]right to remain with the author—and the *profits* to be settled on a fair basis.—

yrs. ever & affectly.

N B

My dear Douglas—I have received the enclosed letter from young Hanson—and shall refer him to you for an answer.—If you think the proposed mortgages eligible—we can agree.—I have also yrs. of the 17th.—I am willing to retain Counsel (at my expence) and the best going—for Mr. J. Hunt.——I am also willing to be *both ostensible* and *responsible* for the poem—and to come home and face the consequences on the *Author*—though I did *not* wish the publication of the V. and indeed particularly warned him to pause—or erase passages likely to be obnoxious.—But I never said nor say—that he is to have *the profit* of what I have written—meaning I suppose the unpublished D[*on*] *Juans*—on the contrary I have particularly prescribed to you the *terms* on which it is to be published.—All this outcry is merely *temporary*—it's very violence will defeat itself—and shows the alarm & weakness of those who use it—but be this as it may—I will not be bullied—and I would rather come home to be calumniated & persecuted than receive the adulations of a dastard and slavish people.—Such I think you.—With regard to "the Liberal"—I merely said that I should not call on him for any accounts on *my* behalf—till the profits (if ever) became sufficient to make him and his brother comfortable—but that *then* I would or might receive a decent proportion, according to the value of the articles contributed.—I also *reserve* to *myself* the copy-right of my own articles—that they may afterwards form a volume—(if I like) to class with those published by Murray—for which Mr. H[unt] may or may not treat—as hereafter may seem good.—With regard to the D[on] Juans I wish them to be published—and *soon*—(now that they bully, the Slaves!) but with all due precaution that the publisher *accounts* for the profits periodically and fully and fairly—including the 12th. Canto sent on the 14th. They will form *two vols.*—*Three* in the first—and *four* in the second.—For "the Liberal" as I said—I have no present call on Mr. J[ohn] H[unt] and I will fee Counsel in his behalf—choose the best—& I repeat that if he will give me up instead—*I* will come and face it.—

I am very glad of old Goëthe being pleased having a great esteem and admiration of that illustrious patriarch of European Letters.—I am also pleased that Mr. Deardon will come to some explanation on the Rochdale business—if he will go to *Arbitration*—I *choose Burdett*—which I presume is the highest Compliment which I can pay to *my* opinion of his conduct on the late Arbitration.—My anger with the the lawyers & *trustees* had nothing to do with the Arbitrators.—If Burdett will accept—it will save time—that he should do so without my writing to him—as a month would be lost by the post.—If he will *not*—I know not whom to choose—*you* are my trustee &c. &c. Hobhouse is just & shrewd—but he has too little sympathy for any thing but politics—to enter into private affairs heartily and I have no other friend able or willing that I know of.—As I said before—I am very willing to terminate the suit—Mr. D[eardon] will perhaps give a fair explanation of the value of the points litigated—which you may verify by other means——is there no way—by which either in disposing of my part of the Manor—or of having it *surveyed*—and working the *whole* in *partnership* with him—he making some sacrifice also on his part—of uniting the concern—& healing all differences? I should be willing to make some outlay—were there any prospect of the collieries (of the unworked portion) being a safe and moderately profitable concern—I hope that you will do all that you can to bring the matter to a termination—I assure you and Mr. Deardon also—that I am *"bona fide"* in earnest—and would rather have him for my friend than triumph at his material expence.——

In the mean time I am reducing my expences—selling horses carriages &c. &c.—I *have* (as I told you I should probably) saved rather better than three thousand three hundred pounds to begin the year with—which is *three hundred* more than I calculated upon—and probably *three thousand* more than you did.—This with the new year's income (if realized) will be upwards of Nine thousand pounds—add five hundred pounds for the Rochdale tolls which I transmitted to you lately—and say—I know not what—but something surely for Werner —and the 7 Cantos of the D[on] J[uan]s—& we ought to be able to face the current expences.———Of the *new Jew* claim started by Bellamy & Massingberd—as was said before—I neither recognize the legality—nor the equity—whenever all other and *just* claims are settled—I may be disposed to make them a *moderate* advance by way of arrangement—they have already had more than the principal.—— And why start up *now* at the end of eight or nine years? I remember their telling me that If I would make a certain advance—I should hear no more of Miss M[assingberd]—old [Fozard?] of Pimlico was her envoy—I *did* make the advance—and now they are trying again.—I will allot a portion according to our net receipts for the gradual extinction of the *just* claims—Baxter's as a bond debt is first—& the whole or a portion should be liquidated this year.—Also a portion of each of the others—I mean those *you* stated—& *not* the new Jews.——[1]

As I have more money here than is actually required—if you will invest a thousand pounds for me in Exchequer bills or on other *low* but *safe* and easily re-convertible in to Cash Security I will return you Circulars for the amount.—Your letter of Credit I shall not use except in case of some unexpected emergency.—I have still at the present writing two thousand seven hundred pounds of your Notes in my hands—and six hundred and thirty pounds in bank at Mr. Webb's Leghorn. Thus—if our receipts (including what I have saved i.e. three thousand three hundred pounds) be nine thousand pounds for the ensuing year—adding the income of this I can pay off debt to the amount of two thousand—spend twelve or [fourteen] hundred—(I hope less) and save the rest—and *invest* it as it arrives in Exchequer bills at interest.—You see that neither the Rochdale tolls—nor Werner—nor the D[on] J[uan]s are included in this estimate.—I am particularly anxious that you should begin immediately to *invest* some of my monies—the interest however trifling—would be something— and the *bond debt* is my only debt bearing interest—and can be reduced or liquidated in the course of the year.—Of course the insurances are first to be considered—carry them up to twenty thousand or twenty five thousand.—And pray do what you can with Deardon—I am ready

[1] For a clarification of the complexities of Byron's debts and financial situation see Doris Langley Moore, *Lord Byron: Accounts Rendered.*

to refer the affair to Arbitration—or settle it on amicable terms without
—as soon as I know the *real state* of the case.—

Yrs. ever & truly
N B

[TO DANIEL ROBERTS?]   *Decr. 30, 1822*

Mr. Trelawny never arranged anything with me on the subject of
Frost—*subsequent* to the sequestration,—on the contrary what he said
was rather in favour of *Bees*.—I have also to add that it was in consequence of Mr. Trelawny's *former* representations of the *very bad
conduct* of *Frost* towards himself—that I did not allow him to retain the
dress—as well as Gaetano and the boy.—*Bees* was impertinent and I
treated him accordingly—but Frost was not so to *me* at least—but I
had such an account of him from Mr. T.—as did not in my opinion
entitle him to any indulgence on my part.

N B

[TO CHARLES HANSON]   *Genoa. 10bre. 30th. 1822*

My dear Charles—I also was about to write to you on the subject of
the mortgages—In the mean time I receive your letter.—I have forwarded it to Mr. Kinnaird to whom I refer you—and can only say—
that if *he* thinks the proposition [is eli?]gible—I shall be very w[illing]
to close with it—but do pray be a little quicker than usual as a lawyer
—and it may be better for us all—. . . .

[TO DOUGLAS KINNAIRD]   *Genoa—J[anuar]y 1 o 1823*

My dear Douglas—The enclosed letter from Mr. Hanson—with the
Counsel's opinion which it contains is for serious consideration.—The
business must, I doubt, go before the Chancellor.—Of course you conceal nothing from me—but it is strange that you have never lately even
alluded to *Crabtree*[1]—although your letters before yr. accident were full
of him and his promised report—and *promising* statement—neither of
which have appeared.——May I hope that we can settle with Deardon
—I am willing to go to Arbitration—(Burdett being mine if he accept
—or if not—Sir William Grant—the once Master of the rolls) or by

[1] Crabtree was an agent recommended by Kinnaird to look into the Rochdale
business affairs.

some arrangement so as to unite the manor and collieries—in *partnership* with Mr. Deardon—(on proper guarantees) and work *over* or rather *under* the *whole*—after a proper survey.——It was surveyed some years ago—& favourably reported upon, if money could be advanced in outlay.—Or I would sell the remainder of the Manor—at a Valuation—on Deardon making some sacrifice on his part.—Or—what you think fair.—Let me have proofs of the 7 D[on] J[uan]s. I shall greatly extend the preface—and say some grand things.—Retain Counsel for Mr. J. H[un]t on my guarantee—believe me

yrs. ever and truly
N B

P.S.—I have written to you lately a good deal on business—which I hope arrived safely.—

[TO R. B. HOPPNER]   *Genoa, J[anuar]y 2d. 1823*

My Dear Hoppner—Your friend Mr. Ingram[1] called on me some time ago, and gave me a tolerable account of you and Mrs. Hoppner, to whom I present my respects. I have had letters from Cicognara[2] and Aglietti[3] on the subject of subscribing to Canova's monument, and have answered in the affirmative, but am undecided to *what amount*, being afraid of giving too much or too little, as it might disgust the Subscribers or the Subscribees, to err on either side. I should like to hear your consular opinion.

I think (if I mistake not) that you received from [illegible] or [illegible][4] some Turkish articles (a dozen in number) and six telescopes (of which I have received *two* since), now four, which you were good enough to take care of for me in my absence. As my return to Venice is very problematical, I could wish you to dispose of them for what they will fetch, and remit the same; they are quite unused and therefore as good as new, and I should think not unlikely to be marketable for the Trieste or Levant trade, as I originally brought them out with the intention of proceeding to Turkey, where they would have served as acceptable presents to the natives.

I do not know that any acquaintances of yrs are here except the Ingrams (I believe you do not know the Guiccioli) and Mrs. Shelley,

---

[1] See May 11, 1821 (Vol. 8, p. 113).

[2] Conte Leopoldo Cicognara. See Oct. 28, 1822, to Cicognara.

[3] Dr. Francesco Aglietti, a famous Venetian physician with whom Byron had been on friendly terms in Venice.

[4] Probably Missiaglia or Siri and Willhalm, Byron's Venice bankers.

who is living at some distance. I see very little of her—about once a month. She is staying with the Hunts, friends of Shelley's, but I see very little indeed of either. Shelley left me his executor, but his will is not at present available, if indeed it ever will be, and his father Sir Timothy will do nothing for the widow as yet, so that it is difficult to decide what is to be done,—she will probably return to her father in the Spring.

I am staying at Albaro on a hill overlooking Genoa, cold & frosty but airy,—only *one chimney* in the whole house, which is spacious enough for twenty. I had been very unwell, but am better and hope to continue so—at least I am temperate enough—much more so indeed than in Venice, where I did not exceed in my eating department, but I find that the greater the abstinence, the better the health. An old, but not often regarded truism. I should have written to you before but I thought that the Congressors would occupy your whole time, and Mrs. Hoppner's toilet. I hope we shall meet again some day and that you will be merry and I be wise. Believe me

ever & truly yrs
NOEL BYRON

P.S.—If you go to Switzerland this Spring, I would make an effort to meet you there.

[TO DOUGLAS KINNAIRD]   *Genoa—Jy. 6 o 1823*

My dear Douglas—You are "a broth of a boy"[1] for business.——
I do not see how or why the reference of the Counsel's opinion to the Arbitration should necessarily conduct to a Chancery Suit—because it may or may *not* happen that I should have no wish to *act* upon that opinion—but I have a natural curiosity to have all possible information on the subject.——I am very glad to hear that anything has been done with Deardon towards an adjustment.—But please to recollect that They & We should be *speedy*—as the Cause will come on next Session —what is to be done—or proposed to be done should be in train therefore without further delay.—You have not sent me the promised communication from *Goëthe* which I would willingly see.—You talk of the *half* year's rent due at Michaelmas—that is *three* thousand pounds—of this do *we* receive half—or only a quarter—or what?—The ensurances are heavy—but these are paid now—for nearly a year I believe—it is a

1 A colloquial Irish expression: the essence of what a boy should be; a downright good fellow.

heavy but expedient deduction.—I trust that Hanson's bill is not to be *taxed*—by a Gentleman of *his nomination* only.—I trust that you have all the *receipts* & necessary documents of all payments made since the Sale of N[ewstea]d—that we may not be come upon *twice*—by the same claimants of any kind.——

I have so far succeeded in my economy as to have saved *three* thousand three hundred of the year 1822—and of this I think of remitting a thousand back to England——I wish my superfluous [moneys?] (however inconsiderable) to be placed at interest—on some safe but *convertible* security—at a moderate interest—on condition of the principal being readily recoverable.—I have reduced and am reducing still further my establishment and expences[.] I presume that "Werner" will be worth something—and even the D[on] Juans—be it small or great—I do not feel disposed to relinquish whatever may arise from them.——If you will put a thousand of *my present* money—(i.e. of 1822—the three thousand so often alluded to) out at usance—I will remit to you the Circulars of your bank—for the amount—untouched.——You may depend on my using every exertion *short* of *sordid*—to continue the temperate system which I have lately adopted —and I hope that you will second me at home.—I think you will allow that the better half of the year 1822—I have been not unsuccessful— thus far at least.—Believe me

ever & truly yrs.
N B

P.S.—I am much pleased with what you say of Crabtree—but I trust that he will not delay on account of the Suit.

P.S.—Please to read and forward the enclosed to Charles Hanson.— I think you will approve of part of it.—I pass everything through *you* —that you may *know* it—as it is useless to consult a friend—and conceal anything at the same time.——

[TO SIR TIMOTHY SHELLEY] *Genoa, Jan. 7, 1823*

Sir,—I trust that the only motive of this letter will be sufficient apology, even from a stranger—I had the honour of being the friend of the late Percy B. Shelley, and am still actuated by the same regard for his memory and the welfare of his family—to which I beg leave to add my respect for yourself and his connections. My Solicitor lately made an application to Mr. Whitton a gentleman in your confidence, in favour of Mr. Shelley's Widow and child by his second marriage both being left by his untimely death entirely destitute.

My intimacy with your late son and the circumstances to me un-known 'till after his decease—of my being named one of the Executors in a will which he left but which is of no avail at present—and may perhaps be always unavailable—seemed to justify this intrusion through a third person. I am unwilling to trouble you personally, for the subject is very painful to my feelings and must be still more so to yours—I must now, however, respectfully submit to you, the totally destitute state of your daughter-in-law and her child, and I would venture to add—that neither are unworthy your protection. Their wishes are by no means extravagant, a simple provision to prevent them from absolute want now staring them in the face is all that they seek—and where can they look for it with propriety—or accept it without bitterness—except from yourself?

I am not sufficiently aware of Mr. Shelley's family affairs to know on what terms he stood with his family, nor if I were so should I presume to address you on that subject. But he is in his grave—he was your Son—and whatever his errors and opinions may have been—they were redeemed by many good and noble qualities.

Might I hope, Sir, that by casting an eye of kindness on his relict and her boy it would be a comfort to them—it would one day be a comfort to yourself, for if ever he had been so unfortunate as to offend you, they are innocent; but I will not urge the topic further and am far more willing to trust to your own feelings and judgment, than to any appeal which may be made to them by others.

Mrs. Shelley is for the present residing near Genoa—indeed she has not the means of taking a journey to England—nor of remaining where she is without some assistance. That this should be derived from other sources than your protection, would be humiliating to you and to her—but she has still hopes from your kindness—let me add from your Justice to her and to your Grandchild.

I beg leave to renew my apology for intruding upon you, which nothing but the necessity of so doing would have induced, and have the honour to be,

Your most obedient, Very humble Servant,
NOEL BYRON

[TO JOHN HUNT] *Genoa. Jy. 8 o 1823*

Sir—I have written more than once to Mr. Kinnaird—to sanction his employment of the best Counsel in your defence—and I forwarded a note to the same Gentleman (to the same purport) to your brother.—

This he was to enclose to you in his own letter—and you were to have the goodness to deliver it in person.—I understand but little of the jargon—but you have every thing to apprehend from the abuse of these factions.———I offered to your brother to stand the trial instead—& to go over to England for that purpose—but he tells me that this would be of no use to you—nor would probably be permitted by the Gang.[1] With regard to the arrangements for the publication of the D[on] J[uan]'s—Mr. Kinnaird is my trustee in all matters of business.—I am not very sanguine on the subject—and would not have *you* to be so— for you must be aware how violent public opinion is at this moment against myself—& others—besides the combination against you which you may expect from "the trade" as it is called.———I sent a 12th Canto to Mr. K[innaird] on the 14 of Dec. 1822. The whole *series* would form two vols. of the same size as former ones—and I ought to have the proofs soon—that they may be correct or at least corrected.[2] —With regard to "the Liberal"—perhaps towards the middle of the year you might collect any pieces of mine from the past numbers—and republish them in a volume correspondent to my other works.—How far such a plan may be useful—I know not at present, but I trust that no time will be lost. Mr. K[innaird] is providing you with the best Counsel—and seeing the question at least *fairly* tried—it is an important one in a general point of view—or there is an end of History. *Southey's* vision ought to be cited in your defence—and also it ought to be *stated how* the obnoxious passages (at least some of them) came to *remain* in the published text.—But all this is for yr. Counsel's consideration.— Let them lose no time.—I have the honour to be

very truly yrs ever &c. &c.

N B

P.S.—The principal object for you in "the Liberal" is to employ good writers and to pay them handsomely. I have no personal objections to any Gentleman you may wish to engage—nor if I had—would I allow such to weigh with me a moment—when it can be of service to you.—

---

[1] The Constitutional Association.

[2] While Byron was still hesitating to give the publication of *Don Juan* to John Hunt because he had no capital to pay for the copyright, he nevertheless requested him to set up the cantos in type so that he could read the proof. This Hunt was willing to do, for he rightly conceived that it would eventually lead to his being the publisher.

[TO JOHN CAM HOBHOUSE]   *Genoa. Jy. 9 0 1823*

My dear Hobhouse—I have written to you once at some length since I heard from you at Turin—and I now enclose you the Sagrati's[1] letter in answer to that of C[ountess] G[uiccioli] on the subject of your introduction;—the latter part alludes to Madame G[uiccioli]'s differences and law-suit with her husband.—You will see by [it] what she says of her illness &c. which occasioned her not seeing you.——I hope that you are arrived and flourishing—pray—let me hear from you—

yrs. ever & truly
N B

[TO LEIGH HUNT]   *Jy. 10th. 1823*

Dear H.—It appears to me that your brother might direct his Counsel to cite from "Wat Tyler" and ask *why that* is not prosecuted? Also a little from *his* Vision.—And it would be as well to send off your *Collectanea* quickly that they may have time to prepare them for the Court and Courtiers.—I have sent to Mrs. S[helley] for the benefit of being copied—a poem of about seven hundred and fifty lines hight— the Age of Bronze—or Carmen Seculare et Annus mirabilis—with this epigraph—"Impar *Congressus* Achilli".[1]—it is calculated for the reading part of the Million—being all on politics &c. &c. &c. and a review of the day in general—in my early English Bards style—but a little more stilted and somewhat too full of "epithets of war"[2] and classical & historical allusions[;] if notes are necessary they can be added.—If it will do for "the Liberal" it and the Pulci will form (in size that is) a *good* half number.—But of this you can judge.—It is in the heroic couplet measure—which is "an old friend with a new face["].[3] I congratulate you on the weather.

yrs. ever
N B

[1] See Dec. 14, 1822, to Hobhouse.

[1] This motto, possibly adapted from Virgil (*Aeneid*, I, 475), meaning that the Congress of Verona was an empty menace, was on the title page when John Hunt published the poem.

[2] *Othello*, Act I, scene 1.

[3] Possibly a proverbial saying. John Wilson ("Christopher North") used it as a pseudonymous signature for some of his savage reviews in *Blackwood's Edinburgh Magazine* in 1821. But Byron quoted the phrase as early as 1807 (see April 16, 1807, to Long. Vol. I, p. 115).

Dear W.—I have not been unwell seriously—but I am at present so tormented with chilblains—as to be nearly unable to move.—None of the books you wish are in my possession or they should be at your service—but I have two of your own (the translation of O'Meara)[1] which after a month's delay and *three* livres expence—(for the binding —and not dear—for they are decently bound) your Genoese Abbé or whatever he was at length forwarded.—I suppose that he handed them to his friends till tired—& then condescended to direct them to their owner's temporary destination.——I should be glad to detain them a little longer, for they are in great request with all natives of my acquaintance—although all the principal part is omitted in the translation.—I will send down for you if you are disposed to venture into this Arctic region—my own *chilblains* (*fact* I assure you) defy Opodeldoc and Turpentine—and seem f[or the] moment as effectual as [paper torn] in making me a fixture [here.?] However the first practicable day —I shall essay to mount on horseback—believe me

very truly yrs.
N B

My dear Hoppner—"Your fault"—*no*—nor anybody's fault that I know—except that of my own laziness, which pardon.—I saw Ingram & a brother Consul of yrs. a day or two ago—and Mrs. Ingram has promised me a *minced pie*—a dainty I have not seen these seven years. ——I am waxed a good deal thinner within the last year—for I made myself ill swimming—and have since been obliged to be temperate even to abstinence.——Your letter has saved me several louis for I shall modestly regulate my subscription by the precedent of those wary diplomatists whose conduct I applaud.—That is to say I will give about the same with any Individual of that cautious corps.—With regard to the watches and telescopes I do not remember the exact price—but you can have them valued by two or three rogues—so as to get at a modicum—and dispose of them for me as you best can,—we must do as well as we can and at any rate be content.—The telescopes by the famous Berge or his successor cost from five to six guineas each—and the watches I cannot even guess at, but they will be more

---

[1] *Historical Memoirs of Napoleon*, 1815. Translated from the original manuscript, by B[arry] E[dward] O'Meara, 1820.

easily estimated.—They are only for the Levant market—as you will see by the figures.—I hope Canning will do what you desire—I am not at all sorry that *he* is in power—for he is worth all the rest in point of talent—and of course will hardly be fool enough to go very far wrong. —I write to catch the post—with my best remembrances to Mrs. H. believe me

ever & truly yrs.

N B

[TO I. INGRAM]   *Albaro. Jy. 16 o 1823*

Dear Sir,—I have made a sumptuous meal on your minced pies— which were worthy of the donor and of his table. I congratulate you on your Cook.——Seven years have elapsed since I saw a minced pie— and time and distance had not diminished my regret for those absent friends to "a merry Christmas and a happy new year"—both of which I augur for you and your family, although the congratulation for the former is somewhat of the latest.—I sent you by your messenger— "Bracebridge Hall" Irving's recent work—which is I believe equal to his former—and both good in their way—and deservedly popular.— The Countess D'Ison[1]—(is that the name?) has sent me Madame Saluzzo's poesies—I shall thank her soon—but I am a reluctant letter-writer—and an epistle in a foreign tongue is no diminution of the difficulty in replying.—If you see the Lady will you present my respects—and say for me—that I shall acknowledge her gift as speedily as a lazy being can.——I have the honour to be

your obliged & very faithful humble Servt.

NOEL BYRON

[TO LEIGH HUNT]   *Genoa. Jy. 16 o 1823*

My dear H—Your parody is *super*excellent—I hope that it will be in time—and I shall desire Lega to ensure it at the Post Office.—— *Don't fag* yourself too much—but take care of your health—as I have sent (with the Age of Bronze) what will be sufficient with the English and Italian Pulci for about eighty or a hundred pages of [the] next Number—you can [send only?] a little on your own—[& let] your home friends pull a little for the present.——I send you Pope—and Warton's essay also—it is perhaps better as more condensed than his Notes to the formal Edition.—Will you tell Mrs. S[helley] that the

1 The Contessa Borgarelli d'Ysone. See letter of June, 1823, to the Contessa.

Compass—turned out *not* to have been our late friend S[helley]'s but to have always belonged to the other vessel—or I would have sent it—but there are some of his books here which I will look out and send.—

yrs. ever & truly

N B

Genoa. Jy. 16 o 1823

My dear Douglas—Your letter is very kind (of the 3d.) and full of what Braham calls "Entusimusy" and I need hardly say how sincerely I feel it.——I trust that I can bear *their* applauses (if they can be called so in the bloom of a three days dawning) no worse than their opposite —perhaps both are of equal value—though it is difficult for a man to think so—and folly to pretend it if he does not.—I am afraid that Prosperity is likely to prove a man's greater temptation of the two—especially on Authors.——I have perused Mr. D[earden]'s statement with some attention.—Of course it must be taken "cum grano Salis" particularly on coming from an Adversary—and being quite contrary to other accounts.[1]—But this does not diminish my wish to accommodate the business—by ending the litigation.—Neither *he* nor *I* can be proper Judges of the value—nor fit Surveyors of the part in or out of litigation.—The value of the unlitigated part—a Manor of 40–000 Acres —over uninclosed ground—depends also in some measure on the part to be alloted to the Lord of the Manor—in case of enclosure—and you know that they cannot enclose without his Sanction.——This has been represented to me as not an *inconsiderable consideration.*——

The Statement of the Suits is also garbled—I beat him—at Lancaster —and in the Court of King's Bench out and out.—He says he offered to give up the property on being repaid his purchase money (about two thousand pounds more or less) would he *do so now?*—He has uniformly refused to account for or state the profit of the last twenty five years— the time from which the *claim* relates—as the years prior to 1798 (i.e. from 1794 to 1798) are not litigated on our part.—But as I said before —I merely state this "en passant"—you can get some accurate information—have the whole honestly surveyed by chosen people, and put an end to the lawsuit if possible.—I repeat that I would rather take Mr. Deardon by the hand—(at some expence)—than go on with bickering lawsuits—which embitter every thing—and every body.——

As to Hanson['s] account—I trust that the Mr. Metcalf of *his*

[1] Of the value of the Rochdale property.

choosing—is not to be the *sole* referee—and I also expect that his *whole* account from 1812 is to be submitted to strict investigation.—It is strange that he *never* names his *bill*—but *always payment*—when he writes to me—what can I think of this? a *careful man* would be anxious to have his *items* canvassed—or at least inspected.——As to the Kirkby referee—I have written to you about [it?] fully—enclosing Hanson's letters &c. &c. &c.—I have come to no decision on the subject but would rather settle it amicably.——Besides I have enough of regard for a friend's advice and my own interest to prefer good counsel (not at law) to a Chancery Suit at any time.——Also, in literary and copy-right matters—you are the lad to deal with the worldlings—and I do not recollect that I have ever appealed from your advice on those points either.—I may have stated what I thought points for consideration—but—perhaps I am refining too much—for I suppose both Murray and the Kirkby Proceeds are likely to prove sufficiently illusory.—Of this you should be the best judge—is the deceased Lady Noel also to eat up a *whole* year? as well as a half year?—She died in January and supposing her Appetite to last till August there ought still to be 1500 in January—for the remaining half year—this would make added to the former—

Kirkby	3168
My own	2715
From Murray	2100
Supposed Surplus of my own of this year	2000
Half year *not* devoured by the defunct	1500
	11483

Indeed by rights—Murray ought to pay more than 2000 g[uinea]s it ought to be three—or two thousand five hundred—but as this may depend upon a mere caprice of the public or the bookseller—and the other upon Lady B[yron]'s life—it would be idle to calculate upon either.—Suppose I were to sell to them or others *my* interest in the moiety of the Kirkby estates? what would they give me?—it would at least pay my debts—I presume—but let me know what you think of these matters—& believe me

yrs. ever
N B

Address to me at *Genoa*—Villa Saluzzo. I wish to have these things settled as I think of going to Greece perhaps to America. What has been done with Claughton's and with the Rochdale Money! and if I mistake not a four hundred pounds (to keep down interest or otherwise) at the time of your remitting to me in the beginning of the year. Is Hanson nearly liquidated—you said *yes* before—but is it so?—You also kept up 81. 0 pounds for sundries with which please to balance accounts for books &c. with Murray—as I want no more of his long bills—at the end of three or four years.——

P.S.—Will you just say if you have received the Rochdale Market deed &c. and the 7th. (i.e. 12th. from the first inclusive) Canto of D[on] J[uan].—You do not positively say that you have—though the Context indicates about as much.—I should be glad to know if (supposing I could now save a few thousand more or less within the year) I could not invest in *land* & good security for an annuity on my own and Sister's life—(she to have it if the Survivor) and would like to know how much per Cent we might expect—I am nearly thirty five—she about two or three years ahead—though I suppose that she don't own so much.—Or perhaps it would be better to retain any surplus principle [sic] and invest it on *safe* and *readily convertible* security at a reasonable interest.—

P.S.—I have stated in all my letters that I am willing to invest in a mortgage on good security at four per cent if better cannot be had.——With regard to the R[ochdale] business you will recollect that Farebrother told you what sum was offered (a pretty good one) of "bona fide" bidding at his former auction for even the unlitigated part of the Manor.——The various contradictory statements so entirely opposite of even indifferent persons—shows that there is something uninvestigated and odd about the whole thing.—As for D[earden]'s statement—however he may really believe it fair—it must naturally be partial, and mine the same.—Two Surveyors of Skill and integrity should go over the whole—(of *his* part with *his* permission) that is—and I am then willing either to settle it by arbitration—or by contract—or by partnership over the whole—or any other honourable method or mode of proceeding.—You will please not to forget—that in case of enclosure—a large allottment of land must come to the Lord of the Manor—as is the usual claim and custom on such occasions—the Manorial rights are over nearly forty thousand acres.—There are also some other privileges and pickings (besides the right of sporting &c. &c. &c.) as the Rochdale Market toll payment shows.———I hope that you received the deed and the other parcels of ye 12th. of D[on] J[uan] and that you will safely receive the packet accompanying this also.

Genoa. Jy. 18th. 1823

My dear Douglas—By ye. post of yesterday—or rather of ye. 16 o —I forwarded a packet to you containing a letter—the revise of [Don] J[uan] and certain poeshies for any ensuing number of "the Liberal"— to be transmitted by you to Mr. J[ohn] H[unt] in time.—This is merely a line of Advice to your Honour.—I have already written more than once to express my willingness to accept the—or almost any mortgage—anything to get out of the tremulous funds of these oscil- latory times.—There will be a war somewhere—no doubt—and wherever it may be the funds will be affected more or less—so pray— get us out of them with all proper expedition.—It has been the burthen of my song to you these three years and better and about as useful as better Counsels.——With regard to Chancery—Appeals—Arbitra- tions— Surveyings — Bills— fees — receipts — disbursements — copy- *rights*—manorial ditto—funds—land—&c. &c. &c.—I shall always be disposed to follow your more practical—and practicable experience.— I will economize—and *do* as I have partly proved to you by my surplus revenue of 1822—(which almost equals the ditto of the United States of America—vide—President's report to Congress—in proportion) & do *you* second my parsimony by judicious disbursements of what is requisite—and a moderate liquidation,—also such an investment of any spare monies—as may render some usance to the owner because how- ever little—"every little makes a mickle" as we of the North say with more reason than rhyme.—I hope that you have *all receipts* &c. &c. &c. and acknowledgements of monies paid towards liquidation of debts,— to prevent confusion and ⟨prevent⟩ hinder the fellows from coming *twice*—of which they would be capable—particularly—as my absence would lend a pretext to the pretension.——

You will perhaps wonder at this recent & furious fit of accumulation and retrenchment—but—it is not so unnatural—I am not naturally ostentatious—although once careless and expensive *because careless*— '—and my most extravagant passions have pretty well subsided—as it is time that they should on the very verge of thirty five.——I always looked to about thirty as the barrier of any real or fierce delight in the passions—and determined to work them out in the younger ore and better veins of the Mine—and I flatter myself (perhaps) that I have pretty well done so—and now the *dross* is coming—and I loves lucre—

for one must love something. At least if I have not quite worked out the others—it is not for want of labouring hard to do so—but perhaps I deceive myself.—At any rate then I have a passion the more—and thus a feeling. However it is not for myself—but I should like (God willing) to leave something to my relatives more than a mere name; and besides that to be able to do good to others to a greater extent. If nothing else—will do—I must try bread & water—which by the way —are very nourishing—and sufficient—if good of their kind.—

yrs. ever
N B

[TO LEIGH HUNT]   Jy. 20 o 1823

My dear H.—would you have the goodness to indorse—or re-indorse—the enclosed to your brother, and at the same time apprize him that the poem to which it is an addition was sent to Mr. K[innaird] on the *16* o and may be obtained when he pleases to require it.—If you could do this by a line for to-day's post—I would send it by Lega.—

yrs. ever
N B

P.S.—Here is an epigram *anonymous*—on Mr. Coke's Philo-genitiveness—I trust that it is decent.—

> When youthful Keppel's name was lost in Coke's
> That Union promised fewer births than jokes,
> Long live the old Boy! he makes to every Jeer
> The best retort, an heir within the year!—
> <div align="right"><i>Philo-Genitiveness.</i>[1]</div>

[TO DOUGLAS KINNAIRD]   Genoa. January 22, 1823

[Part of letter quoted in catalogue]

Enclosed is a letter from Mr. Deardon with my answer, which I trust that you will approve and forward to the address. I could wish something to be arranged that the suits may be expedited [word torn out with seal]. The lawyers (slow as they are) may get the start and push them forward. I put a seal to the letter, but leave it open, the wax being a little above the puncture, where you may place a wafer. You

---

[1] Thomas William Coke (1752–1842), a Whig M.P., married at the age of 70 (in 1822) Lady Anne Amelia Keppel and fathered a child by her. He was created Earl of Leicester in 1837, a few years before his death at the age of 90.

will have had several epistles from me lately, rather for your attention, than an answer.

[TO DOUGLAS KINNAIRD]   *Genoa. Jy. 23d. 1823*

My dear Douglas,—By yesterday's post I sent you a letter from Mr. Deardon—with my answer—both for your perusal and one for your transmission.—As he seems very eager for an interview— I have said that I will meet him in April—that is—if it be absolutely requisite to conclude the negociation.—I would rather not have the expence of the journey—but will keep the appointment if need be.— What do you think? I referred—& still refer him to you (as my letters show) all along—as to myself;—and I see little difference—for I should in the event of meeting Mr. Deardon—take no step without your advice and approbation.—You may state this from me—adding that *if it be necessary*—(as to sign and seal for instance—) I will none-theless come—as I have said.—Recollect—that I shall come (if at all) as strictly *incog.*—as is possible in an age of tittle tattle and news-papers.—Let me have your answer and opinion thereanent.—It would be towards the close of April that I should set out.—There is also another business or two of a different kind—which I can settle at the same time—and which have been on my mind this many a day—and lately re-imprest by some circumstances which there is no leisure to detail here at present.[1]—I do not know whether you will approve what I mean to do though I think that you will—when you know all; but if you don't—I must find somebody that will—at least so far as to do a common office on such occasions.—You will write to me—as—with regard to Mr. Deardon's business—something should be done to stop the lawsuits—Believe me

yrs ever & truly
N B

[TO LEIGH HUNT]   *Jy. 25th. 1823*

Dear H—I sent you all the books I could lay hands on—and will send further.—As I did not look over the transcription till yesterday I did not perceive yr. *penciled* remarks on the thing which I am about at present.[1]——You are kind in one point—and right in the other.—

1 Byron still nurtured his bitterness toward Brougham and Southey and intended to challenge them to duels if he came to England.

1 *The Island*, a poetic narrative of the mutiny on the *Bounty*. Byron had at first intended it for *The Liberal*, but it was published independently by John Hunt in June, 1823.

But I have two things to avoid—the first that of running foul of my own "Corsair" and style—so as to produce repetition and monotony—and the other *not* to run counter to the reigning stupidity altogether—otherwise they will say that I am eulogizing *Mutiny*.—This must produce tameness in some degree—but recollect that I am merely trying to write a poem a little above the usual run of periodical poesy—and I hope that it will at least be that;—You think higher of readers than I do—but I will bet you a flask of Falernum that the most *stilted* parts of the political "Age of Bronze"—and the most *pamby* portions of the ⟨South Sea⟩ Toobonai Islanders—will be the most agreeable to the enlightened Public;—though I shall sprinkle some *uncommon* place here and there nevertheless.—"Nous verrons"——I am going on with the poeshie—and in the mean time I send to Mrs. S[helley]—a few Scenes more of the drama[2] before begun—for her transcriptive leisure.—

yrs. ever & affectly

N B

[TO DOUGLAS KINNAIRD]   *Genoa. Jy. 27th. 1823*

My dear Douglas—Yrs. of the 13th.—Has Hanson's bill since 1817 received any liquidation—is it the 1400—that I have to pay?—or the balance of 6—or 700—as mentioned in yr former letters as about the *whole now* due.—Pray clear up this—an important point.—I enclose you a letter from young Hanson on whose Contents you will have to decide—as I am always willing to go along with yr. opinions, on that and other matters.—You see there *will* be a Spanish war.—As to publishing matters—you can decide on them too—I shall not appeal from yr. tribunals—"to Philip fasting."[1]——Remember me to Hobhouse—whose letter I have—he will have had a second from me by this time.—

ever yrs.

N B

Decide for me about the Kir[k]by reference to the Arbitrators. I will abide by yr. decision—am I not tractable. Will you ask young Hanson what this *Scotch discharge* is? and *what money* is to be received upon it? he will tell ye fast enough if it is to go to his bill.—I have not answered Hanson—and he knows nothing from me of our negociation with

[2] *The Deformed Transformed*, which was published by John Hunt on Feb. 20, 1824.
[1] Valerius Maximus, *Facta et Dicta Memorabilia*, Book vi, chapter 2: "Appeal from Philip drunk to Philip sober".

Deardon.—This Spanish war will be preventive to selling out of the funds which I greatly regret, as you may well suppose.——Before investments you will of course deduct *all you have paid* for insurances &c. let me know what half year's fee *exactly is*—since the four thousand of Sir R[alph] N[oel] was placed in the funds also.—Would we were well out of them!—

[TO DOUGLAS KINNAIRD]   *Genoa. Jy. 29th. 1823*

My dear Douglas,—By this post (in a packet separate from this letter—and insured at the office here—) I remit to you the sum of twelve hundred pounds in your own circulars of August—which are untouched.—Of this I would request you on receipt—to purchase Exchequer bills for one thousand pounds and apply the other two hundred to liquidate the remaining claims.—This will make with the thousand of Jy. 6th. from the funds—which you state as invested in Exchequer bills—two thousand.——You do not say what the actual half year's amount from the funds—really is—the whole year was (or ought to have been) *£2515*—and since then—Sir R[alph] N[oel]'s— payment of the four thousand must have added something to the interest—how much in all I know not—but not to mistake—let us say —*2600* for the whole year—*half* year—*1300*.——The balance then of the sum now remitted—added to that from the funds—will be after the exchequer investments—*five* hundred pounds—the whole of which may go to pay off any debts of mine still extant—i.e. of *those you* have stated—as Baxter—Hanson—or Mealey's relict,—the very names of the others are strange to me—nor will I recognize their claims till fully proved.——

You mention two thousand now in your hands (from the trustees) from Kirkby—and a thousand to be paid shortly.—Am I to understand by this—that fifteen hundred pounds of this Michaelmas rent of 1822— comes to me?—or what—or how much?—If it be so—I could wish a thousand to be invested in a *third* exchequer bill or other safe and easily reconvertible security—and the five hundred pounds to go to liquidation also.—These two Sums of five hundred pounds—added to the like sum for the Rochdale Market tolls—make fifteen hundred pounds to be applied in re-imbursement for the insurances effected and in liquidation of debts.———Of course I speak hypothetically as to the Kirkby receipts—which are not clearly stated—as far as regards 1822. ——I shall still have (at this present writing) besides the twelve hundred remitted to you for the purpose specified—fourteen hundred pounds of your circulars—for my expences here—besides the six hundred pounds in Webb's hands of Leghorn—which latter pays four per cent—and I have now a half year of it due—and ready to be paid.——

All these details will seem trifling to a large dealer in Assetts—but they are "great to little men",[1] I cannot afford to let a few thousand pounds float about without rendering interest of some kind——and I think when I assign fifteen hundred pounds—at the very beginning of the year 1823 to the payment of outstanding debt &c.—I may be allowed to invest the three thousand mentioned (including the 1200 now sent) in such a way as to obtain me at least a trifling increase.—I do not despair of being able to remit even *more* from *hence*—for the same purpose—(when I hear from you in reply) and I will live—or starve—on the rest, for *starve* I *will*—rather than go on longer in this vexatious labyrinth of lawyer's bills.—Besides this I have a *letter unused* of credit for Leghorn &c.—for two thousand pounds,—shall I *return it?* as it is quite gratuitous—and *you* have no funds for it—at least will not—when the monies are invested in Ex[chequer] bills.—

P.S.—You will perhaps be surprized—that after the enclosed epistle —somewhat lengthy—I have not re-manded the subject (the Circulars of August) on which it treats.—But on second thoughts—or *third*—I have postponed their mission till I hear from you again,—as I wish to know whether you think my scheme of investment proper?—or whether the sum ought not to be applied otherwise? or whether I had better keep it by me—as a fund in case of unlooked for emergencies?—You will therefore not suppose that the Circulars are on their tour as yet a *second* time—as when originally transmitted by your house in August, when they described a circle of their own, before arriving at their address.—When I hear from you—I shall probably do—what you think most requisite, i.e. forward or retain them.—With regard to the D[on] J[uan]s—in addition to what I have stated within—I would add that as much rolls (in them) upon the White Bears of Muscovy—who do not at present dance to English Music—it is an appropriate moment to introduce them to the discerning public—in all their native intract-ability.——Besides—they and the Turks form at the present the farce after the Congress melodrame upon Spain.—Their names & qualities are become more familiar household words—than when the D[on] J[uan]s were written.—I am aware of no inferiority in the four succeed-ing cantos i.e. the 8th. 9th. 10th. 11th. 12th. but all these things—like most things are a lottery—it may be as well at least to have the ticket

[1] Goldsmith, *The Traveller*, line 42: "These little things are great to little man."

92

drawn.—It is true—the adventures are kept in abeyance—but if I err not—there is some morality and perhaps poesy—and it may be wit—to keep them as fresh as salt can make them.

yrs. ever
N B

[TO COUNTESS TERESA GUICCIOLI (*a*)]   [*Feb.–July?*] *1823*

A. M.—Sai tu ove è quella piccola edizione Americana colla traduzione da [di] Da Prato [Da Ponte?] della P[rofezia] di Dante?

t. t. in e.[1]
N B

[TRANSLATION]   [*Feb.–July?*] *1823*

My Love—Do you know where that little American edition of the *Prophecy of Dante* is with the translation by Da Prato? [Da Ponte][1]

Wholly yours to eternity
N B

[TO COUNTESS TERESA GUICCIOLI (*b*)]   [*Feb.–July?*] *1823*

Amor Mio,—Son arrivato senza ritardo o disturbo.—Sta tranquilla e credimi sempre il tuo

A. A. in e.
N B

[TRANSLATION (*b*)]   [*Feb.–July?*] *1823*

My Love,—I have got home safely without delays or difficulties. Don't be anxious and believe me always your

Friend and Lover for ever
N B

---

[1] Tutto tuo in eterno.
[1] Byron doubtless intended to refer to L. Da Ponte, *La Profezia di Dante*, Nuova-Jorca, 1821, which also contains Da Ponte's "Letter to Lord Byron" in Italian and Latin, (with a translation into English by his daughter), and his Italian version in ottava rima of "The Apostrophe to the Ocean" from *Childe Harold*.

My dear Douglas—On the 16th. Ultimo I sent you a packet containing the corrected proofs of D[on] J[uan] Canto 6 o and also a poem of seven hundred and forty lines or so entitled "the Age of Bronze"— will you please to have inserted in the latter the following lines *after* the line (which closes the paragraph on the Country Gentleman)

> "And share the blessings which yourselves prepared"
> (Continuation)
> Thou sold'st thy birthright Esau! for a Mess,
> Thou shouldst have gotten more, or eaten less—
> Now thou hast swilled thy pottage, thy demands
> Are idle, Israel says the Bargain stands!—
> Such landlords! was your appetite for war,
> And gorged with blood you grumble at a Scar.
> What[!] would ye spread your Earthquake even to Cash?
> And when land crumbles must even Paper crash!
> So rents may rise bid banks and nations fall
> And ⟨Change becomes⟩ found on Change a *Foundling* Hospital!
> Lo! Mother Church while ⟨true⟩ all religion writhes,
> Like Niobe, weeps oer her firstborn, Tithes,
> The ⟨Bishops⟩ Prelates go to—where the Saints have gone,
> The proud pluralities subside to *one*—
> Church, State and Faction wrestle in the dark—
> Tossed on the Deluge in one common Ark
> Shorn of her bishoprics and dividends—
> Babel begins indeed, but Britain ends.—[1]

By the way—this poem was intended for a third number of H[unt]'s publication—but as that will not be published—and this is a *temporary* hit at Congress &c.[2]—(as you will have seen by the poem if you have received it) perhaps it had better be published *now alone*—it is long enough about 760 lines or so—(as long as the first edition of E[nglish] Bards was) but this is for your consideration—let me have a proof to correct.—You perceive that there *is a War* and a fall of the funds— notwithstanding your pacific prophecies;—as the funds are below *my par*—I can not afford to sell out now—with a loss perhaps of thousands —for the sake [of] a paltry *four* per *cent* interest,—and must run the

---

[1] These lines, slightly altered, appeared in the published poem (lines 632–649).
[2] *The Age of Bronze* satirizes the Congress of the Allied Powers at Verona in November, 1822, which accomplished nothing and was, as the motto suggests "Impar Congressus Achilli", an empty menace.

risk of remaining—with this proviso—[for?] Bland and [Cobourne?]—trustees—i.e.—[that?] as for four years—I have done all in my power to get out of the funds—and *they* by their opposition have placed my property in the common peril—and *they only*—whenever the Crash does happen—and mine goes by their obstinacy——I will as assuredly blow out the brains of one or both of those two persons—as they deserve it —it is hard to be injured on all sides—through the agents of that fiend of a woman.

yrs. ever

N B

[TO JAMES WEDDERBURN WEBSTER]   *Fy. 2d. 1823*

My dear W—The picture which you sent will accompany this note. ——It is indeed a sad remembrance and I can with difficulty trace any resemblance—at least to my memory of the Original.[1]—The letters will be also enclosed—which are still more melancholy—but I see nothing in them to prevent a reconciliation if both parties would but condescend a little to their own eventual happiness—and to that of their children.—By Thursday's post I wrote to Paris—and my letter was sealed before I had received your packet.—I trust that I have said nothing that can offend—or militate against the interests of either party.—I think the *painter's* is the greatest calumny against her hitherto—which is unpardonable—for the infant in the same miniature is much better done, though I am no great judge of such matters.—I send you some books—but the one you mention is not in my present possession—nor have I had, nor am likely to have any copy for some time to come.—The works of that Author are not often in my library[2] —nor have I read many of them—indeed hardly any—since their publication.—"Werner" came to me in a parcel from London—without my direction—and except the French translation (required by M[adam]e G[uiccioli]) and a scurvy ten-franc English Edition published at Paris—and sent as an index of Piracy—by the indignant Galignani (to persuade me to let *him* have a copyright) I have not a line—but—I err—there are two or three stray volumes—but they are of an old date—and scattered, I believe, amongst my other books— and I know not their place.——You have no great loss—however—I

[1] Webster had sent Byron a miniature of his wife, Lady Frances, from whom he was then separated, and had asked him to try to effect a reconciliation. Byron had not seen her since his brief unconsummated affair with her in 1813. See his letters to Lady Melbourne, Sept. to Nov., 1813, in Volume 3.

[2] Webster had asked Byron for some volumes of his poems.

believe,—for the poem is not of great repute—nor is likely to be so.—
So much for scribbling—but it is your own blame—since you entered
upon the subject.—I hope that my negociation will be more successful
—it at least deserves to be so.—

yrs. always & affectly.
N B

[TO DOUGLAS KINNAIRD (*a*)]   *Genoa Fy. 6 o 1823*

My dear Douglas—I return you your D[rury] Lane [warrant?]—
signed & sealed I hope correctly—if not return it.—I have no intention
to renew my correspondence with Messrs Hanson except through
your medium—as you knew before never have I—nor shall I communicate with them through any other channel.—I wish to know the
exact balance now *due* to *them*—after the Rochdale advance.—I perceive
in the accompt (Banker's i.e.) Griffith's and the devil knows who—
who was not in the list of Creditors sent by you in Novr.—I suppose
the Scoundrels will swallow up what little there is one way or the other,
but pray don't pay them too readily—for I suspect some of their pretensions [words torn out with seal] or double what they ought—of this
I am sure at least that I see "Banger" and "Madison" and names that I
never even [heard] of in my existence—*not even* as *duns* and that's
strange.—With regard to Kirkby—what is the Michaelmas payment?
is the sum to be received on our part 1500—or 700—or 100—for on
this I am quite in the dark—or even if it be *three* or *two* or *one*—if it be
like the last—it will be hardly worth a Chancery Suit.——I must
positively remit some of your Circulars back and convert them into
cash—or we shall never get on with lawyers or other rogues of
[fechting?].—This was proposed in a recent letter—and I only wait
your answer to send you 1200 £ in your own paper.—I return the
D[on] J[uan] *corrected*—I say that it is *good* and will *do*—if M[urray] is
playing tricks—through Davison[1]—or there is any further difficulty—
publish boldly on my *own* account—I feel no fears as to the circulation
at least.—The whole 7 *Cantos*—publish, I say.—Call Murray to a
reckoning for *Werner*—and please to recollect—that it is not upon
present sales we are to account with him altogether—but that the fellow
has *eight* and *twenty* years to treat for of Copyright—if he has already
sold six thousand (as you say) he will perhaps sell some more within
28 years.—

yrs. ever
N B

[1] Murray's printer.

My dear Douglas—I have found the enclosed—and signed and had it witnessed.—It must go to the Hansons directly—as it must be returned to Scotland within *sixty days* of the Signature.——The money to be received upon it is £133—12—4.—I also enclose two *old* letters of the Hansons—as they may perhaps let you into some of their affairs with me.—The enclosed could not be signed till yesterday—as it was mislaid—it ought to have been signed three years ago.—You will receive the money & place it to our Items.—

The first witness is William Fletcher my *Valet.*—

The second John [*Davy?*] *an English Gentleman at Genoa—he is of* [*Burwash?*] *in Sussex.*—

The place *Genoa*—the Date Fy the sixth 1823.
You will see by the instructions *that this statement* of the witnesses' derivations are exacted particularly.

yrs. ever
N B

P.S.—I have returned your D[rury] L[ane] paper and the D[on] J[uan] by another packet.

My dear W.—The Bankers have answered that as yr. own Banker had declined—and also another (Quantana—by name) it could hardly be expected that they should run the risk for a Stranger not recommended by their Correspondents.—I shall however send down again to them enclosing your book which proves the sums paid or received by you in 1822—through Hammersley—and so far indicates yr. correspondence with that House.—I have added whatever I could say on the occasion but I regret that I cannot myself either endorse bills nor cash them—nor advance the amount after the heavy expences of last year in England—and the many claims of different kinds which I have had to satisfy—and some (I am sorry to say) to refuse—I assure you that it [sic] at this very moment—I have *five* different *letters* before me—all requiring *money*—by the last two days posts—on one pretext or another—and they are but *five* of fifty of the same kind—my own interference therefore is out of the question.—I have no doubt that the bill is a good bill but I really have not the amount to spare even for a week—and I have already become responsible for two hundred and fifty drawn on England by J[ohn] H[unt] besides having to fee lawyers for his Counsel in his coming on Cause, in London.—Within the last January I have [had] to pay upwards of one thousand pounds in London —the greater part a lawyer's bill.—You may imagine then how far I am in a situation to turn banker.—

yrs. ever & truly

N B

[TO DOUGLAS KINNAIRD]   *Genoa. Fy. 12th. 1823*

My dear Douglas—I have received yrs. of ye 31st. Jy. "You have heard nothing from Davison" you say—and you *will* hear nothing. —He is a mere Spy of Murray's depend upon it—think a little—is it likely that he should be otherwise—connected as they are?—He was merely sent to see what we were about—that M[urray] might be as mischievous as he could.—You had better publish the Cantos on my account—taking such precautions as may be eligible against piracy.—I am not at all clear that the poem is not a *Copyright*—at least all but the *two* first cantos—it is *not* sedition—it is *not* blasphemy—if Murray chooses to try the question before a jury with the former cantos—I *will* with the present ones—indeed I should like to have a legal opinion on that point at any rate—as I am disposed to try it at any rate.—If they pretend that they are *indecent*—let their Counsel read the passages from Fielding Smollet—and the *Bath Guide*—i.e. Miss Blunderhead's hymn—Earl's [*sic*] Strutwell's defence of Petronius—and Fielding's night Scene of Slipslop and Adams—and Mrs. Waters and Molly Seagrim in the thicket—and Square in the garret[1]—all these are quotations for a *Jury*[;] it is useless to go to the Chancellor—better to a Jury at once.—If the Bridge Street Gang *fail*[2]—then the Vision becomes a Copyright—and Hunt should *then* prosecute the pirates.— In the mean time—let the Cantos be published on my account—it is hit or miss—and may as well be tried.—You say "as for Rochdale wait for Crabtree"—but if Crabtree waits—the *Cause* will be heard in

---

[1] In Christopher Anstey's *New Bath Guide* (Letter XIV) Miss Prudence B—N—H—D informs Lady Betty that she has been "visited" by a very fleshly vision. In Smollett's *Roderick Random* (chapter 51) Lord Strutwell defended Petronius Arbiter's handling of homosexual scenes and the practice itself, but later confessed that he was merely trying out the hero's opinions and was in accord with his indignant rejoinder. The scenes in Fielding are in *Joseph Andrews*, Book IV, Chap. 14 (Slipslop and Parson Adams); and *Tom Jones*, Book V, Chap. 5 (Square in the garret); Book V, Chap. 10 (Jones and Molly in the thicket); and Book IX, Chap. 2 (Jones discovered in Mrs. Waters' bed).

[2] The Constitutional Association.

the appeal—and where are we then?—The House is now met.—I sent you some time ago—a letter of Mr. Deardon's to me—with my answer—the letter to be forwarded.—I am willing to take what the Manor may fetch—and he seems disposed to purchase though at a low estimate—let us hear his offer—it will at least be an Index for us.— Hanson in the mean time is pushing on the appeal—and I want something to be done—that I may order him to stop.—You do not say *what* I owe him still—nor whether it be seven hundred or fifteen hundred—or any hundred that we are to have from Kirkby of present payment.——With regard to the arsenal—if lawyers say that it is not legal—only let it be made so—so that I be not involved in present or future litigation——Lushington and the others may be all very well— but suppose anything happen to them and there succeeds to them a truculent trustee. By the way could you not get sold (at any discount) Wedderburn Webster's bond with interest of ten years due upon it— it is in Hanson's hands—and has a judgement and is good against property or person—and it seems that he has the former still—I'll tell you who would buy it—his own Attorneys or mine?—The Youth is here—has been [Jewing?] Diddling his landlord &c.—and wanted me to endorse a bill for *seventy* pounds—I refused—but at last he bored me into the endorsement of a smaller one for *thirty* pounds of which I know not what will be realized—it is on Hammersley's house.—And all this time the fellow owns to the possession of twenty thousand pounds and the receipt of many thousand since I lent him the thousand in 1813— and now there is ten years interest due—try what it will fetch (his bond that is) I will take what it will bring.——I wrote to you by an express of the Consul General's here the other day enclosing your D[rury] L[ane] paper—D[on] J[uan] Canto 7th. corrected and a Scotch law paper of my own—which if properly signed—entitles me to £133. 12 S. 0 D. of good and lawful money of Great Britain.—

yrs. ever
N B

P.S.—Where is Goëthe's letter *twice* promised?—is not Murray to give anything for Werner? As it is a farewell transaction it may be as well to conclude it.—My letters from and to Mr. Deardon were sent on the 23d of Jy.—

yrs ever again

I would rather not come to England if it can be helped—but let me know. The 8th. C[ant]o of D[on] J[ua]n announced to be sent by this post is not yet arrived.—

A. M. Il Medico mi dice che potrebbe durare qualche tempo il mio incommodo—ma che passerà, la gonfiezza sotto l'occhio è diminuito.— Ti rispondo sopra questo perche tu lo desideri.—Io non posso esprimerti il dolore che mi cagiona la mancanza di tua sorella—ma Ella è felice—sono i viventi che meritano la compassione—e la simpatia.— Non sono venuto da te—perche so dalla trista esperienza—che nei primi momenti il dolore aborrisce egualmente la consolazione—la società—ed anche l'amicizia stessa—e le parole! cosa sono? Ti compiango in silenzio—e ti raccomando al' Cielo ed al' Tempo.—

t[utto] t[uo]

My Love—The Doctor tells me that my discomfort might continue for some time, but that it will pass. The swelling under the eye has diminished. I reply concerning this because you desire it.

I cannot express to you my sorrow over your sister's death—but She is happy—it is the living who deserve compassion and sympathy— I have not come to you because I know—by sad experience—that in the first moments sorrow shrinks alike from comfort—from society— and even from friendship itself. And words—what are they? I pity you in silence—and recommend you to Heaven and to Time.

Entirely yours

Dear W.—I cannot keep the book and take [J's?] money too, for the bindings, and if I do not keep it, I have still less right to it. I therefore return it & request that you will not remand it on pain of proscription —My "chilblains" are I assure you no joke & I can scarcely move for them—To be sure the weather is not very inviting for this assistance. I beg your pardon for altering your nomenclature,[1] but old recollections are apt to float uppermost. Believe me

yrs. ever & very truly
N B

[1] Byron probably forgot to address him by his new title. Webster had been knighted.

My dear Cousin—Your letter arrived as I was on the point of answering the former—not forgotten—nor neglected—but my acknowledgement was postponed from day to day till I was afraid that a dilatory reply might look worse than none at all—especially as I thought you might return by the same route—and I could gossip by word of mouth, instead of puzzling you with my hieroglyphics.—That "your Speech is of broken bones"—I thought that you broke nothing but hearts—but you see how the Gods avenge harmless Flirtation.— The subject however is too serious for buffoonery—I rejoice—that I did not hear of your accident till your recovery—I am enough acquainted with,—and too impatient under pain myself—not to sympathize with sufferings less than what you must have undergone—but women bear these things better than men—an additional proof whereof—is— that you have fought through the Carnival with your arm in a sling—a General would have been carried off the field—and not returned quite so gallantly perhaps.—I hope that your Valour—like Virtue—has been it's own reward—and that the arrival of Lent has found you equally able to sustain its privations.————Your Chevalier[1] errant is here and more errant, though still stationary—than usual—and that is much.—He has embroiled himself with two absent friends—a Sir F. V. —and some Caledonian Chiefs of the race of Diarmid,—Mr. Campbell of Glensaddle—I believe—both of whom have *Cut* him by letter—for reasons—which—as I have nothing to do with—I cannot pretend to explain.—There are also some high and doubtful questions with his landlord of the ["]Croix de Malthe"—his tailor—his shoe-maker— and finally his Valet—also his banker—and two other Bankers—who have manifested an unaccountable aversion from his bills—unless guaranteed by an amicable endorsement—"a *backing* of one's friends" which Pylades himself would probably have avoided.—All these woes —to say nothing of others—he lays to *your* door—for having lured him with deceitful hopes to this mercenary country—where a Man must actually pay for his provisions.——To console himself for your rigour,—on his return he paid his court to a very pretty Madame Quantana—the wife of a rich banker—but his bills seemed no less unacceptable to the Lady than her husband—for neither of them would cash his love or money at whatever discount.—Messrs Gibbs were equally inexorable in the pecuniary part, but we will see what is to be done and get him back to Lausanne, and if possible to his wife—which

[1] Webster.

is an important episode by the way—for he is moving Heaven and Earth—for a reconciliation.—She is at Paris.———I knew her soon after their marriage—and him some years before—when he was in the Hussars—and I was a Collegian.—She was very beautiful—and more romantic than wise—and that unlucky kind of woman—who can do nothing without an Eclât—so that the wonder is that they were not separated before.—He has bored me—into being a Mediator in his behalf—attracted doubtless by my own signal success in amicably arranging my matrimonial affairs.———I have consequently addressed the Lady—in a respectful and conciliatory epistle—representing with all the eloquence of common place—that very trite truism—that all quarrels are bad—but those of holy Matrimony the very worst of all.— I do not know that it will do any good but at least it can only hurt myself—if they make it up—well and good,—if not—they will both fall upon the Pacificator according to the ancient custom.—You ask me as to the prudence of coming by Sea to Genoa—if I had the direction of the Winds like the Philosopher in Rasselas—I should know how to answer.—The passage is made from Leghorn daily and with safety— but I know not how far the presence of an Admiral's Consort—might tempt the Ocean—who was very gallant in the old time.—But you might come by the good (*not* the *new*) road as far as Lerici overland— and embark either from Lerici (on the Gulph) or Spezia—for Sestri or Genoa—and arrive at the former (at least) in a few hours—under sail with a tolerable wind—or by dint of rowing—in a cabin.—There is nothing very formidable in either. I made the passage—after being laid up for four days on a sick bed in a sordid Inn—got to Sestri by twilight—(with oars by the way) and came on to Genoa by land which I reached before dawn—and recovered on—and I believe, *by* the amphibious journey.—But you had better—if you decide on the Sea— avoid the Equinox—which will occur about the period of your proposed departure.—I would send round my Goletta for you—but She is laid up in the Arsenal—and is too small for the accommodation of a family—though She is a great "Summer Bark" as the poets say.—I hope however you will pass this way,—though your Escort is departed— I dare say you have relays upon the road.——I have not received Lord Dillon's book but am equally obliged—pray—say so.——I hear very little of Mr. Taaffe—and it would have been as well if that little had been less.—He involved me and some other Englishmen—in a squabble with a drunken dragoon and the Guard on *his* account entirely—and then kept aloof on pretence of having lost his *hat.*——This happened at Pisa.—One was wounded—another arrested—myself and the fourth rode through the Guard—and the affray closed in the Dragoon's being wounded—for some time supposed mortally—but the rascal recovered. —Mr. Taaffe—never made his re-appearance—(after having been the *first* insulted—and the first to complain) till the Squabble was over— and finding that the Pisans took the part of their Scoundrel—(I need not add that he was a *Pisan* himself)—did all he could to shuffle out of any responsibility.—He—Mr. Taaffe—is under some small obligation to me—for I prevented Mr. Trelawny—a truculent Cornish Gentleman —from breaking his bones—for his conduct on this occasion—and I assure you it was no easy matter—I speak of facts sufficiently notorious at the time—to Mr. Dawkins the then Minister at Florence. I am penetrè[?] with the bounties of Lady Jersey though I do not know when I shall be able to avail myself of them,—I was sick of the "Salons" long before I left England—and I have seen enough of the foreign Monde since and before even, to exclaim with Solomon—that "all is vanity— and that there is nothing new under the Sun"—there may be something *new* to the *new*—but I am not in that predicament—and I am glad of it —since it leaves me without ambition or curiosity.——Siate Felice— my Cousin—and let me know that you are so—and I shall be content. —Come this way if you can—or will—or at any rate let me know how far you are from

yrs. ever and most affectly.
N B

[TO MESSRS. WEBB & CO.]   *Genoa. Jy* [*Fy.*] *20 o 1823*

Gentlemen—This letter will be delivered by Signor Giuliani Intendant of the Russian Count Battailin now at Florence.—He thinks that some of his acquaintances are likely to be Purchasers of some of the Snuff boxes or the watch.—You will therefore have the goodness to allow him to look at them or *show* them—but at *your residence only*— you will not allow them to go out of your hands—until you hear further from me. The boxes which I would part with are those which do not contain *portraits*—those with portraits I retain.—The largest box has a Mosaic painting on enamel—but as it is merely a fancy groupe does not come within the description—and may be sold with the Agate and other stone boxes—as also the watch.—I cannot fix a price—as prices vary in different countries—but you can [have] them estimated *fairly* if possible—and let me know the result. I have the honour to be

yr. very obedt. & humble Servt.
NOEL BYRON

P.S.—Would you have the goodness to let me [know] the amount of the *Principal* in your hands on my account—it is stated in your Leghorn way of exchange (which I do not understand exactly) at ⟨£⟩ 3283 of Sp[anish?] Gold——but I would be glad to know what that is in Francesconi—or rather in Italian livres or French Francs.[1]—

[TO DOUGLAS KINNAIRD]   *Genoa. Fy. 20th. 1823*

Dear Douglas/—I enclose the 8th Canto of D[on] J[uan] corrected. —You will have discovered by this time that you have been jouè [sic] by Davison a mere Spy of Murray's to do what harm he could.——You must have them published on *my* account—by somebody or other— taking such precautions—as may seem feasible against the piracies.—I have completed a thirteenth Canto (of 111 one hundred and eleven stanzas) which will be sent when fairly copied over.—This will make with the 7 in your possession—eight in all.——When these three are published—you can have announced the other *five* as in the press—or ready to be so.—John H[unt] who wrote to me the other day seemed to think the *small* additional edition—a balk to the pirates—or at least some check—you may perhaps know better than I can.—But the Season will be over if you do not hasten—it is hit or miss—throw— and let us see what the dice will offer.——I shall also collect my other stray poesies into one or two volumes in the Spring—and do not mean to part with the Copyright——by and bye this will tell.

yrs. ever
N B

[TO COUNTESS TERESA GUICCIOLI]   *F[ebbrai]o 20. 1823*

A. M.—Per dio! ne ha ragione la zia—e voglio anche io avere la vita di S. Cattarina—e la conoscenza dei *"amorosi Gesuiti"*—Ella (la divota di S. Cattarina) ha trovato la Felicità—La dice—e la credo—e cosa è dunque che noi cerchiamo?—Alle dieci spero di vederti—

N B

---

[1] The Italian coinage of the time was complicated and different in each province. Byron had dealt in francesconi in Pisa, but had to deal in crowns or scudi or livres in Genoa. See Doris Langley Moore, *Lord Byron: Accounts Rendered*, p. 250.

February 20, 1823

My Love—By God! your aunt is right—and I too would like to lead the life of Saint Catherine—and make the acquaintance of the "loving Jesuits". She (the devotee of St. Catherine) has found Happiness. She says so—and I believe her—and what else are we all seeking? I hope to see you at ten.

N B

[TO THOMAS MOORE] *Genoa, February 20th, 1823*

My Dear Tom,—I must again refer you to those two letters addressed to you at Passy before I read your speech in Galignani, &c., and which you do not seem to have received.

Of Hunt I see little—once a month or so, and then on his own business, generally. You may easily suppose that I know too little of Hampstead and his satellites to have much communion with him. My whole present relation to him arose from Shelley's unexpected wreck. You would not have had me leave him in the street with his family would you? and as to the other plan you mention, you forget how it would *humiliate* him—that his writings should be supposed to be dead weight.[1] Think a moment—he is perhaps the vainest man on earth, at least his own friends say so pretty loudly; and if he were in other circumstances, I might be tempted to take him down a peg; but not now, —it would be cruel. It is a cursed business; but neither the motive nor the means rest upon my conscience, and it happens that he and his brother *have* been so far benefited by the publication in a pecuniary point of view. His brother is a steady, bold fellow, such as *Prynne*, for example, and full of moral, and, I hear physical courage.

And *you* are *really* recanting, or softening to the clergy![2] It will do little good for you—it is *you*, not the poem, they are at. They will say they frightened you—forbid it, Ireland! Believe me

Yours ever
N B

---

[1] Moore had urged Byron not to ally himself with Hunt in *The Liberal*, "where the bad flavour of one ingredient is sure to taint all the rest".

[2] Moore had taken fright at the objections of the pious to his *Loves of the Angels* and was considering changing the Angels to Turks and God to Allah.

[TO DR. JAMES ALEXANDER (a)] *Fy. 20th. 1823*

Dear Doctor—You tell me nothing of the house which you mentioned some time ago—and my Steward either appears not to have understood or not to wish to understand you upon the subject.—Can you let me know the fact as it stands.

> yr. obliged &c. &c.
> N B

[TO DR. JAMES ALEXANDER (b)] *Fy. 20 o 1823*

Dear Doctor—Thanks for your trouble—the Steward is at your disposal when required.—The swelling in the face is gone almost— but the *pills* have lost their effect—I pray you strengthen them.—I do not know the cause—but they ceased *not* gradually—but all at once— without any change of diet to account for it.

> yrs. ever & truly
> N B

[TO LADY FRANCES WEDDERBURN WEBSTER] *Genoa. Fy. 21st. 1823*

My dear Friend—I saw your husband soon after receiving your letter and the enclosed statement which I need not say shocked me very much—neither did I conceal the impression it made upon me from himself.—As he expressed a strong wish to see your letter I availed myself of your permission to show it, more particularly, that he might not take any fancies into his head—which is a Windmill of suspicions of all kinds.—I then put *your three queries* to which he answered *"Yes"* —expressing at the same time [gre]at attachment to yourself.—He is gone to Lausanne. Since his departure I have received from him a note desiring me to delay writing—except *"in courtesy"*—therefore this present epistle is not to be considered as committing *him* &c. &c.—I really do not know exactly what he would be at—nor do I think he knows himself.—He is to write to me from Turin—more explicitly he says—and requires on your part something *"still more explicit as an expression of your sentiments to justify his answer in the affirmative to your queries."* I certainly think that you should soften a little—I do not mean to say that you have not been injured—but when a reconciliation is proposed—resentments must of course be forgotten.—He wishes to know in case of a renewal—if you would live at Lausanne as he cannot stay at Paris—on account of his affairs.——I still do not despair of your reunion—and, as to his Self-love—about *who* should yield first &c. &c.—these are mere weaknesses—and may be indulged without any great harm.—But I do not wish you to act precipitately—or without consulting your friends—though I trust that you will reckon me among the number.—You can write to me what you wish to be done—or said—or *un*said—and I will scrupulously follow your directions as I have done.—I began this sheet intending to enclose his note —but perceive on looking at it—that I am not authorized to do so.— He certainly answered the three queries—contrary to your expectation but his note leaves them again in abeyance.—I will address you when I have anything to interest you.—Pray believe me in all events as one most truly and affectionately yrs.

N B

[TO COUNTESS TERESA GUICCIOLI]   *F[ebbrai]o 21. 1823*

A. M.—Ti rimando la tua lettera di Giuliani insieme colla sua indirizzata a me.—Spero che Il Sr. Ugolini si mostrerà galantuomo— se no—sarà una birbanteria ed ingratitude di più—che mi farà credere li Italiani anche peggiori degli Inglesi—un' degno della nazione Britannica mi ha già rubato l'altro jeri 50 Luigi—e mi sarebbe incommodo—che un bravo Romagnuolo prendesse esempio di un' tal' soggetto.

S[empre] t[uo]
N B

[TRANSLATION]   *February 21, 1823*

My Love—I return Giuliani's[1] letter to you together with his addressed to me. I hope that Sr. Ugolini[2] will show himself to be a man of honour—if not, it will be another instance of roguery and ingratitude —which will make me think the Italians still worse than the English. One [Italian] worthy of being an Englishman stole 50 Louis from me the other day—and I would be chagrined that a brave Romagnolo should follow the example of such a fellow.

Always yours
N B[3]

[1] Giuliani was an old friend of the Gambas who lived in Florence. He visited Byron in Genoa in January, 1823.
[2] Paolo Ugolini was a Carbonaro of Ravenna.
[3] Translated by Ricki B. Herzfeld.

Dear M.—I enclose Sir T[imothy] S[helley]'s reply.—Would you have the goodness to request L[eig]h Hunt to return the two vols of Napoleon (if finished) as Sir J[ames] W[edderburn] promised to lend them to the Countess D'Isson of Cannes.[1]—I would also thank H[unt] for "the Blues" as I have something to do at them.—I have no other news—but on business—and continual declamation against the Liberal from all parties—literary—amicable—and political—I never heard so persevering an outcry against any work—nor do I know the reason for not even dullness or demerit could authorize the extraordinary tone of reprobation.——

My dear Douglas—I am not going to Naples—nor have any intention of continuing Ch[ild]e H[arold]e.—I told you before that it was impossible for Davison to be sincere without involving himself with M[urray]—let them say what they please—you know that of *me*—they will say anything.—You do not appear to have received—at least you do not notice—two letters sent a month ago enclosed to you by me *from* and *for*—Deardon—viz. his letter and my answer—in which I stated that if he absolutely required it—I would meet him on business in England.—I have no wish for this journey unless absolutely necessary.——You can have the three Cantos published in the way you think securest—but I am inclined to think that *though not* at first—in the *long* run—the retaining the copyright in my own hands would be the best.—Mr. Wright's offer is inadequate—there will be no better probably—but it need not be accepted.—

As to the run against me—I fully believe it—but what is a man good for if he cannot face such things?——Whatever motives may be attributed to me on the score of the Hunts—*you* know the only *real* one—viz. a wish to assist them in their distress.——As to the delay you propose in the publication—I see no advantage in it—and I shall not write any more Ch[ild]e H[arol]ds—in the interim.—Publish them on my account—with *whom* you please—as likeliest to be honest—and leave the notion of profit out of the question.—I have sent back the three corrected cantos.—I am very anxious to hear that you have received and forwarded my letter to Mr. Deardon—(enclosing one of his to which it was an answer) as your not mentioning it keeps me not

---

[1] The Countess D'Ysone was a friend of Mr. Hill, the British Minister in Genoa.

only in the uncertainty of it's arrival—but of whether I am or am not to go to England to meet him.

yrs. ever & truly
N B

P.S.—The promised epistle of Goëthe? Do not forget that the *lawsuit is going* on—and may come to a head before we are aware—unless something is settled that may authorize me to stop the proceedings which I sincerely wish to do—I speak of Deardon and the Appeal. It is my intention to collect my *own* poems out of the liberal—and publish them in one volume—(I have some *unpublished* by me to be included) the profit upon works already published may be trifling—but there is the *twenty eight* years of Copyright ahead—for the bookseller (whoever he may be) and they may be worth something to complete the series of my other works.——I have now in all eight Cantos of D[on] J[uan] (one completed the other day and not yet copied) the thing in "the Liberal" and one or two still in M.S.S.——If you find any one to bid on the whole—so—if not—no matter.—As to popularity—Voltaire was reduced to live in a corner—and Rousseau stoned out of Switzerland—and banished France.—I should never have thought myself good for any thing—if I had not been detested by the English.——You see I know this better than *you*—for when you wrote to me in *raptures* with the *success*!! of "Heaven and Earth" I told you that your joy was kind but premature.—You can tell me nothing of hostile or oppressive from the English—which I have not contemplated—and such is my feeling towards their national meanness—that I would not wish it otherwise— except as far as it gives my friends pain.——But Courage!—I'll work them.——

[TO JAMES WEDDERBURN WEBSTER]   *Genoa, Feb. 27, 1823*

[Part of letter quoted from catalogue; part from MS.]

I do not quite understand your letter—if I have *full* power I can treat. The proposition must come directly from you. I cannot become involved in a long correspondence to determine who is to write first, etc. —the only thing to be said is will you make it up? and then *She* will give her answer. I wrote to her since your departure; if her answer is favourable, you shall hear . . . . I cannot go from the point to wander into sentimental discussions—that were childish.

My dear Douglas—Many thanks for yrs. of ye. 14th.—It is strange that in your three last you never even allude to my *answer to Deardon* (enclosed with his letter to me) which I forwarded to you on the *23d.* of *Jy.* and which required particular notice as upon it depends a good deal.—Have they arrived?—I insured the letter at the office here———I should be very willing to *pay* Baxter[1] off—but how?—I cannot leave myself bare—all my views have been disappointed.—From the Noel property—only 900—in all—as yet—and of that 600 for insurances.— Hanson and others have had a good deal of the rest including the Rochdale money.—Baxter must wait—at least a year—for I see little for my subsistence—but my own economy of last year.—From litera- ture—I have derived nothing.—Murray lies—when he says he loses by Werner—did he not sell 6000?—now make all deductions whatever for *trade* price—to the trade—&c. &c. how *can* he have lost?—And supposing that he *had*—are the *eight* and *twenty* years of Copyright *nothing*? Will he say that he will not be able to sell it with my other works?—But he is capable of anything—we are well rid of him—but I'll expose him before all's over.———As to the D[on] J[uan]s—they must be published and take their chance.—I wish the "Age of Bronze" to be published *alone* and *immediately*—and on *no* account to go into "the Liberal".—The publisher to account to *you* for the proceeds.— Recollect—*it has* a copyright.———I wish also that you would state to Mr. J[ohn] H[unt] that as long as I thought "the Liberal" could be of service to him and to his brother—I was happy to conduce to it— though I *opposed* it from the beginning—knowing how it would end— but that as it answers little to them—and is highly injurious to me in every way—I wish to retire from it.—They will carry it on as well without me.—For his next number he has a translation from Pulci of mine which he may have if he pleases—but the Age of Bronze I wish to appear *alone*—you may choose *him* or what publisher *you* please.———

With regard to Hanson—if you do not stop the law-proceedings— he will have another bill in no time—is it the outstanding balance which is *600* or *what?*—is *this after* the payment of the 500 R[ochdale] Money—or before?—Of Lushington's account I can chiefly understand that out of £4314—I have received £900—very equitable I dare say— but certainly a scanty *half* of 6000 a year.———Do not think I *blame you.* —or indeed any body—but I am out of luck on all sides;—it don't much matter—for my health is far from good—and will not probably

---

[1] Baxter was the coachmaker from whom Byron ordered his Napoleonic carriage before he left England in 1816. The bond debt was still unpaid.

last very long.—I confess I could wish that something was done with Deardon—what *will* he give for the Manor?—*It must* produce something—I am anxious to get a few thousand pounds together—to pay off remaining debt—and invest any little remnant—for my Sister's family—after my demise.——But I can not pay Baxter—till after Kirkby produces something less aerial than is furnished by these Sylphlike trustees—or till I can sell Rochdale (surely it should produce a few thousand pounds) the lowest bidding was 7000—and the highest about 17—or 18000—in 1816–1817—and it must be an object to Deardon—I speak of the undisputed part.——If Baxter were paid *now* —I should not have a sixpence hardly in your bank—as the money now paid by Lushington merely exceeds by a few hundreds—monies paid previously &c. &c. I shall keep the *Circulars*—and letter of Credit for the present—you are quite right on those points—it is as well to have a sum in hand; but I have paid largely enough this half year already to desire to hear no more of Baxter.

yrs. ever
N B

P.S.—You need not send *proofs* of the Age of Bronze—only *correct* them carefully—I shall want proofs of the remaining cantos of D[on] J[uan]—9—10—11—12.—

[TO AUGUSTA LEIGH] *Genoa. Fy. 27th. 1823*

My dearest Augusta—Your informant was as usual in error—Do not believe all the lies you may hear.—Hobhouse can tell you that I have *not* lost *any* of my *teeth hitherto,*—since I was twelve years old—& had a back one taken out by Dumergue to make room for others growing—and so far from being fatter—at *present* I [am] much thinner that when I left England, when I was not very stout, the *latter* you will regret—the *former* you will be glad to hear—Hobhouse can tell you all particulars—though I am much reduced since he saw me—and more than *you* would like.—I write to you these few lines in haste—perhaps we may meet in Spring—either *here*—or in England.—Hobhouse says your coming out would be the best thing which you could do, for yourself & me too—[1]

ever yrs. most affectly
N B

[1] Augusta, who was passing on Byron's letters to Lady Byron, had made excuses and, when pressed further by him, commented that they might find each other much changed. See also Oct. 20, 1822 and Dec. 12, 1822 to Augusta.

My dear Hoppner—We must take what we can get—but you will tell Father Pasqual that he might have known that the value is triple what he proposed—and that I did not think him a dishonest man— when I printed at my own expence an Armenian Grammar in 1816—to oblige his Confraternity.—You will take the best price you can get (would an *auction* do?) and remit the amount on my account to Messrs. *Webb & Co.*—my *bankers* at Genoa—if possible without expence save postage.—I would take Siri's bills—at a month—or two as they pleased.—The whole Sum at present offered is 64 Sequins—by the rogue of an Armenian.——I rejoice to see you in Spirits and should be glad to meet you any where on the face of the earth—even in England; —but I am far from well—have had various attacks—since last summer —when I was fool enough to swim four hours in a boiling Sun—after which all my skin peeled off—then a fever came on—and I have never been quite right from that time—August.—I am as thin as a Skeleton —thinner than you saw me at my first arrival in Venice—and thinner than *yourself*—there's a Climax!——However that may be temporary —but all my *humours* are topsy turvy—and playing the devil—now here now there—and putting me to my patience—which is not exuberant.—Excuse haste—my best Comts to Mrs. H[oppner]—write when you like—and can—and believe me

ever and truly yrs obliged & affectly.

N B

[Fragment]

. . . I have been very unwell—these last three days—with a swelled face—painful as if it were more perilous.—I do not know what to suggest at present on the subject of Sir T[imothy]'s communication— but will think over the affair—and let you know.—

yrs. ever
N B

My dear Douglas/—In my letter of ye. 27th. I forgot to allude to the Mortgage at 4 per cent.—I only take it because you say *more* cannot be obtained at present. I agree with you that we must have nothing to do with Lord Mountnorris[1]—who is a litigant and bad debtor—but if we go on rejecting proposition after proposition how are we to end?——Pray—do not forget to tell me if you received Deardon's letter with [my] answer—I cannot tell till I hear from you—whether I shall have to meet him in England or not. I would rather avoid the expence of the Journey—if he will negociate with you instead. You can hardly have *not* received the letter—and you will see the contents as I sent my answer to him under cover (open) to yourself.——I always told you 1. that there would be a *war*—secondly that the funds would fall—and thirdly that they would attack public Credit *sooner* than you expected. —As to my paying off any more debt—Baxter or others—at present— it is out of the question—till Autumn—or even later.—The Noel proceeds have not as yet paid their way through the Herald's and Insurance offices—Lushington's account shows Lady R. Manners (or Lord R.)— a Mr. Ford—and the Noel Trustees to be the proprietors—or at least the receivers of any income from that property.—I shall see the account at the Audit—and if it is to go on in this way—I will put the Arbitration into Chancery—the Chancery Lawyers may as well have it—as this goodly Company—since it seems that anybody may be better for it than the nominal holders.——

When I know what I really can depend upon—and the exact amount of outstanding debt—I can then decide in what proportion and at what periods the debt is to be liquidated.—You will recollect too in the present state of the Currency that I am paying at a considerable loss— when that is more equitably settled I shall be more disposed to settle the principal.—Baxter can have his interest duly.—Were I to pay him now—my present funds in your bank would be reduced to a few hundred pounds—since of the recent 600– 300 must have gone to replace what was already overdrawn.—You forget how *much*—Griffiths— Hanson—Naylor &c. have already received this current year.—It is true I have my Circulars (2600) and six hundred pounds in Webb's bank—but I agree with you that those sums ought to be kept available "in these times".—I shall keep the letter of Credit too in case of emergency—it has no *fixed period* however but is "a volante" but is only for Florence Leghorn—and Pisa——but I could [have?] cash for it here if needed.—You may reconvert the Exchequer bill as a *fund* for that letter of Credit—if you choose—and reserve all incoming payments to make it up good to the amount (£2000) for your security.—But I particularly request that you will make no further payments till I have

[1] Arthur, first Earl of Mountnorris and 8th Viscount Valentia, was the father of Lady Frances Webster.

113

a good sum in reserve.—You know the Creditors are safe in any event ——but I cannot leave myself bare—I do not calculate on any property in England as secure—and must try to save something in case of a national convulsion.—If my health gets better and there is a war—it is not off the cards that I may go to Spain—in which case I must make all "Sinews of War" (monies that is to say) go as far as they can—for if I *do* go—it will be to do what I can in the good cause. But these are reveries—pray is Sir R. Wilson[2] going there? Do not forget Deardon's affair—time presses—law is a tortoise but she gains ground—I wish to know what he would give for the manor?—The very least would perhaps pay my debts—but I wish I knew what they really were.—As to the Jews I disown them like a good Christian.——I will have no more to do with the Liberal.—The Age of Bronze must be published alone.—The Liberal was a bad business—see what it is to do a *good* action. Had I not assisted Hunt after S[helley]'s demise he might have starved in the Streets—and my reward has been universal abuse.— Never mind—we may beat them all yet.

yrs. ever
N B

Have you received a packet by a Courier of the English Consul's (of Genoa)—containing a Scotch deed signed—on which we receive £133. 12 S. 0 D.

[TO DOUGLAS KINNAIRD]   *Genoa.—M[arz]o 3. 1823*

My dear Douglas—Another letter and yet *no* acknowledgement of my letter to Deardon through you sent on the 24th. of *January!*—What does this mean? I shall send you the 13th. and 14th. Cantos of D[on] J[uan] shortly.—They are to be published in this way—6th. 7th. 8th. *one* volume—9th. 10th. 11th.—2d vol.—12th. 13th. 14th.—3d. vol.— they will perhaps be a little smaller than the former two—but no great difference.——We have now been a year in presumed possession of Kirkby Mallory,—Deducting a £1000 in the interim to Master Ford[1] and Lady Manners (which is to be repaid—it seems—but *when?*)

---

[2] Sir Robert Thomas Wilson (1777–1849), a general in the British army who had fought in the Napoleonic wars, was dismissed from the army for intervening to prevent bloodshed when the household cavalry encountered the mob at Queen Caroline's funeral in 1821. In 1823 he went to Spain to aid the insurgents. Byron considered him an independent and revolutionary character. He was later reinstated and became Governor of Gibraltar in 1842.

[1] John Ford was a partner with G. B. Wharton in a law firm which had represented Sir Ralph Noel.

there remains 5000 and odd pounds—of these Lady Noel's executors have had 950.—and Lady B[yron]—900—and I 900

Add

1000 Ford and Manners
 950 Lady N. B.'s E[xecutors]
 900 Lady B.
 900 Lord B.

3750.

What becomes or is to become of the remnant of the 6000—and odd?

Say

From—6000
Subtract 3750

2250—this seemeth the remainder to my simple eyes——whereof 1125 Sterling ought to be in [my?] exchequer—but we shall see.—Since I wrote to you Hunt has been to beseech me *not* to quit the liberal at present—as it would wound him. —I wish to wound nobody—and will do what I can—but the *"Age of Bronze"* *must* appear *alone*—I insist upon *that*—he has a Pulci translation of mine for his next number.—You *must* publish the Juans—*now* is the time for the warlike Cantos—especially as we hate the Moscovites.—Publish them taking what precautions you can against piracy (publish them on my account) and with whom you please.—

yrs. ever
N B

P.S.—You must postpone further payments and liquidations till Autumn or winter[;] it will be time enough when Ford repays us to pay others—

[TO BRYAN WALLER PROCTER]   *Genoa, March 5th, 1823*

My dear Barry,[1]—I have just got your poem and letter, of which more anon. You must blame the post and not *me*, for I wrote and sent to the address indicated a very long answer to your letter of a year ago —true, upon my honour! so much so, that I rather wondered at having heard no further from you; not that it required notice in itself—but merely as the link of as much correspondence as you chose to tie to it.

---

[1] Barry Cornwall was Procter's pen name.

Why don't you try the drama again? there is your *forte*, and you should set to work seriously; you will have the field to yourself, and are fully able to keep it.

As for myself—neither my way of thinking on the subject as an art— nor probably my powers—are at all adapted for the English drama— nor did I ever think that they were. With regard to "Don Juan," there are nine cantos, seven of which are in England. The reason of the delay is a quarrel with Murray (on Hunt's account originally) and a demur with the *trade* in general—excited by the Arimaspian[2] of Albemarle Street. The said John M[urray] Esq., who is powerful in his way and in his wrath, has done and will do all that he can to perplex or impede. As to what D[on] J[uan] may do in England—you will see. If you had had the experience which I have had of the *grande monde* in that and other countries, you would be aware that there is no society so intrinsically (though hypocritically) *intrigante* and profligate as English high life.

I speak what I do know—from what I have *seen* and *felt personally* in my youth—from what I have undergone and been made to undergo— and from what I know of the whole scene in general, by my own ex- perience, and that of others; and my acquaintance was somewhat ex- tensive. I speak of seven years ago and more; it may be bettered now.

In no other country would the Queen's and similar trials have been *publicly* tolerated a moment.

They mistake the object of "Don Juan", which is nothing but a satire on affectations of all kinds, mixed with some relief of serious feeling and description. At least this is the object, and it will not be easy to bully me from "the farce of my humour."[3]

I have prosed thus far in answer to your inquiry. "Patience and shuffle the cards."[4] L[eigh] H[unt] who is resident in this district, has carried off your "Flood" (by the way, we had one of our own this winter, which carried away bridges, cattle and Christians) before I had time to read it. What little I gleaned I liked extremely. Moore has allowed the priests to menace his angels into Mahometans—a con- cession which I suspect will not stand him in stead. They will merely boast that they have threatened him out of his propriety. As to "The Liberal," I do not know how it is going on; but all my friends of all

---

[2] *Paradise Lost*, Book 2, line 943. See also Sept. 13, 1821, to Kinnaird (Vol. 8, p. 208, note 1). According to Herodotus (IV, 27) the Arimaspians had only one eye. They were Scythians who fought with the griffins for gold. The epithet was applied to Murray, who was also one-eyed.

[3] Unidentified.

[4] *Don Quixote*, chapter 23, Sancho Panza speaking.

parties have made a portentous outcry against the whole publication, and so continue, which is a great encouragement. However, my conscience acquits me of the motives attributed to me by the serviles of Government. What *I* have done to displease my aristocratic connections I can quite understand—in this matter; but what the two H[unt]s are guilty of to sanction their invectives is not quite so clear.

We have only seen the first number hitherto.

I hope that you are better. I am far from well myself; but I won't make this a medical epistle.

Write—when disposed—and tell of your doings and intentions.

Am yours very truly,
N B

Genoa. March 5th. 1823

[TO JOHN HUNT]

Sir,—I have received the proof of the A[ge] of B[ronze] and returned it to Mr. Kinnaird.—It is full (the earlier part) of the worst kind of printer's blunders *viz*—transposition of the verses in every direction so as to form a complete jumble.—I have corrected this as well as I can—but I fear uselessly—unless the Manuscript is carefully referred to.—The poem will be published alone—and by whom I know not—as I leave these things to Mr. K[innair]d.——Your brother is tolerably well—but surprized at your silence.—I have the honour to be.

yr very obedt. humble St.
N B

P.S.—The proof is called "a *proof* in *Slips*" and certainly the "*slips*" are the most conspicuous part of it—I pray you represent as much to your *Faust*[1] on this occasion.—

[TO DOUGLAS KINNAIRD]

Genoa. March 8th. 1823

My dear Douglas/—You will have received by a late post two packets—one containing the Age of Bronze (proof sheet)—the other the 13th. Canto of D[on] J[uan]. The 14th. will be sent when copied out fairly.——In the mean time I send another poem in four cantos called the "Island &c."—it is about 1337 lines—and 100 longer than Lara.—It is too long for "the Liberal" and not in the same style with my former stories—not good enough perhaps to publish alone—but

---

[1] i.e., "your printer", in reference to Johann Fust (or Faust), the inventor of printing.

117

too good to throw away——it will make a respectable figure in any future collection of my writings.——Perhaps you can dispose of it thus —firstly—the Age of B[ronze] alone—and then in a *volume* with the addition of this story—which will make together—upwards of 2100 lines.—As to terms or publisher I know [not?] what to say—you will think and arrange as you can—(subject to a reference to me) but the Age of Bronze should be published alone—and immediately.—There is a translation from Pulci in H[unt]'s hands for his Journal—which is quite as much as is requisite.——

With regard to paying Baxter or others it must be postponed—probably for a year.—*Who* pays me?—Out of £6336 per annum of the Noel estate *my* moiety for 1822 has amounted to £900!—This has just paid the Herald and Insurance offices.—It may be all right—and *come* right again—but "while the Grass grows"[1] you know the proverb.—From literature—I have derived nothing—that is to say about two thousand a year less than heretofore.—You will say this is not *your* fault—assuredly it is not—and it may most likely be mine—but the diminution is not the less.—From my own income I have saved about 3000 or better—but this must be kept in reserve to meet emergencies and usual expences.——As soon as I have realized a sufficient sinking fund—I will pay the remaining Creditors—a great deal has already been paid—as you know.—The rest must wait.—I do not choose to leave myself bare.—Every sixpence which can be saved (after deducting my requisite credits with your bank) must be laid out in Exchequer bills—or at other interest—and *that interest* again at Compound interest—we shall then soon be able to cover the interest of Baxter's bond.——Indeed I can already—with the interest of the Exchequer bill[s]—and that of about 17000 Francs at 4 per cent in Messrs Webb's bank—which I remind you of so frequently—that it may be claimed in case of accidents to me.

You most unaccountably decline saying—whether you have or have not received my letter from Deardon and answer—sent Jy. 24th. 1823 —nearly two months ago—and insured as I was anxious to hear the result.—Is nothing done—or can nothing be done in this business?—I am very anxious to get together a few thousand pounds—to be at my own disposal—and to invest where I please—in America—Spain—or any where but in your country.—Rochdale must produce Something—a few thousand pounds—the expectations are not great—but in the mean time the lawsuit eats up money—and does no good—and nothing

[1] The proverb, "While the grass grows, the horse starves [or dies]", appears in various forms. It is in *Hamlet*, Act III, scene 2.

is done to stop it.—You will soon have the 14th. Canto of D[on] J[uan] which will make *nine* in your hands—to be published in three parts or volumes.——As to the Noel arrears—I can make out nothing—for deducting the Ford and Manners and Lady Noel's executors &c.— there still remains upwards of four thousand pounds (between the Holders of the estate) of which I have received 900—and what became of the rest?—I am living as frugally as I can.——

yrs. ever.

N B

[TO JAMES WEDDERBURN WEBSTER]   *March 9th.* [*1823*]

Dear W.—Part of your news is rather interesting—as I was *present* at the *marriage* of the Earl[1] by request of the father in law & thought

[1] The Earl of Portsmouth was from an early age mentally unstable. Byron's solicitor Hanson had been appointed one of his trustees and acted as a kind of guardian. The Earl could appear perfectly sane in some circumstances, but his erratic and sadistic behaviour broke out frequently. He whipped his servants, and bled and beat his horses unmercifully. He was fond of attending funerals and caused his servants to carry logs on their shoulders as if they were coffins. These were what he called his "Black Jobs". He helped to drive cattle to the slaughter house where he would dispatch them with an axe, shouting "That serves them right, ambitious toads". He had married the daughter of Lord Grantley, a woman of 47 (a marriage encouraged by his younger brother, the Hon. Newton Fellowes who did not want an heir of the Earl to spoil his chances of succeeding to the title). When she died in 1813, Hanson, who had been the Earl's guardian and legal adviser since 1799, saw an opportunity to make his daughter a countess and incidentally to gain control of the Earl's property, which amounted to £17,000 or £18,000 a year. He hurriedly and secretly arranged a marriage with his daughter Mary Anne without the knowledge of his co-trustees and the Earl's brother. He asked Byron the evening before to give the bride away the next morning early (March 7, 1814). Byron had written, at Hanson's request, an affidavit of his recollections of the marriage, which effectively assured the dismissal of the charge of insanity brought by the brother in the autumn of 1814. But Newton Fellowes had gathered numerous witnesses and much evidence when a second trial began in February, 1823, which brought out many sordid facts about the treatment of the Earl by Mary Anne and her sisters and her lover, William Alder, who fathered her children. According to the servants the sisters spat upon the Earl and horse-whipped him when he struck back. These facts and worse came out in the trial. In the end the Earl was found to have been insane since 1809 and the marriage was later annulled and Mary Anne's children bastardized. A judgment of costs of more than £40,000 was awarded against her. It is probable that she escaped abroad to avoid going to prison. Byron protested on various occasions that he knew nothing of the Hansons' conniving and cruelty. He found the story brought by Webster of the trial "amusing" for he then had an animus against Hanson for his past ineptness, delays and greed. For more details see E. Tangye Lean, *The Napoleonists* (1970), pp. 74–75, 87–89; and Doris Langley Moore, *Lord Byron: Accounts Rendered*, Appendix 3, The Hanson–Portsmouth Scandal, pp. 459–471.

that all had been very regular—I suppose there is some statute against his marrying any but a woman past bearing which his last wife was—& his brother intended his next to be—but he chose for himself very perversely.—Pray step over & tell me more of these fine things—which are vastly amusing.—

ever yrs.
B

[TO JOHN HUNT] *Genoa M[arch] 10th. 1823*

Sir—I do not know what Mr. Kinnaird intended by desiring the stoppage of "the Liberal" which is no more in his power than in mine. —The utmost that Mr. K[innaird] (who must have misunderstood me) should have done—was to state—what I mentioned to yr. brother— that my assistance neither appearing essential to the publication nor advantageous to you or your brother and at the same time exciting great disapprobation amongst my friends and connections in England —I craved permission to withdraw.—What is stranger is—that Mr. K[innair]d *could* not have received my letter to this effect—till long after the date of yr. letter this day received.—The Pulci is at your service for the third Number if you think it worth the insertion. With regard to other publications I know not what to think or to say—for the work even by yr. own account is unsuccessful—and I am not at all sure that this failure does not spring much more from *me* than any other connection of the work.—I am at this moment the most unpopular man in England—and if a whistle would call me to the pinnacle of English Fame—I would not alter it.—All this however is no reason why I should involve others in similar odium—and I have some reason to believe that "the Liberal" would have more success without my intervention.—However this may be—I am willing to do every thing I can for yr. brother or any member of his family—and have the honour to be

yr. very obedt. humble St.
N B

P.S.—I have to add that no recession will take place on my part from "the Liberal" without serious consideration with your brother.—The poems which I have desired to be published separately required this for obvious reasons of the Subject &c. and also that their publication should be immediate.—

My dear Douglas/—Enclosed is the 14th Canto of D[on] J[uan]—the thirteenth was sent a few days ago—also—the Age of Bronze (proof to be compared carefully with the M.S.S. by the publisher)—and a poem in 4 Cantos called the Island—this makes the *fourth packet.*—Please to acknowledge arrivals of the same.—Mr. J[ohn] H[unt] writes to his brother that you desired him to *stop* the L[iberal].—You forget that we have no power to stop the publication of a work over which we have no control—there is the Pulci translation for his next number if he pleases.—The things I have sent to *you*—are *not* to be inserted in the Liberal—but it does not follow—that that Journal is to cease—and L[eigh] H[unt] says that it will do him great harm if that Journal stops.—If there must be a sacrifice—I would rather risk myself than other people.—As to D[on] J[uan] you have now *nine* Cantos in hand—I sent the proofs of the last six;—I care nothing for outcry &c.—they *shall* be published and that speedily if I were to print them myself.—

yrs. ever

N B

P.S.—I know no reason for further delay of the publication of the 6th. 7th. and 8th. Cantos and the others need only wait till I can revise them.—Never mind *me*——and do not allow yourself to be swayed by any temporary oppression—if *I* don't—why should *you?*—Anything from Deardon? it is very strange that you never did answer whether you received my letter and his sent on the 24th January 1823.—I have asked twenty times.—It was ensured.—

My dear Hobhouse—I strongly recommend to yr. acquaintance and good offices the Count Giulio Rasponi[1] (of that ilk) a rich and respectable Nobleman of Romagna whom you will find intelligent and gentlemanly.—Whatever you can do in the way of introduction or otherwise will confer a great favour on

yours ever & truly

NOEL BYRON

---

[1] A friend of Teresa Guiccioli and her family whom Byron had known in Ravenna.

[TO LORD HOLLAND]   *Genoa. March 12th. 1823*

My dear Lord Holland—After so long an interval as seven years of (transportation) separation you may perhaps have almost forgotten me—but [requested?], I intrude upon you and Lady Holland (to whom I present my respects and remembrances) for the purpose of presenting to you the Count Giulio Rasponi (now at Paris but shortly to proceed to London) of a noble and very wealthy family in Romagna—and extremely esteemed both for his character and acquirements.—I should not wish a respectable foreigner to leave England without knowing Lord and Lady Holland.—Any attention to him will be very agreeable to me—and I would trust not irksome to yourself who are the Soul of hospitality.—I will not trouble you much about myself. I have been very unwell but am better.——I sometimes dream of returning to England for a short time on business—which an absence of seven years rather accumulates.—But this is uncertain.——I wish you all good things—and am ever

yrs. most affectly
NOEL BYRON

[TO I. INGRAM]   *M[ar]ch 12th. 1823*

Dear Sir—Any kind of coin which is passable in Genoa—will be the same to me—and I will give a receipt on Sr. Hoppner's account and your own.[1]——Two o'clock will suit me very well—and I believe I need not say that I should have been extremely glad to see you even without the accompaniment.—I have only to regret that you should have so much trouble.—

yours (in haste) ever & truly
N B

[TO JOHN HUNT]   *Genoa, M[arc]h 17th. 1823*

Sir,—Your brother will have forwarded by the post a corrected proof of *The Blues* for some ensuing number of the journal; but I should think that ye. Pulci translation had better be preferred for the immediate number, as *The Blues*[1] will only tend further to indispose a portion of your readers.

[1] Probably payment sent by Hoppner for the articles Byron had asked him to sell.
[1] Hunt did nevertheless publish *The Blues* in the third number of *The Liberal*. The Pulci translation appeared in the fourth and last number.

I still retain my opinion that my connection with the work will tend to any thing but its success. Such I thought from the first, when I suggested that it would have been better to have made a kind of literary appendix to the *Examiner*; the other expedient was hazardous, and has failed hitherto accordingly; and it appears that the two pieces of my contribution have precipitated that failure more than any other. It was a pity to print such a quantity, especially as you might have been aware of my general unpopularity, and the universal run of the period against my productions, since the publication of Mr. Murray's last volume. My talent (if I have any) does not lie in the kinds of composition which is [*sic*] most acceptable to periodical readers. By this time you are probably convinced of this fact. The Journal, if continued (as I see no reason why it should not be), will find much more efficacious assistance in the present and other contributors than in myself. Perhaps also, you should, for the present, reduce the number printed to two thousand, and raise it gradually if necessary. It is not so much against *you* as against me that the hatred is directed; and, I confess, I would rather withstand it *alone*, and grapple with it as I may. Mr. Murray, partly from pique, for he is a Mortal—mortal as his publications, though a bookseller—has done more harm than you are fully aware of, or I either; and you will perceive this probably on my first separate publication, no less than in those connected with *The Liberal*. He has the Clergy, and the Government, and the public with him; I do not much embarrass myself about them when *alone*; but I do not wish to drag others down also. I take this to be the fact, for I do not recollect that so much odium was directed against your family and friends, till your brother, unfortunately for himself, came in literary contact with myself. I will not, however, quit *The Liberal* without mature consideration, though I feel persuaded that it would be for your advantage that I should do so. Time and Truth may probably do away this hostility, or, at least, its effect; but, in the interim, you are the sufferer. Every publication of mine has latterly failed; I am not discouraged by this, because writing and composition are habits of my mind, with which Success and Publication are objects of remoter reference—*not causes* but *effects*, like those of any other pursuit. I have had enough both of praise and abuse to deprive them of their novelty, but I continue to compose for the same reason that I ride, or read, or bathe, or travel—it is a habit.

I want sadly *Peveril of the Peak*, which has not yet arrived here, and I will thank you much for a copy; I shall direct Mr. Kinnaird to reimburse you for the price. It will be useless to forward *The Liberal*, the insertion of which will only prevent the arrival of any other books in the same parcel. That work is strictly prohibited, and the packet which came by sea was extracted with the greatest difficulty. Never send by sea, it is a loss of four months; by land a fortnight is sufficient.

Yours ever,
N B

[TO JOHN CAM HOBHOUSE]   *G[eno]a M[arc]h 19th. 1823*

My dear Hobhouse—Before my affairs can be extracted from the Attorno—Douglas K[innair]d must condescend to complete the negociation with Mr. Deardon of Rochdale.—On the 24th of January I forwarded to K[innair]d a very amicable answer of mine to a letter of Deardon's and also the said letter—the former for him to forward to Mr. D[eardon] and the latter for his own inspection.—I have since repeatedly pressed him at *least* to *acknowledge* the receipt of these—but not one word of reply on that point.—In the mean time—the suits are going on—and of course expences and anxieties proportionate.—Few of my friends can be more anxious to get rid of law and lawyers than I am.—As to the Portsmouth business—all I know or could know of it was from Mr. H[anson]'s own statement.[1]—He told me that old Lady First Portsmouth was dead—and that Portsmouth's brother wanted him to marry *another old* woman—that he might have no children, but that Lord P[ortsmouth] wished to marry a *young* woman—and seemed inclined to one of H[anson]'s daughters.—I saw nothing very unnatural in this—nor lunatical—of Ld. P. himself I saw nothing till the day of his marriage.——On the evening previous to the ceremony I received an invitation from Mr. H[anson] begging me as a friend of many years acquaintance with his family to be present at the marriage—which was to take place next morning.—I went—I saw no appearance of entrapment or compulsion.—The Ladies and other witnesses—went in a Carriage.—The Carriage being full—Lord P[ortsmouth] and myself walked to the Church.—On the way he told me that he had long liked Miss Hanson—even during the life of the first Lady P[ortsmouth]— and asked me if I did not think she would make a very good wife.——

[1] See March 9, 1823, to Webster. Hobhouse wrote to Byron on March 2, 1823: "You see what a mess Hanson has made of the Portsmouth business. The jury returned unanimously on Friday last a verdict of lunacy since 1809 . . . . You recollect what a pretty smock-faced girl Laura Hanson [Lady Portsmouth's sister] was in our time, who looked as if butter would not melt in her mouth. Well, it turns out that she used to beat and whip and spit upon this poor crazy creature, and joined in all the cruelties against him." Marchand, I, 441n.

The Ceremony passed without any thing remarkable—the women cried a little as usual—but Lord P[ortsmouth]'s deportment was quite calm and collected.—After the ceremony I went home—and the family I believe went into the Country.——I did not see the couple again till long afterwards—and then but rarely.—I went as I would do to any other marriage—it was no affair of mine to interfere in—and I thought that if Ld. P. got a good plain quiet homekeeping wife—*young* too—instead of the tough morsel prepared by his brother—it was no bad bargain for either party.—I could not foresee Horsewhipping—and the like of that there.——I could not foretell *Venality*—for I was told that Lord P's property was in *trust*, well secured—and that Lady P. could only have a jointure of a thousand a year.—I could not foresee *Lunacy* in a Man who had been allowed to walk about the world five and forty years as Compos—of voting—franking—marrying—convicting thieves on his own evidence—and similar pastimes which are the privileges of Sanity.—I could have no interest of my own for I never performed with the Miss Hanson's nor whipped Ld. P.——I had nothing to acquire from Mr. Hanson—as the state of his bills do show—being about ten thousand pounds—(most part paid—) since that epoch.—Had my evidence been called for by either party I could have given it impartially.—There is—or was—an affidavit of mine on the subject—before the Chancellor in 1814. I thought—and still think that the Marriage *might* have been like any other marriage.—Of the Courtship—which (as far as I can recollect from the time Mr. H[anson] first mentioned Ld. P[ortsmouth]'s addresses—and the subsequent day of the ceremony) might be on the tapis about ten days—I can say nothing —for I saw nothing— and all I heard was from Mr. Hanson himself—and that I think once only; I had been many years in the habit of seeing my solicitor on my own affairs.—He had been my Attorney—since I was ten years of age.——"Causa scientiae patet".[2]——It struck me as so little an entrapment for Ld. P[ortsmouth] that I used to wonder whether the *Girl* would have him—and not whether *he* would take the Girl.—I knew nothing of his ignorance of "fuff—fuff—fuff"—as Cheeks Chester called it——but as he was of a robust[i]ous figure—though not a Solomon—naturally imagined he was not less competent than other people.———We owe to him however the greatest discovery about the blood since Dr. Harvey's;—I wonder if it really hath such

[2] A legal expression, probably borrowed from Scott's *The Antiquary*, chapter 37. The literal meaning is "the reason of the knowledge is evident". It was a technical phrase used in Scotland to denote the grounds of knowledge or the reasons on which a witness based his evidence.

an effect—I never was bled in my life—but by leeches—and I thought the leeches d – – – – d bad pieces—but perhaps the tape and lancet may be better.—I shall try on some great emergency.—

I am not very well—from a concoction of humours—for which an English Physician prescribes a "decoction of Woods" (and Forests too I should think from it's varieties of taste) but it seems epidemical in this vicinity—full half a hundred people have got it—in the shape of swelled faces and red faces and all that.—I dined with the B[ritis]h Minister Hill—on Saturday—the Carriage gave way on my return—and I had to walk three miles (about half of the way *up* hill—) in the night—with a bleak wind—which brought on an attack again—otherwise I was better.——I shall be glad to see Blaquiere.—I am *not* going to Naples—I thought of it for an instant—being invited there—and Mr. Murray has set the report afloat—with a story about a New Childe Harold—because I said that *if* I went there—I *might* write another Canto.—All my affairs are going on (in England) not very prosperously—the Noel trustees pay nothing & nobody—we can't get out of the funds—nor accommodate with Deardon—nor publish—(Douglas is afraid—but publish I will—though it were to destroy fame and profit at once—I will not be advised nor dictated to by public or private) I shall have to come home and if I do it shan't be for nothing—for I will bring affairs to a crisis with Henry Brougham directly on my arrival—and one or two more of the same kind—I have nothing on my mind so much as this.——

ever yours & truly & affectly
N B

P.S.—You are mistaken on one point—I am leading a very *chaste* life—and time [too] at thirty five—

> "Long may better years arrive!
> Better years than thirty five!"—

[TO DOUGLAS KINNAIRD]   *Genoa. March 20th. 1823*

My dear Douglas—Hobhouse writes that you are in Leicestershire —hunting I presume—I pray you to have a reverend care of your invaluable neck—and to make the present *leap* year in your accidents— for I think that one has annually occurred to you for the two last.— You have now kept me in warm water—by not acknowledging the receipt of Deardon's letter—inclosed to you with my own answer— and tending to advance the negociation—Crabtree who was to go in February does not appear to have been—the suit advances—and lo—

another lawyer's bill—and the uncertainty of whether I am to make a not very agreeable journey or not.—Hobhouse is very earnest that we should close with Hanson—I am sure he cannot be more than I am—by the way—*why* was I not summoned by either party on the Portsmouth case?—I would and still will—if required—give what I know on the subject in evidence.—In my answer to Hobhouse—I have stated what he will probably show you.—

You will—or should have received various packets of M.S.S.—a proof of the Age of Bronze—another poem M.S.S. in four cantos—and the 13th. and 14th. of D[on] J[uan]—also a Scotch deed for 133 pounds &c. signed in order to receive the money—and forwarded by the Consul's Courier some time ago.—I do not want you to write letters beyond simple acknowledgements of packets received.——I have already stated—that I am determined to publish "Coute qui coute"— neither public nor private shall alter my course in what I think right on such subjects.—As to more Childe Harolds—and Naples—it was a mere hypothetical case—which now that Murray has thought proper to hint it about—I would *not* write—at all—and least of all for such as him.—He went about saying that *"perhaps he* &c. &c.["]—does the fellow think that he is or ever will be on the same terms with me as formerly?—I have been unwell—& better—but relapsed after dining with Mr. Hill the English Ambassador (or minister) here some days ago—my carriage broke down on returning—and I walked home—in bleak wind—after a *hot* dinner——for some miles (as we live, he on one ⟨side⟩ [hill?] outside of the City and I on a high [hill?] outside the other part) and partly up hill—so that being heated brought on some inflammation—however after some days—I am bettering once more.

You will have the goodness *not* to make any further payments of Creditors—till Autumn—or later—when the Noel arrears are paid up and the receipts more regular—it will be time enough—as the Creditors are safe they must be patient—I have already paid a great deal too much—in proportion to my receipts.—I have nearly done a *15th* Canto of D[on] J[uan]—I am aware that those about you—discourage and disparage that work—but I will "keep my threep"[1]—and ten times the more so—for opposition or outcry.—I should be very glad to hear that something was settled with Deardon—to suspend the anxiety and expences of the Appeal—you might at least let me know the valuation and his offer—whatever it may be little or great.——

ever yrs.
N B

---

[1] Obstinate determination. (Variant of Scottish "threap".)

At the end of the year—when I know exactly what I am to have—and what I still owe—I will set apart a fund for liquidation—till then I can not consent to any outgoings whatever. Compare the proofs of the Age of Bronze with the M.S.S. as the printer has made in the three first paragraphs some strange transpositions.

[TO RICHARD BELGRAVE HOPPNER]   *Genoa. March 24th. 1823*

[Part quoted in catalogue]

   ...I have no fault to find with the bargain in itself—though a great deal with Father Pasqual Aucher, but it only confirms my opinion of mankind, especially the priestly portion thereof....

   P.S.—You are right so far, the avarice seems coming—& perhaps my Methodism may follow—you hardly understood me when I took my degree in some portion of dissipation, but it was to *sow my wild oats* so as not to prolong *those* vices beyond a certain period of life— supposing that I lived. In this I think I have succeeded whatever may be said upon the subject. But Rochefoucault says that *one vice is only driven out by another* and it is not impossible that I may have a fit of avarice or bigotry—or both in succession. But they form at least a less hurtful species of profligacy than the others, though perhaps more selfish. "Voilà les hommes!"

[TO LADY HARDY]   *Genoa. M[arc]h 28th. 1823*

   My dear Coz.—I have enquired of Dr. Alexander the best medical authority here—who says that the air of Genoa is as good as can well be—and the bathing sufficiently convenient—but not having been at Leghorn—of course he cannot draw any comparison between their maritime merits for invalids.——I say nothing myself—least [lest?] I should suggest selfishly.——Mr. Hill is here—I dined with him on Saturday before last—and on leaving his house at San P. d'Arena[?]— my carriage broke down.—I walked home about three miles—no very great feat of pedestrianism—but either the coming out of hot rooms into a bleak wind—chilled me—or the walking up hill to Albaro— heated me—or something or other set me wrong—and next day—I had an inflammatory attack in the face—to which I have been subject this winter—for the first time—and I suffered a good deal of pain—but no peril.—My health is now much as usual.—Mr. Hill is I believe occupied with his diplomacy—I shall give him your message when I see him again.—I believe one of the personages you mention was once Bessy Rawdon was she not?—I have never seen nor heard anything of her since she was a very pretty drapery Miss in town—equipped by her milliner for the matrimonial market—and has (I think I heard since) married a younger brother.—Is it not so?—Let me not err on so important a point.—I had an epistle from your Chevalier this morning— he is at Lausanne.—My negociation to reconcile him with his wife— had the luck of a Congress.—It produced a long (married) State-paper from the Lady—full of the most extraordinary charges against your admirer—and invoking discussions—in which I had no wish to enter. —I have therefore written to both parties to decline interfering further in so delicate a matter.—Certes I have not the luck in matrimonial affairs—of reconciling any body.—My name I see by the papers has been dragged into that unhappy Portsmouth business—of which all that I know is very succinct——Mr. Hanson is my Solicitor—I found him so—when I was ten years old at my Uncle's demise—and he was continued in the management of my legal business.—He asked me by a civil epistle as an old acquaintance of his family to be present at the marriage of Miss H.—I went very reluctantly one misty morning (for I had been up at two balls all night) to witness the ceremony—which I could not very well refuse without affronting a man who had never offended me.—I saw nothing particular in the marriage—of course I could not know the preliminaries except from what *he* said—not being present at the wooing—nor after it—for I walked home and they went into the country as soon as they had promised and vowed.—Out of this simple fact—I hear the "Débâts" of Paris—has quoted Miss H.—as "autrefois très lieé avec le celebre &c."—I am obliged to him for the celebrity—but beg leave to decline the liaison which is quite untrue. ——My liaison was with the father—in the matrimonial shape of long lawyer's bills—through the medium of which I have had to pay him ten or twelve thousand pounds—within these few years.—She was not pretty—and I suspect that the indefatigable Mr. Alder[1]—was (like all law people) more attracted by her title than her charms.———I regret very much that I was present at the prologue to this happy state of horsewhipping and black jobs &c. &c.[2] but I could not foresee that a man was to turn out mad who had gone about the world for fifty years as competent to vote and walk at large—nor did he seem to me more insane than any other person going to be married.———I have no

[1] William Alder, reputed father of Lady Portsmouth's children, was a lawyer.
[2] See March 9, 1823, to Webster, note 1.

objection to be acquainted with the Marquess Palavicini[3]—if he wishes it.—Lately I have gone little into society—English or foreign—for I had seen all that was worth seeing of the former before I left England—and at the time of life when I was more disposed to like it—and of the latter I had a sufficiency in the first few years of my residence in Switzerland chiefly at Me. de Stael's where I went sometimes and [in] Italy—till I grew tired of Conversazioni and Carnivals with their appendages—and the bore is—that if you go once—you are expected to be there daily—or rather nightly—I went the round of the most noted Soirees at Venice and elsewhere (where I remained any time) to the Benzona—and the Albrizzi—and the Michelli &c. &c. and to the Cardinal's and the various potentates of the Legation in Romagna—(i.e. Ravenna) and only receded for the sake of quiet when I came into Tuscany.—Besides—if I go into society—I generally get in the long run into some scrape of some kind or other—which don't occur in my solitude.—However I am pretty well settled now—by time—and temper—which is so far lucky as it prevents restlessness.—But as I said before—as an acquaintance of yours I will be ready and willing to know your friend.—He may be a sort of connection for aught that I know—for a Palavicini of *Bologna* I believe married a distant relative of mine half a century ago.—I happen to know the fact as he and his sposa had an annuity of five hundred pounds on my Uncle's property—which ceased at his demise—though I recollect hearing that they attempted—naturally enough—to make it survive him.—If I can do anything for you here or elsewhere—pray order—and be obeyed.—Your acquaintances the Ingrams are still here.—I saw Mr. Ingram a few days ago—his daughter is better.—

Your despairing "W. W. who never more will trouble you trouble you"[4] effected at length his retreat from Genoa—after some not very creditable skirmishes with the Bankers—tailors—hatters—and inn-keepers of this mercenary city—who manifested an unaccountable repugnance to his bills on England.———To extricate him in a small way—I endorsed two of them for him—to no very great amount luckily—for I am given to understand that my virtue in this instance is likely to become it's own reward.—He departed in company with about fifty pounds sterling of mine—a circumstance which by no means diminished

[3] Isabella, daughter of George, fourth son of William, the fourth Lord Byron, married Count Palavicini-Capelli. The wife of the fourth Lord Byron was of the Berkeley family and thus distantly related to Lady Hardy, daughter of Sir George Berkeley.

[4] A line from John Hamilton Reynolds' "Peter Bell", a parody of William Wordsworth.

my regret for his return to a country where they have more Christian faith with an embarrassed traveller.—What he will do next I do not know—but as he attributes his loss of time—heart—and monies—to your having led him by the most aweful coquetry to Florence—I hope that he will discover some Armida more destined to repay his affections —or at least his expences—You see what mischief you have done—— I had a great mind to send you his unpaid bills—enclosed in an ode of my own inditing—with an excellent moral to it—But on second thoughts—considered the subject too serious for poesy.——Donat and Orsi had actually written from F[lorence] to have him *stopped* here for some banking business or other—but the law could not reach him in another state.—

ever yrs. most affectly.
N B

[TO JOSHUA HENSLOW HAYWARD]¹   *M[arc]h 29th. 1823*

Sir,—If you can do me the honour to call at one or two o'clock *tomorrow* I shall be very glad to see you.—It is a pleasure to receive the Citizen of a free country any where—but especially in these wretched countries—as the sight of such a rarity encourages a hope that time may do for the old world—what the better hearts and hands of the Americans have so nobly done for the new.—I have never been one of the wretched and too numerous crowd of jealous compatriots amongst the English who are doing their worst to stifle the natural sympathy between the descendants of the same fathers.—I should not only be mean but ungrateful were it otherwise—for to America only can I look for anything like justice in the appreciation of my real sentiments on the rights of mankind.—I have the honour to be

yr. obliged & very obedt. Servt.
NOEL BYRON

[TO HENRY EDWARD FOX]¹   *M[arc]h 30th. 1823*

My dear Henry—A blunder of mine and of my servants was the cause of my not having the sincere pleasure and *honour* of seeing you

---

1 Joshua Henslow Hayward (1797–1856) graduated from Harvard College in 1818 and took a medical degree in 1821. He was on a European tour when he called on Byron in Genoa. He returned to Boston where he practised medicine for some years, then became a wholesale druggist, and later an official in the Custom House.

1 Henry Fox was the son of Lord Holland. Byron was fond of him because he, like Byron, was lame.

yesterday.—My circumstances with regard to the English in general are such—that I visit none—and receive none with whom I was not previously acquainted.—Thus it was easy for my *Italians* to confound one with the other and it was not till you were gone that I was aware of the punishment of my folly.—The moment I saw your name—I sent to Genoa to enquire to whom I was indebted—and followed immediately to repair what must appear to you not only rudeness but ingratitude.— —Even if I were not—(as I am) under personal obligations to your parents—I should always esteem it a proud distinction to become acquainted with anyone who bore the *name* of your family.—I did not find you at home—but should have sought you again tomorrow—if your personal note had not anticipated my intention.—will *two* suit you? if not, choose your own hour—I shall be at home from twelve till sunset—and I can assure you that few things could afford me so much gratification as to show you how truly I am

ever & affectly yr. obliged & sincere

NOEL BYRON

[TO DOUGLAS KINNAIRD]   *Genoa. March 31st. 1823*

Dear Douglas/—I enclose you the 15th. Canto of D[on] J[uan] and am anxious to know what have become of the others duly sent to you— by the post.—With this there should be *ten* at your disposal for me. — —I have only had proofs of the *three* first— —and want the others to correct.— —I expect that those corrected already are to be published immediately. I care nothing for what may be the consequence—critical or otherwise—all the bullies on earth shall not prevent me from writing what I like—& publishing what I write—"coute qui coute"— if they had let me alone—I probably should not have continued beyond the five first—as it is—there shall be such a poem—as has not been since Ariosto—in, length—in satire—in imagery—and in what I please.—

yrs. ever

N B

P.S.—I say nothing of other affairs—having already written repeatedly and in vain—but I apprize you that the exchange being very much in favour of the drawer—I shall in a day or two—convert 1500 of my Circulars—into Cash—the gain is five per Cent at the present exchange here—besides interest while it lies at the Bankers—and I have need of some such consolation for the various retardments of the Noel payments.—I have particularly to beg that whatever payments

132

small or great you may receive on my account—may be kept in *bank* by you—and not advanced to pay anybody—until the *whole* of the Noel arrears are paid up, or at all events till the close of the year.—I shall then know a little more clearly what I have in hand and what I have to spare for liquidation.——My object is as soon as I have assured a few thousand pounds—to purchase an Annuity for my own life and that of my *Sister*—of course making a provision for the liquidation of outstanding debts—which cannot be *much now*—in England—and I have no debts abroad.——My health ought to make this an easy purchase —and Augusta has two or three years more than me——*what* would they give me per Cent (on good landed security) and these two lives?

[TO JOHN HUNT]   [*April, 1823?*]

[Fragment of a letter]

...Do not forget this—nor treat me as Mr. Murray did about the preface to "the Vision".——*Who* is to be the publisher of D[on] J[uan] I do not know—but I presume you will have no objection to correct it through the press for me—be he who he may.—I also wish a proof of the "Island"—(in 4 Cantos now in Mr. K's hands) I fear that you will overprint the Age of Bronze—I suppose the two thousand are as many as will be called for—and these being now sold—you had better reduce the number in the next edition to 500.—If it is pirated— we must claim our right—it is time that this sort of question should be settled in one way or another.—Believe me

very truly yrs.
N B

P.S.—Please to add as a Note—to the stanzas on Wellington—the extract from "the Soldier's Journal" which headed your brother's poem in the 2d. Number.[1]——With regard to the "Age of . . . .

[TO CAPTAIN DANIEL ROBERTS]   [*April, 1823?*]

[Fragment quoted in catalogue]

It is more than probable that I shall go up into Greece, the sails in question may probably come into play, for it is a squally station.

---

[1] A quotation from the "Journal of a soldier of the 71st. Regt. during the War in Spain" preceded Leigh Hunt's poem "The Dogs", which appeared in the second number of *The Liberal*. The soldier was assigned to break biscuit for Lord Wellington's hounds and got a share of the dog biscuit and was thus better fed than he had been for some time.

Cannot they be repaired for service? I mean to take her up as a tender. Cannot you *take* our mate's demand a little at least till we go to sea. Whatever repairs are wanted I will guarantee . . . .

N B

[TO DOUGLAS KINNAIRD]   [*April, 1823?*]
[Fragment of a letter]

I have a word to say about "Werner". Murray pretends you say to have lost by it—how this is to be reconciled with the sale of six thousand copies—*he* best knows—but the question is *not* the immediate gain—but how far the eight and twenty copyright may be worth purchase—as it will always be united with my other works.——If I go up into the Levant—and any accident happens—these fellows will be sorry enough not to have purchased D[on] J[uan] before—as it would bear a triple price to the heirs—as a last and posthumous production. ——Murray had the baseness never even to thank me for giving to *him* the French copyright for Galignani—which I sent to him gratuitously—refusing to avail myself of it for my own advantage—by this he got some thousand francs—and formed other arrangements with Galignani.——For the letter on Bowles—the Hebrew Melodies— the Ode to Nap[oleo]n—and some other things of the kind—he never advanced anything at all—for Manfred he gave but three hundred pounds—and *now he* pretends to talk of losing! Why even the Liberal has paid it's expenses & put something besides (though no great deal) into Hunt's pocket—with all the outcry against it.——I merely throw out these hints for your consideration—because win or lose—I shall publish the same—the only question is *why* we need necessarily lose— —or what there is to render it inevitable—you yourself praised "Heaven and Earth" at first and said that every body did so—*Since*— you told J. Hunt it was a *failure*;—assuredly it has not been considered such from what I can hear.——

P.S.—It is essential that I should have proofs of all the remaining cantos—and of "the Island" also—to correct—and that soon—in every case.—I have ascertained from a young Man who was in Galignani's office at Paris—that D[on] J[uan] is by far the most popular—so much so—that G[alignani] always prints several hundred extra copies—of *that only*—in addition—when he makes a new edition of the whole works. If you mean to hint that the new C[ant]o's are inferior to the old—I say that they are equal—and in parts superior—you recollect the similarly obliging and erroneous anticipation of worthy friends about the 3d. 4th. and 5th.——Henry Fox says you are quite alarmed about them—you certainly were *not* so when you first received them.—*What* has changed you I do not know—but this I know—that you seem to have got into the very thick of Murray's well known endeavour to destroy every publication of mine—which don't pass through his own medium.——The advice to postpone the publication till I had written a new Childe Harold forsooth!—*could* only come from that quarter and I know it did—for the Man gave out—that *he* perhaps would condescend to publish *that*.——Lady Blessington says you have been a little alarmed about "John Bull" ever since that paper attacked you for becoming the Queen's banker—are you afraid that he should do as much because you are my friend?—If so—I will say in the preface that you did your best to suppress the publication—all that remonstrance will ever obtain from me will be Canto on Canto as long as I can write —do you suppose that I was to sit down and suppress my free thoughts for the Edinburgh or Quarterly? they may have enough of that—if I live to repay them.—

[TO DOUGLAS KINNAIRD]   *Genoa. April 2d. 1823*

Dear Douglas/—Yrs. of the 21st. Ultmo. duly received.—I am glad of the arrival of the packets so far in safety.—I have since sent the *14th*. Canto—and on Saturday the 29th. the *15th*. Canto also—and a poem called ["]the Island" in four Cantos—which I hope have arrived also— a packet was sent too of a *Scotch* deed—by the *Consul's* courier—and not by post duly signed—I shall be glad to know of it's arrival—as it regards money matters.—I am about as the Exchange is high (*very* high) to convert several of the circulars into monies of the Country.— You say nothing about *my* meeting Deardon—will it be necessary?— Probably Crabtree's journey will decide the matter.—I have been unwell after dining with Mr. Hill—the English Envoy here—by overheating myself in a long evening walk home (my carriage broke down) but am well again.—I dine with your friends Lord and Lady Blessington tomorrow.[1]—On monday I saw Henry Fox (Lord Holland's son) and was delighted with him—he seems to me on so slight a glimpse— the ne plus Ultra of the Amiable—even to the even features of his face. —Lady Blessington makes a grand eulogium of you—and your *beauty*

[1] The Earl and Countess of Blessington, along with her sister Mary Ann Power and their travelling companion Count Alfred D'Orsay, arrived in Genoa on March 31, and remained for two months during which time Byron saw them frequently. Lady Blessington (see biographical sketch, Appendix IV) kept notes of their conversations which she published after Byron's death.

(a sign that you wear well) but wishes you would ride quieter horses
—so do I.—Hunt says *you* consider the 2d. No. of the Liberal a failure.
I suppose you mean in sale—for I had a letter from you three days after
it's publication—in raptures with "Heaven and Earth" and it's "*success*"—as not only your own opinion—but of all those whom you
knew.—You can hardly have changed yr. mind so far—without some
reason—I speak as a *composition*—not with regard to it's circulation.—

yrs. ever & truly
N B

P.S.—Please to reflect—that the Appeal—and lawyers' bills are
still going on—and growing—it is now four months since Crabtree
was to go down—how are we to suspend the lawsuit in time—unless I
have an answer of some kind or other?—

[TO THOMAS MOORE]   *Genoa, April 2d, 1823*

I have just seen some friends of yours, who paid me a visit yesterday,
which, in honour of them and of you, I returned to-day;—as I reserve
my bear-skin and teeth, and paws and claws, for our enemies.

I have also seen Henry F[ox], Lord H[olland]'s son, whom I had not
looked upon since I left him a pretty mild boy, without a neckcloth, in a
jacket, and in delicate health, seven long years agone, at the period of
mine eclipse—the third, I believe, as I have generally one every two or
three years. I think that he has the softest and most amiable expression
of countenance I ever saw, and manners correspondent. If to those he
can add hereditary talents, he will keep the name of F[ox] in all its
freshness for half a century more, I hope. I speak from a transient
glimpse—but I love still to yield to such impressions; for I have ever
found that those I liked longest and best, I took to at first sight; and I
always liked that boy—perhaps, in part, from some resemblance in the
less fortunate part of our destinies—I mean, to avoid mistakes, his
lameness. But there is this difference, that *he* appears a halting angel,
who has tripped against a star; whilst I am *Le Diable Boiteux*,—a
soubriquet, which I marvel that, amongst their various *nominis umbrae*,
the Orthodox have not hit upon.

Your other allies, whom I have found very agreeable personages, are
Milor B[lessington] and *epouse*, travelling with a very handsome companion, in the shape of a "French Count" (to use Farquhar's phrase in
the Beaux Stratagem), who has all the air of a *Cupidon déchaîné*, and is
one of the few specimens I have seen of our ideal of a Frenchman *before*

the Revolution—an old friend with a new face, upon whose like I never thought that we should look again. Miladi seems highly literary,—to which, and your honour's acquaintance with the family, I attribute the pleasure of having seen them. She is also very pretty, even in a morning, —a species of beauty on which the sun of Italy does not shine so frequently as the chandelier. Certainly, Englishwomen wear better than their continental neighbours of the same sex. Mountjoy seems very good-natured, but is much tamed, since I recollect him in all the glory of gems and snuff-boxes, and uniforms, and theatricals, and speeches in our house—"I mean, of peers,"—(I must refer you to Pope[1]—whom you don't read and won't appreciate—for that quotation, which you must allow to be poetical), and sitting to Stroelling, the painter, (do you remember our visit, with Leckie, to the German?) to be depicted as one of the heroes of Agincourt, "with his long sword, saddle, bridle, Whack fal de, &c. &c."[2]

I have been unwell—caught a cold and inflammation, which menaced a conflagration, after dining with our ambassador, Monsieur Hill,— not owing to the dinner, but my carriage broke down in the way home, and I had to walk some miles, up hill partly, after hot rooms, in a very bleak, windy evening, and over-hotted, or over-colded myself. I have not been so robustious as formerly, ever since the last summer, when I fell ill after a long swim in the Mediterranean, and have never been quite right up to this present writing. I am thin,—perhaps thinner than you saw me, when I was nearly transparent, in 1812,—and am obliged to be moderate of my mouth; which, nevertheless, won't prevent me (the gods willing) from dining with your friends the day after to-morrow.

They give me a very good account of you, and of your nearly "Emprisoned Angels."[3] But why did you change your title?—you will regret this some day. The bigots are not to be conciliated; and, if they were—are they worth it? I suspect that I am a more orthodox Christian

[1] See Pope's lines "On receiving from the Right Hon. the Lady Frances Shirley a Standish and Two Pens":

> "But, Friend, take heed whom you attack;
>   You'll bring a House (I mean of Peers)
>   Red, Blue, and Green, nay white and black,
>   L———— and all about your ears."

Pope had been threatened with prosecution in the House of Lords for his Satires on personalities. "Red, Blue, and Green" were the ribbons of the orders of the Bath, the Garter, and the Thistle.

[2] "Byron quotes from *The Bold Dragoon*, on which Scott probably founded his *Bold Dragoon, or the Plains of Badajos*." Prothero, *LJ*, VI, 181.

[3] Moore's *The Loves of the Angels* was published in December, 1822.

than you are; and, whenever I see a real Christian, either in practice or in theory, (for I never yet found the man who could produce either, when put to the proof,) I am his disciple. But, till then, I cannot truckle to tithe-mongers,—nor can I imagine what has made *you* circumcise your Seraphs.

I have been far more persecuted than you, as you may judge by my present decadence,—for I take it that I am as low in popularity and bookselling as any writer can be. At least, so my friends assure me— blessings on their benevolence! This they attribute to Hunt; but they are wrong—it must be partly at least, owing to myself; be it so. As to Hunt, I prefer *not* having turned him to starve in the streets to any personal honour which might have accrued from such genuine philanthropy. I really act upon principle in this matter, for we have nothing much in common; and I cannot describe to you the despairing sensation of trying to do something for a man who seems incapable or unwilling to do any thing further for himself,—at least, to the purpose. It is like pulling a man out of a river who directly throws himself in again. For the last three or four years Shelley assisted, and had once actually extricated him. I have since his demise,—and even before, —done what I could: but it is not in my power to make this permanent. I want Hunt to return to England, for which I would furnish him with the means in comfort; and his situation *there*, on the whole, is bettered, by the payment of a portion of his debts, etc.; and he would be on the spot to continue his Journal, or Journals, with his brother, who seems a sensible, plain, sturdy, and enduring person.* * * * *

[TO THE EARL OF BLESSINGTON]   *April 2nd, 1823*

My Dear Lord,—I send you to-day's (the latest) Galignani. My banker tells me, however, that his letters from Spain state that two regiments have revolted, which is a great vex, as they say in Ireland. I shall be very glad to see your friend's journal.[1] He seems to have all the qualities requisite to have figured in his brother-in-law's ancestor's Memoirs. I did *not* think him old enough to have served in Spain, and must have expressed myself badly. On the contrary, he has all the air of a *Cupidon déchainé*, and promises to have it for some time to come. I beg to present my respects to Lady B[lessington], and ever am

Your obliged and faithful servant,

NOEL BYRON

[1] Count D'Orsay kept a journal which Byron admired.

138

[TO EDWARD BLAQUIERE][1]   *Albaro. April 5th. 1823*

Dear Sir—I shall be delighted to see you and your Greek friend—
and the sooner the better.—I have been expecting you for some time—
you will find me at home—I cannot express to you how much I feel
interested in the cause—and nothing but some Italian connections
which I had formed in Italy—connections also in some degree referring
to the political state of this country—prevented me from long ago—
returning to do what little I could as an individual—in that land which
is an honour even only to have visited.—

ever yrs. truly
NOEL BYRON

[TO THE EARL OF BLESSINGTON]   *April 5th. 1823*

My dear Lord B.—How is your Gout?—or rather how are you?—
I return the C[ount] D'O[rsay]'s journal which is a very extraordinary
production and of a most melancholy truth in all that regards high life
in England.—I know or knew personally most of the personages and
societies which he describes—and after reading his remarks—have the
sensation fresh upon me as if I had seen them yesterday.—I would however plead in behalf of some few exceptions—which I will mention by
and bye.—The most singular thing is—how he should have penetrated
not the *fact*—but the *mystery* of the English Ennui at two and twenty.—
I was about the same age when I made the same discovery in almost
precisely the same circles (for there is scarcely a person mentioned
whom I did not see nightly or daily—and was acquainted more or less
intimately with most of them) but I never could have described it so
well.[1]—Il faut être Francais—to effect this.———But he ought also to
have been in the Country during the hunting season with "a select
party of distinguished guests" as the papers term it.———He ought to
have seen the Gentlemen after dinner—(on the hunting days) and the
soireè ensuing thereupon—and the women looking as if they have had
[*sic*] hunted—or rather been hunted—too.———And I could have wished
that he had been at a dinner in town—which I recollect at Lord

---

[1] Blaquiere accompanied by Andreas Luriottis, a delegate of the Greek government, who had come to England to seek British aid for the revolution against the
Turks, stopped in Genoa on his way to survey the situation in Greece for the
London Greek Committee. Blaquiere had served in the British Navy and became a
political propagandist first for the Spanish revolution and then for the Greeks. He
was one of the founders of the London Greek Committee.
[1] Byron had already described English ennui very well in *Don Juan* (canto 13,
stanza 101).

Cowper's[2]—small but select—and composed of the most amusing people. The desert was hardly on the table—when out of 12 of the masculine gender—I counted *five asleep*—of these five—three were *Tierney*[3]—Ld. Lansdowne[4]—and Ld. Darnley[5]—I forget the other two—but they were either wits or orators—perhaps poets.——

My residence in the East and in Italy has made me somewhat indulgent of the Siesta—but then they set regularly about it in warm countries—and perform it in Solitude—(or at most in a tete a tete with a proper companion—) and retire quietly to their rooms to get out of the Sun's way for an hour or two.—Altogether your friend's journal is a very formidable production.—Alas! our dearly beloved countrymen have only discovered that they are tired and not that they are tiresome —and I suspect that the communication of the latter unpleasant verity will not be better received than truths usually are.—I have read the whole with great attention—and instruction—I am too good a patriot to say *pleasure*—at least I won't say so—whatever I may think.—I showed it (I hope no breach of confidence) to a young Italian Lady of rank—tres instruite—also—and who passes or passed—for being one of the three most celebrated belles in the district of Italy where her family and connections reside in less troublesome times as to politics ——(which is *not* Genoa—by the way) and she was delighted with it —and says that she has derived a better notion of English society from it—than from all Madame de Stael's metaphysical dissertations on the same subject in her work on the Revolution.——I beg that you will thank the young Philosopher—and make my compliments to Lady B and her Sister.——Believe me

yr. very obliged and faithful

N B

P.S.—There is a rumour in letters of some disturbance or complot in the French Pyrenean army[6]—Generals suspected or dismissed—and ministers at war travelling to see what's the matter—"Marry! (as David says) this hath an angry favour" [savour?].[7]——Tell C[ount]

[2] The fifth Earl Cowper was the husband of Lady Melbourne's daughter Emily Mary.

[3] The Hon. George Tierney (1761–1830) had been in the government of "All the Talents" and was later a leader of the Whig Opposition.

[4] Lord Lansdowne (3rd. Marquess—1780–1863) was the friend and patron of Thomas Moore.

[5] John Bligh, 4th. Earl of Darnley (1767–1831).

[6] In March, 1823, General Piat and other officers of the Duc d'Angoulême's forces were arrested for plotting against the government.

[7] *The Rivals*, Act V, scene 1. "This, my lady, has an angry savour."

D'O[rsay] that some of the names are not quite intelligible especially
of the Clubs—he speaks of *Watt's*—perhaps he is right—but in my
time *Watier's* was the Dandy Club—of which (though no Dandy) I
was a member at the time too of it's greatest glory—when Brummell
and Mildmay—Alvanley and Pierrepoint gave the Dandy balls—and
We (the Club i.e.) got up the famous Masquerade at Burlington
House and Gardens for Wellington.——He does not speak of the
Alfred—which was the most recherché and the most tiresome of any
—as I know by being a member of that too.——

[TO THE EARL OF BLESSINGTON]   *April 6th, 1823*

It *would* be worse than idle, knowing, as I do, the utter worthless-
ness of words on such occasions, in me to attempt to express what I
ought to feel, and do feel for the loss you have sustained;[1] and I must
thus dismiss the subject, for I dare not trust myself further with it *for
your* sake, or for my own. I shall *endeavour* to see you as soon as it may
not appear intrusive. Pray excuse the levity of my yesterday's scrawl—
I little thought under what circumstances it would find you.

I have received a very handsome and flattering note from Count
[D'Orsay]. He must excuse my apparent rudeness and real ignorance
in replying to it in English, through the medium of your kind interpretation. I would not on any account deprive him of a production, of
which I really think more than I have even *said*, though you are good
enough not to be dissatisfied even with that; but whenever it is completed, it would give me the greatest pleasure to have a *copy*—but *how*
to keep it secret? literary secrets are like others. By changing the
names, or at least omitting several, and altering the circumstances in-
dicative of the writer's real station or situation, the author would render it a most amusing publication. His countrymen have not been
treated, either in a literary or personal point of view, with such deference in English recent works, as to lay him under any very great
national obligation of forbearance; and really the remarks are so true
and so piquante, that I cannot bring myself to wish their suppression;
though, as Dangle says, "He is *my* friend,"[2] many of these personages
"were *my friends*," but much such friends as Dangle and his allies.

---

[1] Lord Blessington's only son, Viscount Mountjoy, died March 26, 1823, in his
tenth year. News of it had just reached the Blessingtons.
[2] *The Critic*, Act I, scene 1.

I return you Dr. Parr's letter[3]—I have met him at Payne Knight's[4] and elsewhere, and he did me the honour once to be a patron of mine, although a great friend of the other branch of the House of Atreus, and the Greek teacher (I believe) of my *moral* Clytemnestra—I say *moral*, because it is true, and is so useful to the virtuous, that it enables them to do any thing without the aid of an Ægisthus.

I beg my compliments to Lady B., Miss P., and your *Alfred*. I think, since his Majesty of the same name, there has not been such a learned surveyor of our Saxon society.

Ever yours most truly,
N B

[TO LORD SYDNEY OSBORNE]   [*April 6, 1823?*][1]

[Fragment quoted in catalogue]

...I pray you be as kind to him [Blaquiere] as your situation will allow....He can tell you anything about me you may wish to know and many things about others much better worth your knowing. Perhaps we shall meet somewhere this summer.....

[TO JOHN CAM HOBHOUSE]   *Genoa April 7th. 1823*

My dear H.—I saw Capt. Blaquiere and the Greek Companion of his mission on Saturday.—Of course I entered very sincerely into the object of their journey—and have even offered to go up to the Levant in July—if the Greek provisional Government think that I could be of any use.— —It is not that I could pretend to anything in a military capacity—I have not the presumption of the philosopher of Ephesus— who lectured before Hannibal on the art of war—nor is it much that an individual foreigner can do in any other way—but perhaps as a reporter of the actual state of things there—or in carrying on any correspond- ence between them and their western friends—I might be of use—at any rate I would try.—Capt. Blaquiere (who is to write to you) wishes to have me named a member of the Committee in England—I

---

[3] Samuel Parr was assistant master at Harrow while Sheridan was there. When Byron met him at Payne Knight's he was renowned for his classical lore and his conversation.

[4] Richard Payne Knight (1750–1821) was a numismatist and connoisseur of antique art. He bequeathed his collection of bronzes to the British Museum.

[1] The date given in the catalogue is April 3, 1823, but since Byron did not meet Blaquiere until the 5th or 6th, this seems a more likely date.

fairly told him that my name in it's present unpopularity there—would probably do more harm than good—but of this you can judge—and certainly without offence to me—for I have no wish either to *shine*—or to appear officious;—in the mean time he is to correspond with me.—I gave him a letter to Ld. Sydney Osborne at Corfu—but a mere letter of introduction as Osborne will be hampered by his office in any political point of view.[1]—There are some obstacles too to my own going up to the Levant—which will occur to you.—My health—though pretty good—is not quite the same as when it subdued the Olympian Malaria in 1810—and the unsettled state of my lawsuit with Mr. Deardon—and the affairs still in Hanson's hands—tend to keep me nearer home. —Also you may imagine—that the "absurd womankind" as Monkbarns[2] calls them—are by no means favourable to such an enterprise.— Madame Guiccioli is of course—and naturally enough opposed to my quitting her—though but for a few months—and as she had influence enough to prevent my return to England in 1819—she may be not less successful in detaining me from Greece in 1823.—Her brother Count Gamba the younger—who is a very fine spirited young fellow—as Blaquiere will tell you—is of a very different opinion—and ever since the ruin of Italian hopes in 1820—has been eager to go to Spain or to Greece—and very desirous to accompany me to one or other of those countries—or at any rate to go himself.—I wish you could have seen him—you would have found a very different person from the usual run of young Italians.—

With regard to my peculium—I am pretty well off—I have still a surplus of three thousand pounds of last year's income—a thousand pounds in Exchequer bills in England—and by this time—as also in July—there ought to be further monies paid to my account in Kinnaird's bank.—From literary matters—I know not if any thing will be produced—but even out of my own—K[innair]d will I suppose furnish me with a further credit—if I should require it—since all my receipts will pass through his bank.—I have desired him *not* to pass further sums (except for the Insurances of Ly. B[yron]'s Life) to the payment of what remaining debts (and they are but few) may be extant till the end of the year—when I shall know more precisely what I am to have—and what I may then still owe.

You must be aware that it would not do to go without means into a

---

[1] Lord Sydney Osborne was Secretary to the government of the Ionian Islands, and the British who governed the Islands maintained their neutrality in the Greek–Turkish conflict.

[2] Jonathan Oldbuck, Laird of Monkbarns in Scott's *The Antiquary*.

country where means are so much wanted—and that I should not like to be an incumbrance—go where I would.——Now I wish to know whether *there*—or (if that should not take place—) *here* I can do any-thing—by correspondence or otherwise to forward the objects of the Well-wishers to the Hellenic struggle.—Will *you* state this to them—and desire them to command me—if they think it could be of any service—of course—I must in no way interfere with Blaquiere—so as to give him umbrage—or to any other person.—I have great doubts—not of my own inclination—but from the circumstances already stated —whether I shall be able to go up myself—as I fain would do—but Blaquiere seemed to think that I might be of some use—even *here*;—though *what* he did not exactly specify——If there were any things which you wished to have forwarded for the Greeks—as Surgeons—medicines powder—and swivels &c. of which they tell me that they were in want—you would find me ready to follow any directions—and what is more to the purpose—to contribute my own share to the ex-pence.——Will you let me hear from you—at any rate your opinion—and believe me

Ever yrs.
N B

P.S.—You may show this letter to D[ouglas] K[innair]d—or to any one you please——including such members of the Committee as you think proper—and explain to them that I shall confine myself to follow-ing their directions—if they give me any instructions——my uncer-tainty as to whether *I* can so manage as to go *personally*—prevents me from being more explicit—(I hear that Strangers are not very welcome to the Greeks—from jealousy) except as far as regards anything I might be able to do *here*—by obtaining good information—or affording assistance.

[TO DOUGLAS KINNAIRD]   *Genoa. April 7th. 1823*

Dear Douglas/—I have to thank you for ye. prompt acknowledge-ment of the arrival of the packets—since which I have also sent the 15th. C[ant]o.—You do not mention the arrival by the Consul's courier of a Scotch deed—which I signed and sent to enable you to receive £133. 12S. 0D. on my account.——I saw Capt. Blaquiere on his [way] to Greece a few days ago—and have written to Hobhouse [by to]day's post on the result of our conversation which [I have] requested Hobhouse to communicate to you.——If I can in person or

144

otherwise do anything for the good cause I will—as far as my means go —but I do not choose to intrude till invited. I have converted £1500 in Circulars into cash—on account of the present great advantage of the exchange here—the gain being between 50—and 60—that is 57 pounds Sterling above par—on the whole sum now drawn.—I have dined with yr. friends the Blessingtons—whom I find very agreeable people—and full of your praises.——*If* I should have to take a turn in the Levant—to investigate the state of things there—you must reconvert the Exchequer bill into Cash in your bank—and let me have— by July next as extended a credit as my means or assetts will justify— yr. prudence in permitting—since every thing will pass through yr. hands during my absence.——You see for many reasons how anxious I must be to have Deardon's business settled in some way;—you will keep up the insurances—that is a necessary expence.—The Creditors must wait another year or so—which they may well do—since happen what may to me—they are eventually secure.—As to Literary matters —they seem hopeless—though I do not see why *you* are so *frightened*— as Henry Fox (Ld. Holland's son) tells me you are—this is to want *moral* courage—which is strange in one who has so much *physical* valour as to be rather too temerarious in most things.——You however might probably dispose of the *ten* Cantos and "the Island" to Somebody or other.

yrs ever

N B

I open my letter to say that I have just seen a young man who was Clerk to Galignani at Paris—he tells me that of all *my* works Juan is by far the most popular and sells best—especially with the women—who send by hundreds slily—for copies.——now pray what is the fright about publishing?—depend upon it you are taken in by some cursed scheme of Murray's and his gang to disgust [me?] and to frighten you— what are you afraid of—the *Newspapers!*

[TO JOHN HUNT] *April 9th. 1823*

Sir—I add a few lines to what I wrote last week to request that you will have ye goodness to mention to Mr. K[innair]d—that is it essential for me to have the remaining Cantos in proof immediately that I may correct the press—as also those of "the Island" a poem in four Cantos—now received in London.—The number of *un*published C[ant]o's of D[on] J[uan] (including the 15th lately sent) is *ten* in all—

forming three series or even three *vols*—with only *nine*—allowing
three for *each*.—

yrs. in great haste
N B

P.S.—I open my letter (so do not calumniate the post) to say that I
have just seen a young man late Clerk to Galignani—of Paris—who
tells me that of all my works D[on] Juan is the most popular—and sells
doubly in proportion—especially amongst the women who send for it
the more that it is abused.——Now what is the motive of Mr. K[in-
naird]'s delay or demur—I cannot tell—he must be taken in by some
plot or circulating lie of the bookselling Leviathan to disgust me—or to
appall him.—I do not know who *may* be or who *should* be the publisher
—but I should see little difficulty in finding one—as to the reviewers—
leave me to fight with them—I have "bobbit it weel" with them *once*—
and "Gin it be na weel bobbit[1]—weel bobbit—weel bobbit—Gin it be
na weel bobbit["]—we'll bob it[.]

[TO THE EARL OF BLESSINGTON]   *April 9, 1823*
My dear Lord,

* * * * * * * * *

P.S.—I salute Miledi, Mademoiselle Mama, and the illustrious
Chevalier Count [D'Orsay]; who, I hope, will continue his history of
"his own times." There are some strange coincidences between a part
of his remarks and a certain work of mine, now in MS, in England, (I
do not mean the hermetically sealed Memoirs, but a continuation of
certain Cantos of a certain poem), especially in *what a man* may do in
London with impunity while he is "a la mode"; which I think it well to
state, that he may not suspect me of taking advantage of his confidence.
The observations are very general.[5]

[TO DOUGLAS KINNAIRD]   *Genoa. April 9th. 1823*

Dear Douglas/—I have received the inclosed note from and seen a
Mr. Jones.—I can only say of the Messrs Howard and Gibbs and Miss
Massingberd—that I have nothing further to do in the business.—The
letter contains a proposal for me to pay the insurance of Miss M[as-

---

[1] Scott, *Heart of Midlothian*, Chap. 39.
[5] Byron's satire on English high society in the later cantos of *Don Juan* had been
written before he met Count D'Orsay.

singber]d's life!—With exactly the same equity as if *I* were to insure *your* life—and ask *you* to pay the insurance.—I have paid at one or another [time] more than the principal and legal interest of the whole sum—if Miss M[assingberd] did not choose to pay them what she received—that is her affair.—In 1814 she proposed to me by a Mr. [Fozard?]—that if I would advance a certain sum—I should hear no more of her—I *did* advance it—and till within this last year—heard no more on the subject.—You are I suppose fully aware what sort of people Howard & Gibbs turned out—and I shall listen to no representations of theirs—I never spoke with Gibbs—or saw him or Howard that I recollect—since I was one and twenty.—Thomas and Riley were my only Jews—and they were paid off in 1818 or 1819.—At least so it was stated in my accounts from Hanson—which I presume you saw verified.——If Mr. Jones calls upon you—I can only say—that you may repeat what is here stated—and what I stated to himself this morning.——I wrote to you and Hobhouse by Monday's post—chiefly on the substance of an interview between Capt. Blaquiere and the Greek envoy—and myself on the subject of the Greek cause.—It is probable—if they send to me (as they seem inclined) that I may go out there—to the provisional seat of Government—or at any rate do what I can for them in the way of correspondence &c.——In that case I shall wish you to reserve all monies to supply me with as ample a credit as you can furnish me with consistent with the sums you may receive or are likely to receive for me.—

yrs. ever
N B

[TO DR. JAMES ALEXANDER]   *April 12th. 1823*

D[ea]r D[octo]r—My steward tells me an unintelligible story about *flags* &c.—for the family of Col. B.—Do they put to Sea—or do they not?—I have heard nothing further since you informed me that they had given up the idea of the voyage being of use to Miss B.—Of course if they require it—they shall have what they desire.—I mentioned in my last note that I had a couple of *Warts* on the face—for which I would thank you to prescribe an unguent—or Caustic—as they trouble the economy of my beard in shaving.—If my handwriting is not de-cypherable—I will try to make it legible—as often as you please, rather than bore you with a visitation—for such trifles.—

ever yrs.
N B

[TO THE EARL OF BLESSINGTON (*a*)]   *April 14th, 1823*

I am truly sorry that I cannot accompany you in your ride this morning, owing to a violent pain in my face, arising from a wart to which I by medical advice applied a caustic. Whether I put too much, I do not know; but the consequence is, that not only I have been put to some pain, but the peccant part and its immediate environ are as black as if the printer's devil had marked me for an author. As I do not wish to frighten your horses, or their riders, I shall postpone waiting upon you until six o'clock, when I hope to have subsided into a more christianlike resemblance to my fellow-creatures. My infliction has partially extended even to my fingers; for on trying to get the black from off my upper lip at least, I have only transfused a portion thereof to my right hand, and neither lemon-juice nor eau de Cologne, nor any other eau, have been able as yet to redeem it also from a more inky appearance than is either proper or pleasant. But "out, damn'd spot"—you may have perceived something of the kind yesterday; for on my return, I saw that during my visit it had increased, was increasing, and ought to be diminished; and I could not help laughing at the figure I must have cut before you. At any rate, I shall be with you at six, with the advantage of twilight.

Ever most truly, etc.

Eleven o'clock.

P.S.,—I wrote the above at three this morning. I regret to say that the whole of the skin of about an *inch* square above my upper lip has come off, so that I cannot even shave or masticate, and I am equally unfit to appear at your table, and to partake of its hospitality. Will you therefore pardon me, and not mistake this rueful excuse for a *"make-believe,"* as you will soon recognise whenever I have the pleasure of meeting you again, and I will call the moment I am, in the nursery phrase, "fit to be seen." Tell Lady B., with my compliments, that I am rummaging in my papers for a MS. worthy of her acceptation. I have just seen the younger Count Gamba; and as I cannot prevail on his infinite modesty to take the field without me, I must take this piece of diffidence on myself also, and beg your indulgence for both.

[TO THE EARL OF BLESSINGTON (*b*)]   *Abril, 14th. 1823*

My dear Lord,—I was not in the way when your note came. I have only time to thank you, and to send the Galignani's. My face is better

148

in fact, but worse in appearance, with a very *scurvy* aspect; but I expect
it to be well in a day or two. I will subscribe to the Improving Society.

Yours in haste, but ever,

Noel Byron

[to john cam hobhouse]   *April 14th. 1823*

Dear H.—Since I wrote to you last week on the subject of Blaquiere's
interview—and on the Greeks—I have heard no more from Blaquiere
—who was to have written to me at length—so I suppose that he has
either exceeded his powers—or repented him—for some reason or
other—"tis a' ane to Dandy".[1]—By the enclosed paper you will see
that *I* was in earnest—and would either have gone to Greece myself—
or sent aid in her cause—besides doing all I could in every way either
here or elsewhere.——Will you request the Honourable Douglas—to
state if anything is paid from Kirkby—I have now been a year and a
quarter in possession—and have received *nine* hundred pounds—from
rents of 6336 *stated* to be *duly* paid!—A Mortgage carried off a thousand
pounds—(to be repaid however it seems on some sale of other property) and Lady Noel—a rather more expensive Spectre than Lucian's
Ghosts—walked over Styx with another—by some kind of honourable
posthumous process.—But still there remained £4336.—to divide (or
account for) between Lady B[yron] and myself—of this she had nine—
I nine—total eighteen hundred

Subtract   4336

1800
———
2536

and there still ought to accrue to each party—a sum of twelve hundred
and sixty eight pounds—if I do not miscalculate.—Luckily I have monies
of my own—three thousand of last years—and my own fund fee of this
—and lucky it is—for by some mismanagement it seems no more is to
be depended upon from any copyrights.—However I will perish piece-
meal—before they shall silence me——I have now eleven unpublished
Cantos of D[on] J[uan] nearly ready in M.S.S. and I mean to make
them a hundred.——I never saw such a set of scoundrels on one hand
—and to say the least—of hesitating Gentlemen (afraid of newspapers)
on the *other*—as the two Mr. Murray's gangs on the one hand—and
my worthy friends on the other.—

yrs. ever

N B

[1] Scott, *Guy Mannering*, Vol. II, chap. 7.

Dear Douglas/—I have received a copy of "the Age"[1] from Mr. J[ohn] H[unt] who seems apprehensive of piracy—if such an attempt is made we must apply for an *injunction*—as there is nothing illegal that I see in the publication.—Tell Hobhouse that I have written twice on the subject of Greece—with a request that you should know what I have written on the subject of my interview with Capt. Blaquiere.— You will in case of it's being necessary—supply me with such a credit as my available funds will sanction—I suppose.—Do not make any more payments—without letting me know—and pray let us stop these Rochdale proceedings.—I suppose that Mr. Deardon would give us *something* for the Manor—a little would be better now—than more at another time. I have now been a year and [a] quarter in possession of Kirkby & we have received nine hundred pounds! out of a (stated as available) rental of six thousand three hundred and thirty six pounds per annum.—Admitting a thousand for the mortgage—(which you say is to be repaid to me eventually) and another thousand for Lady Noel's posthumous perquisite—there still remain 4336. to account for to Lady B[yron] and to myself.——

You have now ten Cantos of D[on] J[uan] (I am writing the eleventh)— and the Island in hand—can you make no arrangement with Wright or others for the publication? I know that the work D[on] J[uan] is by far the most popular of mine.——You may reckon upon eleven or twelve Cantos being forthcoming (the Gods willing) and I shall probably make the work a *hundred* in time—if I live—just to show these fellows that I am not the boy to be put down by their outcry.——As to the merits—I think that the subsequent Cantos will be found as good as the others on the whole—and better in some parts.— You must not mind occasional rambling I mean it for a poetical T[ristram] Shandy—or Montaigne's Essays with a story for a hinge. —I hope that you will not let these lawyers H[anson] and trustees do as they please with my interests in my absence.

yrs ever
N B

Sir—If the attempt at Piracy is made—an injunction must be applied for—I am determined to try that question.———You will probably have

[1] *The Age of Bronze* was published by John Hunt without Byron's name on the title page on April 1, 1823.

to regret publishing "the Blues" which will merely beget more enemies to the Journal.——I have read "the Age" [of Bronze] which with one or two exceptions is correctly printed.—Two thousand were too many to print—but I will make up any loss that may be sustained—I have little notion of it's success.—I have nearly finished a 16th. Canto of D[on] J[uan] and am anxious to have proofs [of] the others to correct—which I will thank you to [send] to Mr. Kinnaird.— As to the 4th. No. of the Liberal you will use yr. discretion—the profits of the work will probably be greater when it's periodical continuation has ceased—as it will then form two volumes of a curious Miscellany. I have the honour to be

yr. very obedt. Servt.
N B

[TO JOHN CAM HOBHOUSE] *April 17th. 1823*

My dear Hobhouse/—Since I wrote I have heard from Capt. B[laquiere] he is at Rome—was refused passage through *Naples* and must go to Corfu—by Ancona—please to state this to the committee. —They [(]i.e. B. and his companion[)] are anxious for me to go up there—and if I can—I will.—I have in the mean time ordered about a hundred pounds Sterling worth of powder—and some hospital supplies to be sent up to the seat of the provisional Government.——I have had the enclosed letter from my banker here (Mr. Barry—the Agent of the house of Webb & Co.—and a very good fellow) but he tells me that we can have a choice of Vessels at any time at a more moderate rate.——Pray tell me what you think that I should do—and please to request Douglas K[innair]d to have the goodness (in case I go up) to let me have credits in the most convenient Italian or Levant places—for the whole of my disposable funds—which ought to be a tolerable sum —including the present year—and as all my monies must pass through his hands—I suppose that he will not hesitate.——I have not broken in upon anything of the present year—and have still three thousand pounds of my income of 1822.—I wish that he could get anything for the Don Juans (he has ten cantos in hand) and an eleventh nearly ready (besides some other M.S.S.) my going up far and away—would neutralize the bookselling hostility against me—as being likely to be my latest work.——That and any arrangement about Rochdale—however scanty in proportion to it's actual value—would enable me to go up with means that might be of some real service—or even whether I go or not—enable me to forward the views of the Committee and the

Greek People.—If I go there—I shall do my best to civilize their mode of treating their prisoners—and could I only save a single life—whether Turk or Greek—I should live "mihi carior"—and I trust not less so to my friends—

ever yrs.

N B

P.S.—I shall send you a copy of B[laquiere]'s letter in my next—

[TO J. WEBB]   *Genoa. April 19th. 1823*

Dear Sir,—I have had a letter from Sr. Giuliani, informing me that he has re-mended [remanded?] the watch, and wants to have a price fixed for the box with the portraits of the Emperor, Empress, and their son. I should like to have it valued out of curiosity—but whatever value may be set upon it, I shall not take less than a hundred Guineas—and it is perhaps worth more, as the portraits, two at least, are original, and the whole of Parisian workmanship.—With regard to the Tortoise-shell box, or whatever box the other is that they are haggling about—I shall not abate a centime of the estimate I fixed upon—they may buy or not as they please. I am sorry to give you this trouble—but it is not altogether my fault—and there is no one else in Tuscany whom I could trust with the deposit. I have had, as you perhaps know, a petty law-suit at Pisa, and one with a fellow called Depuy at Leghorn.[1] During my absence they have gained (at least the Pisan rascal), and you know what kind of justice the Tuscans administer to foreigners. It is possible, I suppose, that they might try to get hold of any property of mine in your hands—in that case, you will, I pray, keep a good look out—and throw it into the sea—or send it off here—or do anything with it—rather than permit these scoundrels to profit by their rascality. I assure you I would rather lose it altogether, than that they should have a six-pence. Recommending this in particular to your attention, I have the honour to be

yr. obliged & obedt. Sert.

N B

[TO DOUGLAS KINNAIRD]   *April 19th. 1823*

My dear Douglas/—Hobhouse will have communicated to you my interview with Capt. Blaquiere—and the substance of the subsequent

[1] Byron also lost the lawsuit with Francesco Dupuy, from whom he had leased the Villa at Montenero from May 1 to the end of October. He left after little more than a month of occupancy.

152

letter which I have had from B[laquiere] (dated Rome) I have not yet sent a copy of the letter to H[obhouse] but merely a summary of the contents.— —If I go up into the Levant—I shall want all the credit you can muster for me—from monies received or to be received—that is— as far as *you* think it prudent to venture.—I should think that you might sell my *ten* Cantos—you had a thousand offered for the *seven*— which is not a fair offer—but with the adjunct of the three new ones— and the four Cantos of the Island—and the permanent copyright of the poems (already published) to be collected into volumes—I think you might get a decent value for the whole.—Firstly—if I go up—there is some risk of not returning—and in this case—my *latest* works would bear some value merely as *such*—2dly.—if I do come back—I shall probably bring some poesy or prose worth the looking for—as I know the Country—and it is an interesting time.—Murray *ought* to pay something for "Werner"[.] I have made enquiries and find that at *Paris* at least—the sale of *four hundred* copies of a work—pays it's *expences*—now M[urray] sold six thousand by his own account—then how can he have lost?— —The question besides is—whether the eight and twenty years copy right are not worth something—as it will sell with the others—as long at least as *they* sell.—What they may do at home—I know not—but abroad—they have a great sale—if I may judge by the number of editions—in France and Germany—and America.— —

Did you get the Scotch deed?—You have never answered about Webster's bond—(in Hanson's hands) I see similar sales (Ld. Moira's bonds for instance) in the papers daily—and I would willingly sell it— for what it may fetch—Rowley & Capron—in Savile Row would be likely to buy it.— —With regard to the Noel payments if they are eventually so secure—you could let me have a credit on those due (I speak in case of my Greek expedition) and also on the Exchequer bill (reconverting it into cash) as well as on my own July dividends—and I must positively require that you do not make any further payments at present either to Baxter or to any one else.—I have occasion for all the floating sums I can collect—and as the Creditors are few in number— not great in amount—and are eventually secure—as I have property to cover all their claims a thousand or five thousand times over—whether I survive or not,—you must really not be complying with every pre- tension of these fellows—till I know better whether they are well founded.— —As to Rochdale—as you do not condescend [to] favour me with the slightest information on the subject—that I may be enabled to stop the process—I am a good deal puzzled what to say—

but I have neither time nor inclination to scold about it—and am besides much

very much yrs.
N B

P.S.—If the present time is let slip by for the publication of the D[on] J[uan]s—it is so much lost;—do not listen to the *Cabal*—that will pass by and bye—and they are only mystifying you to bully me.—

P.S.—I have your letter of Credit for two thousand pounds untouched—and it is only for Tuscany—though I could get money on it here.—I have also a thousand in Circulars still—fifteen hundred I converted the other day—as the Exchange was temptingly in favour—and at the same time likely to alter.—If you send me an extended Credit on Italy and the Levant—I shall return you the *Letter* (for the £2000) untouched as is just and proper.——I have 17000—Francs too—(for the Gold exchanged last year) in Webb's bank in Leghorn—all this is sufficient for my *own* private expences—and more—but if I go up into Greece—I wish to have as great a command of monies of mine as I can—that I might be of some use to the Cause—and you know that Cash is the Sinew of war as indeed of most other things—love excepted and occasionally of that too.——

[TO DOUGLAS KINNAIRD] *April 21st. 1823*

My dear Douglas—By all means send the power of Attorney for you *sole*—or—in case of my going up to the Levant—from whence our correspondence must be slow and uncertain—suppose you make it for you and Hobhouse—lest any accident should occur (you rough rider you!) when I might be for months without any person able or willing to act for me—during my absence.——Send me also correct instructions for the signature—and then you can control and regulate and get me out of lawyers' hands and bills,—you surely know that it is now *eight* years—I have [been] striving to extricate my affairs from Chancery Lane—and Hobhouse can tell you the same thing.——

With regard to the Juans (you will have the tenth by this time) and The Island—and the rest (I mean those published—but not disposed of as to Copyright) you could perhaps arrange with Wright or some one else—for the purchase of the copyrights of the *whole*—they would form five—six or more volumes to match with the former works.— H[unt] writes that he has sold in a week about 2000 of the Age [of Bronze] &c.—which will at least pay it's expences;—you will be able to judge from this matter the truth of Murray's averment about

Werner—of which he sold 6000.—He *ought* to make a deposit for the Copyright of Werner—recollect that it lasts for eight and twenty years.——At Paris—*400 copies* sold—pay the *expence* of publishing a work—how this may be in London—I know not——There is a trickery in these things—no one can understand—though we see and feel it.—After the expences of the *Age*—are settled—the fair way will be for the publisher and author to divide the surplus—if any.——Much they will probably not have to divide—because the work is temporary——and the price small—but much or little—we will take our right;—living on the Continent teaches a man the value of ten pounds—which goes a good way—and cuts an excellent figure in francs—or even in Crowns—Ecus—or Scudi.—I had been too long negligent of the "pence" and not very careful of the "pounds"—it is time to refine a little on these points.—The 133—12—from Scotland and any of the small sums from 100 to [word torn off] [would?] at [least?] help to balance the insurances—and pay postages—and wages—and to set off the "three pounds for the stamps"—as also some of Hanson's Six and eight pences.——If you do not take care however—you will find that whether the Appeal goes on or no—H[anson's] bills will go on the same.—I really think that Mr. Crabtree might have devoted a week to the Survey of R[ochdale]—before now—it would have saved time—and it may be—money.——I merely want to hear the result—and settle the business—time and disappointments—have made my expectations very moderate; but it is hard with Deardon's wish to finish the affair—and mine also—that I cannot get a statement of any kind.—Six months have now elapsed since I first wrote—but like the Noel rent days (which occur on the Greek kalends) with the exception of yr. and Mr. D[eardon']s first epistle—every day seems to put the period further *off*—than it was before—reversing the usual progress of Time.—You must allow—that the Trustees of the Noels are a noble and trusty pair of paymasters—what would you give me for *their* arrears?—or what will *they* give me—to give up the whole reversion of my *own* interest in that property?—I assure you I will sell it to them for a moderate estimate—or put it up to Public sale—realize a small sum—and with that & the produce of [the] Rochdale Manor sale purchase an annuity.——

yrs. ever
N B

Seriously what would the sale of my interest in the Noel property fetch?—two or three years purchase? or what?—We must bring Webster's bond to the hammer.

My dear Count D'Orsay—(If you will permit me to address you so familiarly)—You should be content with writing in your own language like Grammont—and succeeding in London as nobody has succeeded since the days of Charles 2d. and the records of Antonio Hamilton[1]—without deviating into *our* barbarous language—which you understand and write however much better than it deserves. My "Approbation" as you are pleased to term it—was very sincere—but perhaps not *very* impartial—for—though I love my Country—I do not love my Countrymen—at least such as they now *are*—and besides the seduction of talent and wit in your work——I fear that to me—there was the attraction of Vengeance—I have *seen* and *felt* much of what you have described so well—I have known the persons and the reunions so described—(many of them that is to say) and the portraits are so like that I cannot but admire the painter—no less than his performance——but I am sorry for you—for if you are so well acquainted with Life at your age —what will become of you when the illusion is still more dissipated? But never mind—"En Avant!" live while you can—and that you may have the full enjoyment of the many advantages of youth—talent—and figure—which you possess—is the wish of an—Englishman—I suppose,—but it is no treason,—for my mother was Scotch—and my name and my family are both *Norman*——and as for myself I am of no Country——as for my "works"—which you are pleased to mention— let them go to the Devil—from whence (if you believe many persons) they came.—I have the honour to be

> yr. obliged and faithful Sert.
>
> NOEL BYRON

Milor—I received yr. billet at dinner—which was a good one— with a sprinkling of female foreigners—who I dare say were very agreeable.—As I have formed a sullen resolution about presentations which I never break (above once a month) I begged Mr. Hill to dispense me from being introduced——and intrigued for myself a place as far remote as possible from his fair guests—and very near a bottle of the best wine to confirm my misogyny.—After Coffee—I had accomp-

---

[1] Anthony Hamilton wrote the *Mémoires de la Vie du Comte de Grammont, contenant particulièrement L'Histoire Amoureuse de la Cour d'Angleterre sous le Règne de Charles II.* It was first published at Cologne in 1713.

lished my retreat as far as the Hall—on full tilt towards your *Thé*—
which I was very eager to partake of—when I was arrested by Mr. Hill
—requesting that I would make my bow to the French Ambassadress
—who it seems is a Dillon—Irish—but born or bred in America—has
been pretty—and is a *blue*[1]—and of course entitled to the homage of all
persons who have been printed. I returned, and it was then too late to
detain Miss P[ower] over the tea-urn. I beg you to accept my regrets,
and present my regards to Milady, and Miss P[ower], and Comte
Alfred, and believe me

Ever yours,
NOEL BYRON

[TO THE EARL OF BLESSINGTON]   *April 23d. 1823*

My dear Ld. B.—I thank you for quizzing me and my "learned
Thebans".[1] I assure you my notions on that score are limited to getting
away with a whole skin—or sleeping quietly with a broken one in some
of my old Glens where I used to dream in my former excursions;—I
should prefer a grey Greek stone over me to Westminster Abbey——
but I doubt that I shall have the luck to die so happily.—A lease of my
"body's length"[2] is all the land which I should covet in that quarter.—
What the Hon Dug. [Douglas Kinnaird] and his committee may decide
I do not know—and still less what I may decide (for I am not famous
for decision) for myself—but if I could do any good in any way—I
should be happy to contribute thereto—and without *eclât*—I have seen
enough of that in my time—to rate it at it's value.——I wish that *you*
were upon that committee——for I think you would set them agoing
one way or the other—at present they seem a little dormant.——I
dare not venture to *dine* with you tomorrow—nor indeed any day this
week—for *three* days of dinners during the last seven days—have made
me so head-achy and sulky—that it will take me a whole Lent to sub-
side again into any thing like independence of Sensation from the
pressure of materialism.——But I shall take my chance of finding you
the first fair morning for a visit[.]

ever yrs
N B

---

[1] First page (from facsimile) ends here.
[1] *King Lear*, Act III, scene 4.
[2] *Henry VI*, Part III, Act. V, scene 2.

[Part quoted in catalogue]

...I know how difficult it is for a man of good sense to follow a rhyming MS. through with its evolutions—but my distance leaves me no other resource. You have sometimes corrected where it was not necessary—for instance, "bark of vapour" (i.e.: steam boat) was printed rightly, you have corrected it into "bank"; appropriate enough —but not exactly what I meant. I have to request your attention to stanzas 57 and 58 of Canto 11th. I have marked in the proofs that the half of 57, and the whole of 58th. Stanza are to be omitted—and asterisks placed instead of the lines, leaving however the space and numbers of the stanzas the same. Do not forget this—nor treat me as Mr. Murray did about the preface to "the Vision". Who is to be the publisher of D[on] J[uan] I do not know but I presume you will have no objection to correct it through the press for me—so be who he may. I also wish a proof of the "Island" (in 4 Cantos now in Mr. K[innaird]'s hands). I fear that you will overprint the Age of Bronze. I suppose the two thousand are as many as will be called for—and these being now sold you had better reduce the number in the next edition to 500. If it is pirated we must claim our right—it is time that this sort of question should be settled in one way or another. With regard to the "Age of Bronze" and publishing on what is called the author's account, I suppose that the fair way is after the expences are paid for the publisher and author to divide the profits—if any exist. I think of collecting all my works (not hitherto collected) whether published or in MS. into volumes, so as to form a series to the works published by Murray—if Mr. Murray declines purchasing "Werner" I shall add it to the number....

My dear Douglas/—The only will hitherto found of Mr. Shelley's is in England.—So inform your Applicant.—I have written on the subject which is all that an absent man can do—and I have received a not very Clear answer—which is all that an absent man can expect.—— Messrs. Hanson and Godwin can inform you of the particulars—and whether or not his will is available—or when—if ever—it will be so.— This is all that I know of his affairs.———I repeat that I cannot give a clearer account of them—but this is the most satisfactory that I have been able to obtain of his—or of any other person's—including my own—for which latter fact—I refer to your Honourable Worship—

who will I presume confirm this Eulogy of lawyers and trustees. I return you the corrected proofs of D[on] J[uan].—and shall be glad of the others—I presume that the 15th. has arrived also.—I have nearly a hundred stanzas of the 16th. finished.——Perhaps you can arrange with Wright or some other—for the purchase of the whole—and of "the Island" and all poems of mine published or in M.S.S. *not* yet collected into Volumes—the whole would form six or seven——as to publishing on our *own* account—I suppose it is a "pis aller"—but we can form some notion from the "Age of Bronze" though it is a light performance.—The piracy will interfere with D[on] J[uan] probably—but I presume that there is some way of reducing the effect.—— Murray *must* account for "Werner"—it is nonsense to talk of having *lost*—even if he had only sold a *thousand*—instead of 6000—as you and he said.——Enquire—and you will find the truth—besides—there is the time to come (28 years of the Copy right) however I desire nothing but what is fair.—Let him merely account for the sale—if he declines the purchase—and we will collect "Werner" and publish it in the ensuing volumes of my collected works.—I recommend to you earnestly—Rochdale—Kirkby—and

yrs. very truly
N B

P.S.—Pray make no *payments* but keep all in bank—or send to me in credit till you hear from me. I hope you have not been wasting my Exchequer bills on the other items—on Baxter or anybody else.

[TO CHARLES F. BARRY][1]   *April 25th. 1823*

Dear Sir—I have not employed any one to "take up a vessel for me at Leghorn"[.] I have merely requested some information on the subject of a Genoese ship which has been mentioned as adapted for the voyage—in case it should take place. The case of Snuff-boxes—which your Partners of Leghorn have expedited is of some value—considerably more than the insurance—they are of English manufacture—all save one—which is Parisian—I am not aware whether there will or will not be difficulties in the extraction from the Dogana—but as private property—not merchandise—and part of my furniture—I should hope that permission may be obtained—I shall apply to the Consul or to the Minister—if necessary.—Mr. Webb has done well in

---

[1] The Genoa partner of Webb & Co., Byron's bankers in Leghorn. See Biographical Sketch in Appendix IV.

transferring my balance of monies to Genoa.—I wish to know, if it is to remain on the same footing in the bank here—or how? I mean with regard to ye. interest hitherto allowed upon the original sum.—

My Pisa lawsuit was a very trifling one—originally about the discussion of some five pounds sterling—swoln by the scoundrel Pisan Attorneys to about *ten*—more or less.—As it is not agreeable to be cheated by these rascals—or to be exposed to their Chicanery and vexatious proceedings—to which I will never submit—I hope you will not disapprove my having transferred the funds on which they might have tried to fix their claws—to this place.—Had either their pretensions—or the decision of their tribunals (with whose iniquities in all cases regarding a foreigner you may be acquainted by report or experience of their injustice) been in any degree fair—I need hardly add that I would never have disputed the point;—it is not the *amount*—but the mode of their proceedings—which I reclaim against.——Whether they can transfer their cause—or pretended cause here—I know not—but *they* say that they can;—we shall see if it be so—at any rate I will "try conclusions with them".[2]——I have the honour to be

your very obedt. humble Servt.

N B

[TO JOHN HUNT]   *Genoa. April 29th. 1823*

Sir—I have to acknowledge yrs. of ye. 15th. inst.——The principal objections I believe may probably be the want of Capital—and of that mercantile influence by which publishers on a large scale are enabled to (what they call) *"push* a work" added to the political hostility which exists independent of such considerations.—This I take to be the grounds of Mr. K[innaird]'s hesitation—and I cannot take upon myself to decide at this distance—what would be advisable—since I am ignorant of the real grounds of the question—further than the above conjecture.—Whoever may be the publisher eventually—I should think that the smaller edition must be an indispensable appendage to the 8vo.—As to making any alterations (except in a *critical* point of view) to mollify the Self-love and irritation of Bigotry or Corruption —or the insolence of Power in any shape—this is not to be expected from *me*—especially when the *outcry* is *greatest*;—I leave it to Others to *Circumsize* their "Angels"[1] with their "bonnes fortunes" to the drawing room and classical standard;—what *I* have written—I have

---

[2] *Merchant of Venice*, Act II, scene 2.
[1] See April 2, 1823, to Moore.

written.——My whole apprehension and uneasiness upon any point of this kind—has regarded entirely the probable persecution of yourself and family—and it is a serious consideration;——for myself the battle in a worldly point is more equal—and requires less courage in consequence.—Believe me

yrs. truly
N B

P.S.—The "two thousand" is not a bad sale in itself—but comparative with the numbers—from 6—to 9—and once or twice (as in the case of "the Corsair") to 13000—the first day—and 20000 within the fortnight—is a proof of a decline of popularity to a great extent—but "En Avant!" Courage! you were quite right however not to *overprint* —and I would advise the same precaution in any case.——

[TO CHARLES F. BARRY]   *April 30th. 1823*

Dear Sir—I will thank you to apprize the advocate you mention that mine will communicate with him on the Appeal now pending.—With regard to the [Pisacano?]—the plaintiff is a varnisher of carriages— who made an overcharge which was resisted—he brought his action— and obtained a verdict—the latter since my departure—and under unfair circumstances.—I wish to know—1stly. whether the action can be tried over again in the courts here—2dly.—if I can not make a conveyance to some one here; or else a shipment of *my* effects of *all* kinds from hence (as they were only allowed to enter free from duties on condition of *not* being sold here) because though the whole amount of the rascal's charge and sentence &c. is not above twelve or thirteen pounds sterling;—there is no inconvenience or expence I would not undergo rather than submit to it—even to quitting the state or any states—because I *know* the sentence to be an unjust one.—I should like to have an answer as soon as convenient—that I may take steps of some kind accordingly.——Lega can tell you any particulars—as he was employed in some subaltern department of the old tribunal under the former Government in Italy.—I have the honour to be

yr. very obedt.
N B

[TO ?]   [*May, 1823?*]
[Postscript to letter of Count Gamba]
. . . The boats had better be engaged, because if this intelligence is not confirmed, I must sail at any rate, and even if it be, I shall sail as

soon as possible, after communicating with the vessels[1] on their voyage, which, (if my instructions do not err, and I fr[om] them), are committed to my direction. I do not perceive, however, how a ship directed to *Greece* from *London can* touch at Ancona in its proper course, unless it has contrived to pass *the Alps* by *steamer* or a special wind of Providence added to a New Deluge. . . .

[TO DOUGLAS KINNAIRD]   [*Genoa, May? 1823*]

[Fragment of letter—beginning missing]
. . . fair play on my part—I don't know what is.—Believe me
                                    yrs. ever & truly
                                         N B

P.S.—I hope you have retained the best Counsel for the H[unt]s— have you received the 12th. C[ant]o of D[on] J[uan] sent on the 14th. 10bre. 1822?—I do not know what security we can have for H[unt]'s accounting for the profits—but he has a property in the Examiner; ——a fair account of profit or loss—would perhaps be the better way —supposing it to be accurately stated.——I have had a letter from my Sister—wishing me *not* to leave anything by my will to *her* children!! I do not know if I mentioned to you a similar circumstance;—when Allegra died I was going to leave the five thousand pounds which I had originally bequeathed to that infant to Madame La Comtesse Guiccioli —which she declined in the most positive and, indeed, displeased terms—declaring that she should consider such a bequest as not only an injustice to my daughter by Lady B[yron] —and to my Sister's family—but as a posthumous insult to herself—and persisted so—that I have been obliged to leave my will as it was—Is not this odd? *two women* of different countries converging upon the same point! It is true Madame G. has her separate allowance (by the Pope's decree) from her husband—and will have a considerable jointure at his demise, but it is not unhandsome conduct nevertheless.——

[TO MR. HAMLET]   *May 1, 1823*

[Part quoted in catalogue]
    Mr. Hamlet will have the goodness to forward the articles ordered by Lord Byron to Florence[1] as soon as possible.

    [1] Ships to be sent out with supplies by the London Greek Committee.
    [1] Thus in the catalogue quotation. It is strange that Byron should have ordered articles sent to Florence. It could be a misreading for Leghorn, where he stopped on his way to Greece.

My dear Lady Blessington—I must write you a line to thank you for your very kind notice of me. For the cordiality with which you have praised and defended me I am—I assure you—most deeply grateful—and though less alive—I am sorry to say—both to praise and blame—than I used to be—yet coming from a heart and a taste like yours—they cannot fail to touch me very sensibly—Believe me—dear Lady Blessington—

ever faithfully your obliged
BYRON

[TO THE COUNTESS OF BLESSINGTON] *May 3d. 1823*

Dear Lady B.—My request would be for a copy of the miniature of Lady B[yron] which I have seen in the possession of the late Lady Noel.—as I have no picture—nor indeed memorial of any kind of Ly. B.—as all her letters were in her own possession before I left England—& we have had no correspondence since—at least on her part.—My message with regard to the Infant—is simply to this effect—that in the event of any accident occurring to the mother—and my remaining the Survivor—it would be my wish to have her plans carried into effect—both with regard to the education of the child—and the person or persons under whose care Ly. B. might be desirous that she should be placed.—It is not my intention to interfere with her in any way on the subject during her life—and I presume that it would be some consolation to her to know—(if she is in ill health as I am given to understand) that in *no* case—would anything be done—as far as I am concerned—but in strict conformity with Ly. B's own wishes and instructions—left in what manner she thought proper.———Believe me my dear Ly. B.

yr obliged & obedt. St.
NOEL BYRON

[TO JOHN CAM HOBHOUSE] *Genoa—May 5th. 1823*

My dear Hobhouse—This will be presented to you by my friend Capt. T. Medwin—who at my request—will introduce himself to you as Member of the Greek Committee and explain some plan that he has formed with regard to offering his services to the Greeks—a subject on which we are all interested. I need not say more—than that any

attention to him will be appreciated by me as an additional obligation
due to you on the part of

yrs. ever
N B

[TO EDWARD LE MESURIER, R. N.]¹   *Villa Saluzzo. Albaro.*

May 5th. 1823

Sir—I have received with great gratitude yr. present of the Newfoundland Dog.—Few gifts could have been more gratifying—as I
have ever been partial to the breed.——He shall be taken the greatest
care of—and I would not part with him for any consideration;—he is
already a chief favourite with the whole house.——I have the honour
to be

your much obliged & very faithfl. Servt.

NOEL BYRON

[TO MADAME SERGENT-MARCEAU]   *Genova 5 Mag[gi]o 1823*

Stimatissima Signora—La di Lei Lettera m'onora—e niun presente
Ella potea farmi che mi fosse più grato della Operetta in cui sono così
bene descritte le azioni del di Lei Fratello la cui memoria io venero. Io
ho letto questa Operetta col più vivo piacere—ed ho sentito sempre-
più nel leggerla quanto l'omaggio da me reso alla memoria di codesto
Giovine Eroe è ancora ben inferiore a quello che Egli meriterebbe: ma
almeno è sincero.

In quanto poi all'osservazione del Sig.r Sergent-Merceau sopra la
nota 13 [&c. &c.?]—mi faccio un dovere di rispondergli essere io stato
informato di quanto scrissi dal Locandiere dell'Albergo situato sul
Reno—Dirimpetto alla Fortezza: ed Ella m'obbligherà se compiacerà
notificar ciò per parte mia al suddetto Signore. E nel rinnovarle le mie
più sincere proteste di riconoscenza—colla maggiore stima—ho l'onore
di dirmi——Di Lei gentile Signora——

Devot[issi]mo Obb[ligattissi]mo Servitore
NOEL BYRON   Pair d'Angleterre

---

¹ Le Mesurier (1796–1855) entered the navy as a boy. When he left the service
as a lieutenant, he spent the rest of his life in Italy. "Lyon", the Newfoundland dog
which Byron took to Greece, was brought back to England with his corpse.

Most esteemed Signora—Your letter honours me—and no present you might give me would be more welcome than the short work[1] in which the actions of your Brother, whose memory I revere, are so well described. I have read this little work with the greatest pleasure—and I realised more and more in reading it, how much the homage rendered by me to the memory of this Young Hero,[2] is still so inferior to that which he might deserve: but at least it is sincere.

In regard then to the observation of Signor Sergent Merceau[3] on the 13th note [&c. &c.?]—I am making it my duty to reply to him, having been informed of that which I wrote by the Innkeeper of the hotel situated on the Rhine—opposite the Fortress: and you will oblige me if you will be kind enough to report this on my behalf to the above-mentioned Signore. And in renewing my most sincere protestations of gratitude to you—with the greatest esteem—I have the honour of declaring myself——dear Signora, your

Most devoted & grateful Servant

NOEL BYRON   Peer of England[4]

[TO CAPTAIN DANIEL ROBERTS]   *May 5th. 1823*

Dear Sir—The enclosed letters are my first intimation of any proceedings on the subject—and I am very sorry to see you called in question on the occasion.——I believe that you are aware from Mr. Trelawny himself—that from the very first—I doubted the propriety of hoisting a pendant—(though I had always understood that it was a kind of courtesy allowed to Noblemen—and even to others of inferior rank) on board the Bolivar—and that as to the *hostile* correspondence between the acting Lieutenant and Tre[lawny]—I knew nothing of it—(being at Pisa) till it was over—and regretted it for many reasons—more especially as I had been told by T[relawny] that Captain [Jervoise?] had been perfectly gentlemanly in his demeanour.——What

---

[1] Madame Sergent-Marceau, the half sister of the Marceau who was killed in 1796 in a heroic struggle to suppress the Vendean insurrection. She had just read Byron's two stanzas in the third canto of *Childe Harold* extolling Marceau's bravery as told to him by the innkeeper at Coblenz in 1816. Her husband had compiled a little book on Marceau's life and character which she sent to Byron. (Antoine Francois Sergent-Marceau, *Notices Historiques sur le Général Marceau*, Milan, 1820, 228 pp.)

[2] *Childe Harold*, Canto III, stanzas 56 and 57.

[3] Teresa Guiccioli, who wrote the letter which Byron signed, spelled the name "Merceau".

[4] Translated by Ricki B. Herzfeld.

the proceedings are or are to be—I cannot conjecture—nor do I much care—except that I should regret their affecting either yourself or Trelawny—or indeed any body but myself—who knew nothing of the matter.——Can I do any thing in your part of the question that would be of use—if so—pray command me?——I think Trelawny should make a statement—as far as you are *professionally* concerned— that it may not injure you in the service.—

ever yrs. & truly
N B

P.S.—I shall be glad to see you whenever convenient—and should like to know *what* they are likely to do—that I may be ready.—

[TO JOHN HUNT]   *May 5th. 1823*

Sir—I have returned to Mr. K[innair]d the proofs of the Canto and the *half* of another which I have just received.—I should take it as a great favour—if you will carefully collate and correct by the M.S.S.— or by the *sense* (where there is any) for the Copy is sometimes in- correct.——It is my intention to publish the whole of the new Cantos of D[on] J[uan]—also "the Island"—and to collect my recently pub- lished or unpublished scattered poems—into volumes to form a series to my former works.—What do you think of this?—

yrs. ever in haste
N B

P.S.—I dare say my praising Canning will have given umbrage[1]— I praised him because I thought that he deserved it—and I belong to *no* party—and claim the independence of saying what I please of *any* according to their acts.—Canning's at this time promise—or pr[om- ised?] something for the World and his Country?—I see an Edinburgh Review of H[eaven] and E[arth] advertised—is it abusive?—or by Jeffrey—or by whom?—

[TO THE COUNTESS OF BLESSINGTON]   *May 6th. 1823*

Dear Lady Bless[ingto]n—I send you the letter—which I had for- gotten—and the book which I ought to have remembered—it contains

---

[1] Byron had praised the statesman George Canning in a note to the Preface to Cantos 6, 7, and 8 of *Don Juan*, and also in *The Age of Bronze*, lines 548–567. Though Canning was a Tory, he had opposed the foreign policy of Castlereagh, and was generally independent.

—(the book I mean) some melancholy truths though I believe that it is too triste a work ever to have been popular.—The first time I ever read it—(*not* the edition I send you—for I got it since) was at the desire of Madame de Stael—who was supposed by the good natured world to be the heroine—which she was not however—and was furious at the supposition.[1] This occurred in Switzerland in the Summer of 1816—and the last season in which I ever saw that celebrated person. —I have a request to make to my friend Alfred—(since he has not disclaimed the title—) viz.—that he would condescend to add a cap to the Gentleman in the Jacket[2]—it would complete his costume—and smoothe his brow—which is somewhat too inveterate a likeness of the original,—God help me!——I did well to avoid the water party— *why*—is a mystery—which is not less to be wondered at than my other mysteries.—Tell Milor that I am deep in his M.S.S.—and will do him justice by a diligent perusal.——

The letter which I enclose[3]—I was prevented from sending by my despair of its doing any good—I was perfectly sincere when I wrote it —and am so still—but it is difficult for me to withstand the thousand provocations on that subject—which both friends and foes have for seven years been throwing in the way of a man whose feelings were once quick—and whose temper was never patient.—But "Returning were as tedious as go oer"[4]——I feel this as much as ever Macbeth did—and it is a dreary sensation which at least avenges the real or imaginary wrongs—of one of the two unfortunate persons whom it concerns.—But I am going to be gloomy—and so "to bed to bed—to bed"[5]—Good night or rather morning——one of the reasons why I wish to avoid society is—that I can never sleep after it—and the pleasanter it has been—the less I rest.——

Ever and truly yr. obliged and faithl. Sert.

N B

[TO THE EARL OF BLESSINGTON]   *May 7th. 1823*

My dear Lord,—I return the poesy, which will form a new light to lighten the Irish, and will, I hope, be duly appreciated by the public. I

---

[1] Benjamin Constant's novel *Adolphe,* which Byron had earlier sent to Teresa. (See Volume 7, p. 163.)

[2] In none of the known drawings of Byron by D'Orsay was a cap added.

[3] One of a number of letters which Byron wrote to Lady Byron after the separation but did not send.

[4] *Macbeth,* Act III, scene 4.

[5] *Macbeth,* Act. V, scene 1.

have not returned *Miledi's* verses, because I am not aware of the error she mentions, and see no reason for the alteration, however, if she insists, I must be conformable. I write in haste, having a visitor.

Ever yours, very truly,

NOEL BYRON

[TO JOHN CAM HOBHOUSE]   *Genoa. May 12th. 1823*

My dear H.—Enclosed is my answer to Mr. Bowring,—I am truly anxious to be of use if I can.—I send the létter open—and will write more by and bye—the moment I am aware of anything to the purpose.

yrs. ever

N B

P.S.—If I go up—the Douglas K[innair]d must furnish me with all the Credit my own resources can justify as available——I have written to him to send me a joint power of attorney for *you* and *him*—to act during my absence—so that all monies would pass through yr. hands —and I assure you there is a tolerable sum due from the Noel property —and still going on—I have not touched my *own* income either of this year—and have nearly three thousand still of last year's in hand—but the more the better—as I would righteously expend it on the furthering the good Cause.—

[JOHN BOWRING][1]   *Genoa. May 12th. 1823*

Sir,—I have great pleasure in acknowledging your letter and the honour which the Committee have done me.—I shall endeavour to deserve their confidence by every means in my power.—My first wish is to go up into the Levant in person—where I might be enabled to advance—if not the cause—at least the means of obtaining information which the Committee might be desirous of acting upon,—and my former residence in the Country—my familiarity with the Italian language (which is there universally spoken—or at least to the same extent with French in the more polished parts of the Continent) and my *not* total ignorance of the Romaic—would afford me some advantages of experience.—To this project the only objection is of a domestic nature—and I shall try to get over it,—if I fail in this—I must do what I can where I am—but it will be always a source of regret to me —to think—that I might perhaps have done more for the cause on the

---

[1] Secretary of the London Greek Committee, who wrote to announce that Byron had been made a member of the Committee. See Biographical Sketch, Appendix IV.

spot.—Our last information of Capt. Blaquiere—is from Ancona where he embarked with a fair wind for Corfu on the 15th. Ult[i]mo—he is now probably at his destination.—My last letter *from* him personally— was dated Rome—he had been refused a passport through the Neapolitan territory—and returned to strike off through Romagna for Ancona. —Little time however appears to have been lost by the delay.— The principal material wanted by the Greeks appears to be—1st. a park of field Artillery—light—and fit for Mountain service—2dly. Gunpowder—3dly. hospital or Medical Stores——the readiest mode of transmission is—I hear—by Idra—addressed to Mr. Negri[2] the Minister.—I meant to send up a certain quantity of the two latter—no great deal—but enough for an individual to show his good wishes for the Greek success—but am pausing—because in case I should go myself—I can take them with me.—I do not mean to limit my own contribution to this merely—but—more especially if I can get to Greece myself—I should devote whatever resources I can muster of my own— to advancing the great object.——I am in correspondence with Signor Nicolas Karvellas[3] (well known to Mr. Hobhouse) who is now at Pisa —but his latest advice merely states—that the Greeks are at present employed in organizing their *internal* government—and the details of it's administration—this would seem to indicate *security*—but the war is however far from being terminated.—The Turks are an obstinate race—as all former wars have proved them—and will return to the charge for years to come—even if beaten—as it is to be hoped that they will be.——But in no case can the labours of the Committee be said to be in vain—for in the event even of the Greeks being subdued—and dispersed—the funds which could be employed in succouring and gathering together the remnant—so as to alleviate in part their distresses—and enable them to find or make a country (as so many emigrants of other nations have been compelled to do—) would "bless both those who gave and those who took"[4]—as the bounty both of Justice and of Mercy.—

[2] Theodore Negris had been the Ottoman chargé d'affaires at Paris, but gave up his post to join the Greek revolution. George Finlay called him "an active, able, intriguing, ambitious, and unprincipled Phanariot." (History of Greece, ed. 1877, VI, 237.) He later (1823–1824) became the principal adviser of the equally cunning and unprincipled Odysseus in Eastern Greece.

[3] Nicolas Karvellas and his brother Francis had first met Byron in Geneva. They were studying in Italy and had first hand information about what was going on in the revolutionary circles in Greece. See also May 14, 1823, to Karvellas; and May 24, 1823, to Hobhouse.

[4] Cf. *Merchant of Venice*, Act IV, scene 1: "It blesseth him that gives and him that takes."

With regard to the formation of a brigade (which Mr. Hobhouse hints at in his short letter of this day's receipt—enclosing the one to which I have the honour to reply) I would presume to suggest but merely as an opinion—resulting rather from the melancholy experience of the brigades embarked in the Columbian Service—than from any experiment yet fairly tried in *Greece*—that the attention of the Committee had better perhaps be directed to the employment of *Officers* of experience—than the enrolment of raw British Soldiers—which latter are apt to be unruly and not very serviceable—in irregular warfare— by the side of foreigners.———A small body of good officers—especially Artillery—an Engineer—with a quantity (such as the Committee might deem requisite) of stores of the nature which Capt. Blaquiere indicated is most wanted—would I should conceive be a highly useful accession.—Officers who had previously served in the Mediterranean would be preferable—as some knowledge of *Italian* is nearly indispensable.———It would also be as well that they should be aware—that they are not going "to rough it on a beef steak—and bottle of Port"[5]—but that Greece—never of late years—very plentifully stocked for a *Mess* —is at present the country of all kinds of *privations*,—this remark may seem superfluous—but I have been led to it—by observing that many *foreign* Officers—Italian—French and even German—(but *fewer* of the latter) have returned in disgust—imagining either that they were going up to make a party of pleasure—or to enjoy full pay—speedy promotion and a very moderate degree of duty;—they complain too of having been ill received by the Government or inhabitants, but numbers of these complainants—were mere adventurers—attracted by a hope of command and plunder,—and disappointed of both;—those Greeks that I have seen strenuously deny the charge of inhospitality— and declare that they shared their pittance to the last Crumb with their foreign volunteers.——

I need not suggest to the Committee the very great advantage which must accrue to Great Britain from the success of the Greeks—and their probable commercial relations with England in consequence—because I feel persuaded that the *first* object of the Committee—is their *emancipation*—⟨[when the?] fruitful and important [boughs?] of the tree of Liberty have been⟩ without any interested views—but the consideration might weigh with the English people in general—in their present passion for every kind of speculation——they need not cross the American Seas—for one much better worth their while—and nearer home.—The resources even for an emigrant population—in the Greek

[5] Unidentified.

Islands alone—are rarely to be paralelled [sic]—and the cheapness of every kind of not *only necessary*—but *luxury*—(that is to say—*luxury* of *Nature*) fruits—wine—oil—&c.—in a state of peace—are far beyond those of the Cape—and Van Dieman's land—and the other places of refuge—which the English population are searching for over the waters.———I beg that the Committee will command me in any and every way———if I am favoured with any instructions—I shall endeavour to obey them to the letter—whether conformable to my own private opinion or not———I beg leave to add personally my respect for the Gentleman whom I have the honour of addressing—and am Sir—

yr. obliged & very obedt. Sert.

NOEL BYRON

P.S.—The best refutation of Gell[6]—will be the active exertions of the Committee;—I am *too warm* a controversialist—and I suspect that if Mr. Hobhouse has taken him in hand—there will be little occasion for me to "encumber him with help".[7]—If I go up into the Country—I will endeavour to transmit as accurate and impartial an account as circumstances will permit.——I shall write to Mr. Karvellas;—I expect intelligence from Capt. Blaquiere—who has promised me some early intimation from the seat of the provisional Government.—I gave him a letter of introduction to Lord Sydney Osborne at Corfu—but as Lord S. is in the Government Service—of course his reception could only be a *cautious* one—but as he is an old friend of mine—I should hope not an unkind one.——

[TO THE EARL OF BLESSINGTON] *May 14th. 1823*

My dear Lord—I avize you that the reading Association have received several numbers of English publications—which you may like to see—and as you are a member should avail yourself of early——I have just returned my share before it's time—having kept the book one day instead of *five*—which latter is the utmost allowance.—The rules obliged me to forward it to a Monsieur [Gravot?]—as next in rotation.——If you have anything for England—a Gentleman with some law

---

[6] Sir William Gell in his *Narrative of a Journey in the Morea* (1823) maintained that the Greeks would not benefit from the change brought by the Revolution if it meant that they would free themselves from the Turks and end up under the Russians.

[7] From Johnson's letter to Chesterfield on patronage: "Is not a patron, my Lord, one who looks with unconcern on a man struggling for life in the water, and when he has reached ground, encumbers him with help?"

papers of mine returns there tomorrow (thursday) and would be
happy to carry anything for you.—

> Ever yrs. & truly
> N B

P.S.—I request you to present My compliments to Ly. B[lessington]
—and C[ount] A[lfred D'Orsay] & Miss P[ower].

[TO NICOLAS KARVELLAS] *Genoa—14—Maggio—1823*

Pregiatissimo Sig[no]re—Avrò care tutte le notizie che potrete dar-
mi sulli avvenimenti della vostra Patria—tanto più che ora io debbo
informarne il Comitato, che si è formato a Londra per spedire de'
soccorsi alla Grecia—questo comitato mi ha voluto associare—e in
breve si tratterà se voranno mandare una Brigata, oppure degli
Ufficiali solamente al vostro Governo. Mi hanno chiesto il mio
parere—ed è che siano da preferirsi degli Ufficiali e di artiglieria
provvisti di munizioni e di altri mezzi necessarii; perche penso che
questi potranno rendervi de'servizi più utili. Vi sarò obligato se mi
spiegherete il vostra parere. Io aspetto nuove risposte dal Comitato—e
da Blaquiere già essere arrivato a Idra—poi stabilirò la mia risolu-
zione, che ben facilmente sarà di recarmi in Persona presso al vostra
[sic] Governo, onde farmi utile come potrò meglio alla vostra Patria.
—Fatemi sapere il parere degli vostri compatrioti più istruiti.

> ever yours very truly
> N B

P.S.—My dear Karvellas, You understand *English* I therefore add
a few words—I do *not* know that I shall be able to go up in *person* to yr.
Government—but I will do all that I can—let me have any information
that I may transmit it to the Committee—our friend *Hobhouse* is an
active member—pray write—

> ever yrs.
> N B

[TRANSLATION] *Genoa—May 14—1823*

Honoured Sir,—I shall hold dear all the news that you may be able
to give me about the events of your country—so much more now that I
have to inform the Committee, which has been formed in London to
send aid to Greece—this committee has desired me to join—and
shortly it will discuss whether to despatch a Brigade or only some

Officers to your Government. They have asked me my opinion—and it is that some Officers and artillery provided with munitions and other necessary supplies are to be preferred; because I think that these will be able to render you more useful services. I shall be obliged to you if you will express to me your opinion. I am expecting fresh answers from the Committee—and from Blaquiere who must already have arrived in Hydra—and then I will settle my decision, which very probably will be to betake myself in person to the side of your Government, to make myself useful as best I can to your country.—Let me know the opinion of your best-informed compatriots.

ever yours very truly
N B[1]

[TO LADY HARDY]   *Genoa. May 17th. 1823*

My dear Coz.——My voyage to Greece will depend upon the Greek Committee (in England) partly—and partly on the instructions which some persons now in Greece on a private mission may be pleased to send me.—I am a member—(lately elected) of the said Committee—and my object in going up would be to do any little good in my power—but as there are some *pros* and *cons* on the subject— with regard to how far the intervention of strangers may be advisable —I know no more than I tell you—but shall probably hear something soon from England and Greece—which may be more decisive.——

With regard to the late person—whom—you hear—that I have attacked[1]—I can only say that a bad minister's memory is as much an object of investigation—as his conduct while alive—for his measures do not die with him like a private individual's notions, he is matter of *history*—and wherever I find a tyrant or a villian—I will mark him.— ——I attacked him no more now than I had been wont to do.—As to "the Liberal"—it was a publication set up for the advantage of a perse- cuted author—and very worthy man—but it was foolish in me to engage in it—and so it has turned out—for I have hurt myself by it— without doing much good—to those for whose benefit—it was princi- pally intended.—Do *not defend me*—my Coz—it will never do—you will only make *yourself* enemies—and a pretty woman will have always enough without encumbering herself with the superfluities of other people—mine are neither to be diminished nor softened—but they

---

[1] Translation by H. B. Forster.
[1] In the first number of *The Liberal* Byron published three cutting epigrams on Castlereagh.

may be overthrown—and there are events which *may* occur less improbable than many which have happened in our time—that may reverse the present state of things—"nous verrons."——————

Your Chevalier—whom you do not again allude to—has not closed his career yet.—He has been to Paris—ran away with one of his *wife's* children—(by mistake it is supposed for one of his own) has been taken by the police—ran away again—been *telegraphed* to Lisle—but escaped—bearing away this paternal trophy of his prowess—after having broken his word to a Mr. Fawkes—to whom he pledged himself that he only wanted to *see* the children—and would restore them immediately to Lady Frances—who had recourse to the Ambassador &c. &c. &c.—But this is not all—he involved me—when he was at Genoa—1stly in a correspondence with Lady F. to *reconcile* them—well—he had the impudence to deny to Sir Charles Stuart—having *ever authorized* me to address her upon the subject!——

This comes of peace-making!—2dly. I endorsed two bills for him here—to enable him to get away—*my* banker here says—that they were protested by *his* banker—and of course *I* have had to pay them.——All this has somewhat stirred my meekness.—I have written to England to have him arrested (if he appears there) on a bond for a thousand pounds which I lent him ten years ago—with ten years interest due upon it.——I am tired of [keeping?] measures with such a mauvais sujet.——I remember lending him that sum on condition that he would *not* go to the Jews—he took it—went to the Jews notwithstanding—and never paid me a farthing from that hour to this.————I hope I shant be deemed a *hard* Creditor—in being at length provoked to teach him some articles of faith.—

I have not lately seen anybody who could give me news of you—and your letter was very apropos—as I had begun to think you had quitted Tuscany.—I have dined four or five times with our Minister Mr. Hill—and see occasionally some passing English—amongst others I saw Henry Fox Lady Holland's first born in second wedlock—and I was delighted to see him again—for he was always an especial favourite of mine. There be here—and have been here some time past—the Earl and Lady Blessington—and a Parisian Ami of the family's (a Comte d'Orsay) to all of whom as friends of Thos Moore's—and *Blue* themselves besides—I have been presented—and all that.——The Parisian is very young—and a Beauty—of which last advantage he is fully aware—but he is not at all disagreeable—and I should suspect that the women find him more formidable than dreadful.——Miledi is the Miledi of whom Lawrence made a picture that set all London raving

—as you may have seen in the papers.——She is also an authoress—
hath written three books and will I suppose write thirty in due course
of time and tide.—As they were friends of Moore's and have been very
civil to me—I could not easily (in my usual way—) escape being
occasionally with them—espccially as they are Equestrians—and I met
them frequently in my rides about Genoa.—But this has plunged me
into a pit of domestic troubles—for "la mia Dama" Me. La Contesse G.
—was seized with a furious fit of Italian jealousy—and was as unreasonable and perverse as can well be imagined.—God He knows—
she paid me too great a compliment—for what little communication I
had with this new Goddess of Discord—was literally literary—and
besides that I have long come to years of discretion—and would much
rather fall into the Sea than in Love any day of the week—her Ladyship
was extremely well guaranteed from any presumed aberration of my
inclinations by her Parisian Appendage—and would only have changed
for the worse—which would neither have suited her nor me.——
Madame Gi.—(who *never* saw her—) *won't* allow her to be pretty—
and *will* allow her to be *not* young —I dared not form a judgment on the
subject—before a person who argues with all the insolence of four and
twenty.—I send you this gossip—that you may laugh at it—which is
all that it is good for—even if it were good for so much.—I shall be
delighted to see you again—but it will be melancholy—should it be
merely for a moment.—

Ever yrs. most affly.
N B

[TO ISABEL HARVEY][1]   *Genoa May 19th. 1823*
[Fragments of a letter]

. . .—a painter of the name of Holmes made (*I think the very best*)
one of me in 1815—or 1816—and from this there were some good
engravings taken—I enclose you a note to him for one of these—. . . I
assure you it will be better than any of the thousand things you have
seen as portraits of the same subject.—— . . . . By the way—"Isabel"
has been one of no good omen to me—in former times—but at present
"we defy augury"[2]—

Believe me again and again yrs ever
N B

---

[1] A hero-worshipping young girl who signed herself Zorina Stanley wrote to
Byron from London, asking for his picture. She later confessed that her name was
Isabel Harvey.
[2] *Hamlet*, Act V, scene 2.

P.S.—The "Isabel" neither "died nor was faithless" but she was— *my wife*—Anne Isabella is her name—Is not the coincidence of names in the dramatic personae of "the Fatal Marriage"[3] a strange one—and yet no one has hit on the remark—

[TO JAMES HOLMES]   *Genoa. May 19th. 1823*

Dear Sir—I will thank you very much to present to or obtain for the bearer—a *print* from the miniature you drew of me in 1815—I prefer that likeness to any which has been done of me by any artist whatever. ——My sister Mrs. Leigh—or the Hon[oura]ble Douglas Kinnaird— will pay you the price of the engraving.——

ever yrs.
NOEL BYRON

[TO JOHN CAM HOBHOUSE]   *Genoa. May 19th.1823*

My dear H.—I saw yr. speech which did you great credit—at full length—with Canning's civil reply—"Fas est et ab hoste *laudari*"[1]— I have yr. letter of ye. 6th. and enclose one just received from Blaquiere which will "prate of our whereabouts"[2] to you and all friends to the Cause.—There is no obstacle to my going up—but the "absurd womankind"—and how absurd they are—as well as those under their dominion—thou knowest by all tale and history—and the experience of several of yr. friends.—It is the more absurd in this case—as the *Pope*—and her Grandfather (the oldest Count Gamba) are extremely desirous of her return to Ravenna—her father has been recalled from his exile (on the late rising account in 1820) but been positively told that he is expected to bring his daughter back with him—her husband —*would* forgive—provided that I (a very reasonable condition) did not continue his Subagent—(as the Irish call a middle man)—and her brother who is a fine bold young fellow—(as he has proved himself more than once) is even more anxious for him and me to go up to Greece than anybody else—being a thorough Liberty boy.—However I hope to prevail upon her to accompany her father to R[avenn]a.—but she has it seems a due share of "female punctuation"—as Mrs. Mala- prop calls it—and stands out upon Sentiment and so forth—against the

---

[3] Thomas Southerne's *The Fatal Marriage* (1694).
[1] "It is allowable to be praised even by an enemy." Adapted from Ovid, *Metamorphoses* IV, 428.
[2] *Macbeth*, Act II, scene 1.

will of half the families in Romagna—with the Pope at their head—and all this after a liaison of four years and better—besides at present she has a fit of Jealousy of Lady Blessington, with whom I have merely a common acquaintance as she is an authoress—and all that.——It is besides against her worldly interest in every way—for they (the Pope that is) have proposed to confirm her separate maintenance from her husband—if she will not make it up with him—but then says the Pope —and the "Ultra Santissimo" you must not live naughtily with a heretic—and a Carbonaro—and a foreigner like L[ord] B[yron].—— However I *will* go———("d—n my eye—I will go ashore") an' it be possible—or do all I can in the cause—go or not.—I think of about August or earlier—for the voyage—but much would depend on Blaquiere's future letters.—If I go—I presume the Committee will give me some regular instructions of what they wish to be observed— reported or done—I will serve them as humbly as they please— Believe me

ever yrs.
N B

P.S.—I would tell you (were it not per the *post*) of some *queer* things brooding here—I have had some propositions made to me but I answered—you must first show yourselves more capable than you did in the last events before I can take it upon me to answer either for myself—or for any prospect of assistance from the people of England.

P.S.—Tell Douglas—that when any thing is settled—I will let him know *what* sum I should like to take in Credit and on what houses.— His answer was as handsome as could possibly be; and as usual with him in such matters—I will try not to abuse either the means—or the purpose for which they are intended.—

[TO DOUGLAS KINNAIRD]   *May 21st. 1823*

My dear Douglas/—I enclose you another corrected proof of D[on] J[uan]—and also—a note of Mr. Barry—the acting partner of Messrs Webb—on the proposed Credit—in case I go up—to the Levant.—— I do not quite know what to name as the amount—undoubtedly about 5000—in addition to what I already have in ye. Circular notes—and in Webb's bank—would be more than sufficient for my own personal wants for *good four years*—for my habits are simple—and you are aware that I have lately reduced my other expences of every kind.——But if I go up among the Greeks—I may have occasion to be of service to them

—There may be prisoners to ransom—some cash to advance—arms to purchase—or if I was to take an angry turn some [sultry?] morning—and raise a troop of my own (though this is unlikely) any or all of these would require a command of credit—and require my resources.

——You will let me have what you think proper *not under* the sum above stated—but there is no *immediate* hurry—as I shall not sail till about July—if at all.—It is to be understood that the *letter of Credit for two thousand pounds* which I have *now untouched* is to be *returned* or left to be returned *untouched* in the hands of Messrs Webb—for your house——the moment I receive the more extended credit.—It is also to be understood—that if I receive this extended Credit—and from any circumstances do not go up into the Levant—then that Credit is to be null and void—as it would in fact then become quite superfluous to my present occasions.

I am doing all I can to get away—but I have all kinds of obstacles thrown in my way—by the "absurd womankind"—who seems determined on sacrificing herself in every way—and preventing me from doing any good—and all without reason—for her relations and her husband (who is moving the Pope—and the Government here to get her to live with him again) and everybody are earnest with her to return to Ravenna.—She wants to go up to Greece too! forsooth—a precious place to go at present! of course the idea is ridiculous—as every thing must there be sacrificed to seeing *her* out of harm's way.— It is a case too in which interest does not enter, and therefore hard to deal with—for I have no kind of control—in that way—and if she makes a scene—(and she has a turn that way) we shall have another romance—and tale of ill usage and abandonment—and Lady Caroling —and Lady Byroning—and Glenarvoning[1]—all cut and dry;—there never was a man who gave up so much to women—and all I have gained by it—has been the character of treating them harshly.—— However I shall do what I can—and have hopes—for her father has been recalled from his political exile—but with this proviso—that he do not return without his daughter.———If I left a woman for another woman—she might have cause to complain—but really—when a man merely wishes to go on a great duty for a good cause—this selfishness on the part of the "feminie" is rather too much.

ever yrs.
N B

I add the enclosed letter from Mr. J[ohn] H[unt] which does him credit. ——Also another M.S.S. for a proof from the same.

[1] Lady Caroline Lamb's novel *Glenarvon*.

[TO JOHN CAM HOBHOUSE]   *May 21st. 1823*

My dear H[obhous]e—Only time at present to request you will read
and transmit the enclosed to the Honorary Secretary.[1]—

                                        ever yrs.
                                          N B

[TO THE CHAIRMAN OF THE GREEK COMMITTEE]
                                        Genoa. May 21st. 1823

Sir—I have only just been honoured with your letter dated March
14th. With great pleasure I accept the honour conferred upon me and
shall be happy to contribute by every means in my power to forward
the views of the Committee who have considered me worthy to become
a member of their body.—I have the honour to be

                              yr. obliged and obedt. humble St.
                                        NOEL BYRON

[TO JOHN BOWRING]   *Genoa. May 21st. 1823*

Sir—I received *yesterday!*—the letter of the Committee dated the
14th. of March—what has occasioned the delay I know not—it was
forwarded by Mr. Galignani from Paris—who stated that he had only
had it in his charge four days—and that it was delivered to him by a Mr.
Grattan.—I need hardly say that I gladly accede to the proposition of
the Committee—and hold myself highly honoured by being deemed
worthy to be a member—I have also to return my thanks particularly
to yourself for the accompanying letter which is extremely flattering.
——Since I last wrote to you through the medium of Mr. Hobhouse—
I have received and forwarded a letter from Capt. Blaquiere to me—
from Corfu—which will show how he gets on.—Yesterday—I fell in
with two young Germans—survivors of General Norman's band.[1]——
They arrived at Genoa in the most deplorable state—without food—
without a sou—without shoes.——The Austrians had sent them out
of their territory on their landing at Trieste—and they had been forced
to come down to Florence—and had travelled from Leghorn here—
with four Tuscan *livres*—(about three francs) in their pockets.—I have

---

[1] John Bowring, Secretary of the London Greek Committee.
[1] Charles Frederick Lebrecht, Count of Norman-Ehrenfels had joined the Greeks
at the head of a band of Germans in 1822. On July 16, 1822, he was wounded at the
Battle of Petta near Arta. He died shortly after at Missolonghi of a fever.

179

given them twenty Genoese Scudi—(about a hundred and thirty three livres French money) and new shoes—which will enable them to get to Switzerland—where they say they have friends.—All they could raise in Genoa—besides—was 30 *Sous*. They do not complain of the Greeks—but say that they have suffered more since their landing in Italy.

I tried their veracity—1stly by their passports and papers—2dly by topography—cross questioning them about Arta—Argos—Athens—Mesalonghi—Corinth—&c.—and 3dly in *Romaic*—of which I found (one of them at least) knew more than I do.— —One of them (they are both of good families) is a fine handsome young fellow of three and twenty—a Wirtembergher—and has a look of *Sandt*[2] about him;—the other a Bavarian—older—and flat faced—and less ideal—but a good sturdy soldier like personage.—The Wirtembergher—was in the action at Arta[3]—where the Philhellenists were cut to pieces after killing 600 Turks—they themselves being only 150 in number—opposed to about 6—or 7000.—Only 8 escaped—and of those about 3 only now survive.—So that General Normann has "led his ragamuffins where they were well peppered not three of the 150—left alive—and they for town's end for life."[4]— —

These two left Greece by the direction of the Greeks ⟨themselves⟩—when Churschid Pacha[5] overran the Morea— —the Greeks seem to have behaved well—in wishing to save their allies—when they thought that the game was up with themselves.—This was in September last (1822)[;] they wandered from island to island—and got from Milo to Smyrna—where the French Consul gave them a passport—and a charitable Captain a passage to Ancona—whence they got to Trieste—and were turned back by the Austrians.— —They complain only of the Mainotes—(who have always had an indifferent character—) say that the Greeks fight very well in their own way—but were at *first* afraid to *fire* their own cannon—but mended with practice. Adolfo (the younger) commanded at Navarino for a short time.—The other—a more material person—"the Bold Bavarian in a luckless hour"[6]—seems

[2] Charles Sandt assassinated Kotzebue in 1819 in the belief that he was a Russian spy. Sandt went to execution as to a fête, saying that he died "for the liberty of Germany".

[3] At the battle of Petta.

[4] *Henry IV*, Part I, Act V, scene 3.

[5] Kurshid Pasha was Governor of the Morea. When the Greek Revolution broke out he was besieging Ali Pasha at Jannina. After Ali was killed, he returned to the Morea in September, 1822.

[6] Johnson, "The Vanity of Human Wishes", line 241.

chiefly to lament a fast of three days at Argos—and the loss of twenty five paras a day of pay in arrear and some baggage at Tripolitza—but takes his wounds and marches and battles in very good part.—Both are very simple—full of naiveté and quite unpretending.——They say the foreigners quarrelled among themselves—particularly the French with the Germans—which produced duels.——

The Greeks accept musquets—but throw *away bayonets*—and will *not* be disciplined.—When these lads saw two Piedmontese regiments yesterday—they said "Ah—if we had had but *these* two—we should have cleared the Morea."—in that case—the Piedmontese must have behaved better than they did against the Austrians.—They seem to lay great stress on a few regular troops——say that the Greeks *have* arms and powder in plenty—but want victuals—hospital stores—and lint & linen &c. and money very much.—Altogether it would be difficult to show more practical philosophy—than this remnant of our "puir Hill folk" have done—they do not seem the least cast down—and their way of presenting themselves was as simple and natural as could be.—They said—a Dane here had told them that an Englishman friendly to the Greek cause was here—and that as they were reduced to beg their way home—they thought they might as well begin with me.—I write in haste to snatch the post believe me

ever and truly yr. obliged & obedt. Sert.

N B

P.S.—I have since I wrote this seen them again—Count P. Gamba asked them to breakfast—one of them means to publish his journal of the campaign;—the Bavarian wonders a little that the Greeks are not quite the same with those of the time of Themistocles—(they were not very tractable then by the bye) and at the difficulty of disciplining them —but he is a "bon homme" and a tactician—and a little like Dugald Dalgetti who would insist upon the "erection of a Sconce on the hill of Drumsnab"[7] or whatever it was—the other seems to wonder at nothing.——

[TO JOHN HUNT]   *May 21st. 1823*

Sir—I have by this day's post returned to Mr. Kinnaird—the further corrected proof of D[on] J[uan].—If you are the publisher—as I presume you will be—I shall leave to yr. discretion the mode and form of publication—but I join with you in thinking the *cheap* edition

[7] Scott's *A Legend of Montrose*, Chap. 10.

indispensable.—I suppose you will take care not to overprint.—I sent the 16th. Canto in M.S.S. the other day—there are in all eleven.— These I think would form *three* thick—or *four thin* volumes—I should think they ought to be published one volume a fortnight after another —or all at once—what do *you* think?—Your letter does you great Credit—but the 15 per Cent is *not* enough for yr. portion—if you posi- tively decline the half—you may at least accept a fourth which would be 25 per Cent—or a third rather better than thirty per Cent—think again.[1]—I have no objection to put my name to the "Island" which I returned to Mr. D[ouglas] K[innair]d with an extract from the account of the voyage of the Bounty—as a note to it.———I could wish all that I have *published* or unpublished except the *epigrams* (which are not worth the trouble) to be collected in a series of the size and shape of my former works.—They would form with the D[on] J[uan]s about 7 or 8 vols—including what was published in the Liberal—and the Pulci &c. &c. and the Age of Bronze—"the Island" &c. &c.—I have also *two parts* completed of an odd sort of drama[2]—but I doubt if I shall go on with it.—I sent the two parts by this post—to Mr. K[innair]d—let me have a proof.

> yrs. ever
> N B

P.S.—I *am an orientally scrupulous bather,*[3] both by nature and choice —I wear an easy shoe—as for "gentle friction" I have nearly rubbed the foot off—but still the Corn continues as hard as a king's heart.

[TO CAPTAIN DANIEL ROBERTS]   *May 21st. 1823*

Dear Sir—As it is more than probable that I shall go up into Greece the sails in question may probably come into play—for it is a squally station.—Cannot they be repaired for service?—I mean to take her up as a tender.[1]—Cannot you bate our Mate's demand a little—at least till we go to sea.—Whatever repairs are wanted I will guarantee—so you may proceed—we shall have no difference on that point—nor on any other I hope.—

> ever yours
> N B

[1] Hunt kept to his proposal of 15 per cent. His careful records of sales rendered to Kinnaird are in the Murray MSS.

[2] *The Deformed Transformed.*

[3] See Nov. 9, 1820, to Murray, note 3. (Vol. 7, p. 224).

[1] The *Bolivar* had been laid up during the winter. In the end Byron sold the schooner to Lord Blessington.

My dear Lord—I thought that I *had* answered yr. note—I ought—
and beg you to excuse the omission.—I should have called but I
thought my chance of finding you at *home* in the environs—greater
than at the Hotel. Who can the *"some"* be who will be *"happy that you
are going"*? they are not of my acquaintance. On the contrary the few
people that I have seen—seemed anxious that you should stay—and
Mr. Barry (the banker) was going to look out a house for you.—I
hope you will not take my *not* dining with you again after so many
dinners—ill—but the truth is—that your banquets were too luxurious
for my habits—and I feel the effect of them in this warm weather—for
some time after.—I am sure you will not be angry——since I have
already more than sufficiently abused yr. hospitality.——Do *you* quit
your party—and return alone?——I fear that I can hardly afford more
than two thousand francs for the steed in question[1]—as I have to undergo considerable expences at this present time—and I suppose that will
not suit you.——I must not forget to pay my Irish Subscription—you
will let me know previously to your day of departure—that I may
come and shake hands with you before you start.——I have been a
good deal occupied lately—I find that I was elected a member of the
Greek Committee *in March*—but did not receive the Chairman's
notice till yesterday—and this by mere chance—and through a private
hand.——I am doing all I can to get away—and the Committee and
my friends in England seem both to approve of my going up into
Greece—but I meet here with obstacles—which have hampered and
put me out of Spirits—and still keep me in a vexatious state of uncertainty.——I began bathing the other day—but the water was still
chilly—and in diving for a Genoese *lira* in clear but deep water—I
contrived to imbibe so much water through my ears—as to give me a
Megrim in my head—which you will probably think a superfluous
malady.—

Ever yrs. obliged & truly
N B

P.S.—My remembrances to Miledi and to Alfred—and Miss
P[ower]

[1] Lady Blessington had consented to sell her Arabian horse Mameluke to Byron
to take to Greece with him, but was chagrined that he would not give more than
eighty pounds, but she let him go, though she had paid a hundred guineas for him,
probably because she was eager to supply a mount to the poet whom she admired.

My dear H[obhous]e/—I mentioned to you some little time ago—
that I had heard from Karvellas.—As soon as I was favoured with the
wishes of our Committee I wrote to him again—requesting any information which he thought might be useful to his countrymen that I
might transmit it to the Hon. Secretary.——I enclose you *both* his
letters—the second is a curious one—he says "that he cannot comply
with the request—as he is prevented—" but whether by the Pisan or
Tuscan Slaves in office—or by his own people—he does not state.—
He then concludes by a demand for 100 crowns for *himself*, —which
would be paying high for *no* news.—I really hardly know what to think
of these our worthy friends—but am willing to lend them a hand—
though I could wish to hear something from Blaquiere first—from the
seat of action.—I forwarded to you his letter from Corfu—and wrote
to you a day or two ago enclosing one for Mr. Bowring.—I am ready
to contribute and do what may be deemed best—to any extent in my
power—but I hope that the rest of his compatriots will not like Karvellas—refuse information for his Country's benefit—and demand a
loan for *themselves* individually.——

yrs. ever
N B

My dear Douglas—By this post—I have written to Hobhouse—and
enclosed him a curious letter from a Greek of our acquaintance[1]—who
first *offered*—and now *declines* to give any information—however
simple—in behalf of his Countrymen—out of apprehension apparently
of the Government but whether his own or the Tuscan he does not say
—and then concludes with the demand of a *loan* for *himself!*—I hope
that this is not to be a specimen of their general behaviour.—I have
heard once from Blaquiere from Corfu—and forwarded the letter to
Hobhouse.—I also have had (dated *March 14th!*) the Circular from
the Chairman of the G[reek] Committee—which I have answered
accepting the nomination.—The delay was not my fault.—As I only
had the letter two days ago.—I wrote to you by last post—but shall
not *hurry* for the Credits—till I hear something more positive—either
from the Committee or from Blaquiere of what kind of reception I am
likely to have from the Greek G[overnment] for if it is to be like

1 Nicolas Karvellas.

Karvellas' Correspondence—I may as well wait to know how far I shall be welcome—before I adventure a large sum of money—and my personal safety in behalf of those who may not thank you for either.—But I am ready and willing to fulfil all that I proposed—so that the Committee think it will be of service—and I would even in that case—put it out of the question how far my presence may be acceptable or not to the Greeks themselves.—

yrs. ever
N B

[TO CHARLES F. BARRY]   *May 25th. 1823*

Dear Sir—I cannot fix a value upon the Snuffbox—as it was not estimated nor can I name the maker but it is obviously of Parisian manufacture—and two of the portraits are generally supposed to be originals.—It was sent to me at Bologna—some years ago—and I never knew by *whom*—nor from what quarter——This is all that I can say upon the subject—and it is the one which I would feel least disposed to part with of the number[1]—though as the whole case (with the exception of one or two of the least valuable) is a superfluity in the present probability of my changing my place of residence—I am willing to dispose of the greater part of it's contents.——I can name no price—because I might err on either one side or the other——if an offer is made I can then judge whether it would be such as I would accept.— —

Ever and truly yr. obliged & obedt. Sert.
N B

P.S.—I expect in a few days to go down and take a view of the vessels you had the goodness to enquire after—I am sorry to be so great a plague to you—as I doubt that I am.—I had a letter from a *Greek* from Pisa yesterday—declining (after *offering it first himself*) to send any information for the G[reek] Committee—on account of some apprehensions which he does not explain—and concluding with the request of a loan of 100 Scudi for *himself*!—I have forwarded his epistle

[1] See Sept, 1819, to Teresa Guiccioli, note 1, and Sept. 17 [12?] [actually Sept. 7 in MS. found later], 1819, to Murray [?] (Vol. 6, pp. 221, 223). Barry wrote to a Dr. Wilson of Leghorn the next day asking him to make an offer for the Napoleon snuff box, but adding: "I am rather surprised at his Lordship's parting on any terms with a valuable box that came to him in so mysterious a way but I think this very mystery increases the value of the box. Who knows but Maria Teresa herself may have sent it?" (MS. letter, Barry to Wilson, Carl H. Pforzheimer Library.)

to our Committee.—If the rest of his countrymen are to behave in the same way—it will be a great encouragement to those who are disposed to risk their monies and persons—in behalf of such people.

May 26th. 1823

My dear Douglas—I have to acknowledge a letter of Credit for £4000 sterling received by this day's post.—Last week I sent to you Mr. Barry's (partner of Messrs Webb here who have been particularly attentive throughout—in every respect) Suggestions on the subject of credit on the Levant—which his house would undertake as you will see stated.—I shall reserve yr. present letter till I hear further ——I think about letters for six thousand would be as much as I should need in any case for some time to come—but then I *have* [your] *former* letter of *credit* on Tuscany and Genoa *untouched* for two thousand which with the present four thousand makes up the sum—*this*— (as well as the present 4000) I keep untouched—and meant to sent [send] back the former on receiving a similar credit on other places than Tuscany——if any change takes place as to the houses or places —I shall remit the present letters of course back to you.—In any case —it is understood between us—that I shall not avail myself of them— except in the event of my *personally* going up among the belligerants. —I state this for the purpose of avoiding any mistake as to my object in requiring these letters.—In case you do not think any change necessary of places and houses—it is possible that I may if occasion requires use the letter for 2000—as well as the present one—but *not* without yr. further approbation;—let me know;—if you choose to order the payment of the whole 6000—to be made through my bankers here—then the letters upon other places for the like sum—(viz for the 2000—and the 4000) become void—and shall be returned immediately.——I have heard nothing further (since I wrote lately) from Blaquiere— and a good deal will depend on his intelligence—and on what I hear from Hobhouse and the Committee—

ever yrs.
N B

May 27th. 1823

I do not object to the *quantity* provided the price is not much beyond the statement, which (if I rightly apprehend) is about 1,600 Genoese Livres—more or less—of course the articles *chiefly* required *are* for an army—will you give the necessary orders, and I will be responsible for the rest. I take it there will be occasion for what can be sent up there (as I here at least have authority), and I would wish to do it properly. I send you the books. Any others you may want are quite at your service.

Dear Douglas/—Enclosed is the corrected proof of the 15th. of D[on] J[uan]—and a letter for Hobhouse which you are to read of course also.—I have received yr. letter of Credit—which I acknowledged—but had written before it arrived to say—that as I know Messrs Webb's house well—and that it is a strong one in the Mediterranean I should have liked my business to have gone through their hands directly—under the sanction of your house in London.—But it is much the same—for they say they will give me cash on *your* letters—though not directly addressed to their house.—I am now sufficiently provided—in the *two* letters of Credit—*that is*;—but if you commute them for one on Webb's and the houses at the places indicated in their note of directions for the same sums—viz—6000—these will of course be returned—let me know that I may not act without your approbation —my going up will depend much on what I hear from the Committee —and from Blaquiere.——I have no wish to be officious or to invest myself with authority—but merely to *do as I am bid*—if they will merely say—what will advance their object—or gratify their wishes— I can have—(thanks to your handsome behaviour) resources enough of my own—without in any way interfering with the direction of theirs—and I suspect that I shall not be the most backward in applying them—for the benefit of the people.—

yrs. ever
N B

Dear Sir—Many thanks—it will undoubtedly be very desirable that every information should be obtained from Leghorn on the subject of the Greek cause—and also suggestions of every kind on *what* they want—&c. &c. &c. I beg that you will correct one mistake——I am a member of the Committee—and have been so (though I was not informed till lately) from the month of March last—and I am empowered by the rest to obtain information—and requested to furnish any plan or suggestion for the advantage of the Greeks—to their consideration—but I am not—nor have any reason to think that I shall be their treasurer or distributor—or even their missionary—neither am I aware *what funds* they have in hand——but I have collected as *you know* some not inconsiderable funds of my own (at least for an individual) which in the event of my going up to the Levant—I shall be willing to advance in favour of the Cause—in the mode that may appear best in the circumstances,—the question is—whether my going up may appear either useful [or] agreeable to the Greeks themselves—as I neither wish to be officious or otherwise.—As far as I have yet heard from the Members of the Committee—it seems to be their opinion that I might be of use——but I am *not dependent* on them in any way—though perfectly willing to serve them as far as may be in my power—as a volunteer—reserving to myself of course a certain portion of free [agency?] Believe me

ever yrs.
N B

[TO JOHN CAM HOBHOUSE]   *May 28th. 1823*

My dear Hobhouse—The enclosed notes one from Dr. Alexander an English physician—and the other from Mr. Barry the Banker will show you that I have not been idle in the good cause.—The medical stores "for a 1000 men—for two years" are not very dear since their cost will hardly amount to seventy pounds sterling—and I shall either send or take them up with me—with other things for the service—as I said before—purchased & conveyed at my own expence—of course.——I hear no more of the Committee—except what I see in the papers—and am not aware—whether they have any course of conduct to suggest to me or no—you will let me know I presume——I read your various speeches in the Times.—I shall collect and send what information I can —as directed—and

am ever yrs.
N B

P.S.—The question of the Greeks mentioned in Mr. B[arry]'s note are from some supposition of their own—as I never gave out—that I was to be distributor of the Committee—but merely that I had offered my services in *general* for any purpose in attainment of their object.—

Sir,—At present, [now?] that I know to whom I am indebted for a very flattering mention in the "Rome, Naples, and Florence in 1817, by Mons. Stendhal," it is fit that I should return my thanks (however undesired or undesirable) to Mons. Beyle, with whom I had the honour of being acquainted at Milan in 1816. You only did me too much honour in what you were pleased to say in that work;² but it has hardly given me less pleasure than the praise itself, to become at length aware (which I have done by mere accident) that I am indebted for it to one of whose good opinion I was really ambitious. So many changes have taken place since that period in the Milan circle, that I hardly dare recur to it;—some dead, some banished, and some in the Austrian dungeons.—Poor Pellico!³ I trust that, in his iron solitude, his Muse is consoling him in part—one day to delight us again, when both she and her Poet are restored to freedom.

Of your works I have seen only "Rome", etc., the Lives of Haydn and Mozart, and the *brochure* on Racine and Shakespeare. The "Histoire de la Peinture" I have not yet the good fortune to possess.

There is one part of your observations in the pamphlet which I shall venture to remark upon;—it regards Walter Scott. You say that "his character is little worthy of enthusiasm," at the same time that you mention his productions in the manner they deserve. I have known Walter Scott long and well, and in occasional situations which call forth the *real* character—and I can assure you that his character *is* worthy of admiration—that of all men he is the most *open*, the most *honourable*, the most *amiable*. With his politics I have nothing to do: they differ from mine, which renders it difficult for me to speak of them. But he is *perfectly sincere* in them; and Sincerity may be humble, but she cannot be servile. I pray you, therefore, to correct or soften that passage. You may, perhaps, attribute this officiousness of mine to a false affectation of *candour*, as I happen to be a writer also. Attribute it to what motive you please, but *believe* the *truth*. I say that Walter Scott is

¹ Byron met Henri Beyle, who later took the pen name of Stendhal, a few times at the theatre in Milan in 1816.

² Beyle had some flattering things to say about Byron in this book, but his accounts as a whole (he wrote two other reminiscences of the poet) were so filled with errors that Hobhouse labelled them "a tissue of fictions". See Doris Langley Moore, *The Late Lord Byron*, pp. 372–393).

³ Silvio Pellico (1788–1854) whom Byron had met briefly in Milan in 1816, wrote a tragedy, *Francesca da Rimini* (1818). He was arrested by the Austrian Government in 1820 because of his connection with the liberal newspaper, *Il Conciliatore*, and was held for nine years. After his release he wrote *Le Mie Prigioni* (1831) which contributed to his later fame.

as nearly a thorough good man as man can be, because I *know* it by experience to be the case.[4]

If you do me the honour of an answer—may I request a speedy one —because it is possible (though not yet decided) that Circumstances may conduct me once more to Greece;—my present address is Genoa— where an answer will reach me in a short time, or be forwarded to me wherever I may be.

I beg you to believe me with a lively recollection of our brief acquaintance—and the hope of one day renewing it.—

> your ever obliged and obedt. humble Servt.
>
> NOEL BYRON

I make no excuse for writing to you in English, as I understand you are well acquainted with that language.[5]

[TO CONTESSA BORGARELLI D'YSONE]   *Genova Giugno 1823*

Stimatissima Signora—La singolare bontà ch'Ella mi dimostra mi fà ardito d'indirizzarmi a lei nella circostanza d'abbisognare dell'opera d'una qualche rispettabile Dama[.] Ella non ignora forse l'amicizia che da lungo tempo mi lega alla Contessa Guiccioli, ed il mio prossimo viaggio in Grecia. Ora la suddetta per la mia partenza, e per quella dei Conti Gamba, di lei parenti, richiamati alla loro patria dopo due anni d'esiglio sofferto per politiche vicende; restando qui, si troverebbe in una situazione troppo isolata, la quale non si conviene nè alla sua età, nè alla sue circostanze. La sua abitudine, e il suo gusto per la vita retirata lè avevano fatto preferire l'idea di chiudersi per qualche tempo in un monastero; ma ha dovuto abbandonarla non permettendogli la clausura di codesti luoghi di fare l'uso dei bagni di mare indispensabili alla sua salute. Ora per qualche mese volendo quì rimanere (al che la risalvono varie ragioni che a lei farà note) non la resta che cercare la compagnia, anzi la protezione—non avendo in Genova nè parenti nè amici—d'una Dama rispettabile: ed è perciò che io a lei m'indirizzo. Se questo sarà combinabile, e se non temessi d'esser troppo indiscreto aggiungendo anche se la Contessa Guiccioli potesse venire ad allegiare per qualche mese sotto allo stesso tetto, od almeno vicino a Lei io intraprenderei il mio viaggio con maggiore tranquillità, e la mia riconoscenza per la di lei bontà sarebbe la maggiore di cui il mio animo sia

---

[4] The remainder of the text of the letter is from a facsimile in Medwin's *Conversations* of Byron (Paris edition).

[5] This postscript is not in Medwin but is in the text of the letter in Martineau's *Cent-Soixante Quatorze Lettres à Stendhal,* quoted in *The Late Lord Byron,* p. 375.

capace[.] Frattanto nell'aspettativa del di lei riscontro ho il piacere di protestarmi colla più sincera Stima

Umilissimo, div[otissi]mo Servitore

NOEL BYRON—pair d'Angleterre

P.S.—Mi obbligherebbe ugualmente se per opera sua la Contessa Guiccioli potesse collocarsi presso una qualche dama di sua conoscenza, e in un'abitazione a lei non molto distante, perchè possa aprofittare della di lei valevole protezione, che del resto questa Signora si preggierà di non recargli il più piccolo incommodo. Mi creda nuovamente

U. d. S e

N B

[TRANSLATION]   *Genoa, June, 1823*

Most esteemed Signora—Your singular kindness towards me, makes me bold enough to address you in the circumstances of my needing the help of some respectable Lady.[1] Perhaps you are not ignorant of the friendship that for a long time has bound me to the Countess Guiccioli, and of my impending voyage to Greece. Now, because of my departure, and that of the Counts Gamba, her relatives, who have been recalled to their homeland after two years of exile suffered for political reasons, the aforementioned remaining here, would find herself in too isolated a situation, which would not be suitable to either her age, or her circumstances. Her custom, and her liking for a retired life, had made her prefer the idea of withdrawing for some time to a convent; but she has had to abandon this idea since the seclusion of these places would not permit her to make use of the sea baths which are indispensible to her health. Now, wanting to remain here for several months (having decided this for various reasons which I shall let you know)[2] she is left no choice but to seek the companionship, rather the protection—not having relatives or friends in Genoa—of a respectable Lady: and it is for this reason that I address myself to you. If this could be agreed upon, and, if I were not afraid of being too indiscreet, adding also that if the Countess Guiccioli could come and stay for a few months under the same roof, or at least close by you, I would undertake my journey with much more tran-

[1] Byron had met the Countess d'Ysone through Mr. Hill, the British Minister in Genoa.
[2] Teresa wanted to remain in Genoa and await Byron's return from Greece, but the Countess d'Ysone was not eager to undertake her "protection" and in the end she was forced to return to the Romagna with her father.

191

quillity, and my gratitude for your kindness would be the greatest that my heart is capable of. In the meantime while awaiting your reply, I have the pleasure of declaring myself with the most sincere esteem

Your most humble devoted Servant
NOEL BYRON—Peer of England

P.S.—I should be equally obliged if with your help the Countess Guiccioli might place herself with some lady of your acquaintance, and in a residence not far from yours, in order that she might benefit from your valuable protection, and finally, this Signora will not be asked to suffer the smallest inconvenience. Believe me again

U. d. S e
N B[3]

[TO THE EARL OF BLESSINGTON]   *June 1, 1823*

[Part quoted in Catalogue]

.... I will try to come down in time not to interfere with yr. Opera— only if you are at dinner you will in that case let me in the same. Owing I suppose to bathing again yesterday—when the water was very chill —I am today in a sort of lethargy—which I cannot account for—as I slept very well—but all the morning I have been in a sort of torpid stupor—till within this half hour . . . .

[TO THE COUNTESS OF BLESSINGTON] *June 2d. 1823*

My dear Lady B[lessington]—I am superstitious and have recollec- ted that memorials with a *point* are of less fortunate augury;—I will therefore request you to accept instead of the *pin*[1]—the enclosed chain —which is of so slight a value that you need not hesitate.—As you wished for something *worn*—I can only say that it has been worn oftener and longer than the other.—It is of Venetian manufacture— and the only peculiarity about it is—that it could only be obtained at or from Venice,—at Genoa they have none of the same kind.—I also enclose a ring which I would wish Alfred to keep—it is too large to *wear*—but is formed of *Lava*—and so far adapted to the fire of his years and character. You will perhaps have the goodness to acknow- ledge the receipt of this note—and to send back the pin (for good

---

[3] Transcribed and translated by Ricki B. Herzfeld. The copy of the original letter was made by the Countess d'Ysone's son in 1859.

[1] The pin was a small cameo of Napoleon.

luck's sake) which I shall value the more for having been a night in
your custody.——

Ever and faithfully yr. obliged & sincere

N B

P.S.—I hope your nerves are better to-day—and will continue to
flourish.

[TO ANDREA VACCÀ]   [*June 2–4? 1823*]

Pregiatissimo Signor Vaccà,—Nel viaggio che in breve io imprendo
nella Grecia vorrei in mia compagnia un Chirurgo pel mio servizio
personale e per quello della mia famiglia.

Se fra i giovani usciti dalla vostra scuola si trovasse qualcuno dis-
posto ad accetare questo incarico, io lo accetterei volontieri. Sarebbe
mantenuto di alloggio e cibarie alla mia tavola, col salario di cento
luigi d'oro annuale, e lo fisserei per un anno al certo.

Quando sia stato istruito e raccomandato da Voi, non ho bisogno di
altre garanzie pel suo merito nell'arte e per le altre indispensabili
qualità. Che sia giovane robusto e non sprovvisto di coraggio è da
cercarsi, perchè la natura e la situazione del paese dove vado lo esigono:
non però che egli possa essere esposto mai a maggiore pericolo e
fatiche che non io stesso ed anche meno. Soprattutto si richiede che sia
tosto pronto, perchè io partirò da Genova al 1 o [primo] del prossimo
luglio. Il Brick inglese *Hercules* di *John Scott* che si reca in Livorno
a scaricare alcune mercanzie tornerà sulla fine di giugno qui per
imbarcarmi. In quest' occasione il Chirurgo potrebbe montare a
bordo del Brick a Livorno.

Recapiti al signor Dun[n] negoziante inglese ben noto in quella
piazza, che sarà da lui diretto in tutto. Scusate l'incomodo che vi porgo;
prevaletevi liberamente dell' opera mia, se potesse giovarvi, e crede-
temi

Vostro devotissimo Servo

NOEL BYRON   *Pair d'Angleterre*

[TRANSLATION]   [*June 2–4? 1823*]

Most esteemed Signor Vacca,[1]—For the voyage which in a short time
I am undertaking to Greece, I would like in my company a surgeon for

---

[1] André Vacca Berlinghieri (1772–1826) headed the school of surgery at Pisa.
He had studied with the surgeons Bell and Hunter in London.

my personal service and that of my family. If from among the young men coming out of your school is to be found someone disposed to accept that post, I would accept him willingly. He would be given lodging and would eat at my table, with an annual salary of one hundred louis d'or, and I would guarantee him a year's employment for certain.[2]

If he be instructed and recommended by you, I have no need of other guarantee of his professional capability and other indispensable qualities. He should be young, robust, and not lacking in courage and resources because the nature and the situation of the country where I am going require it; not however that he will ever be exposed to greater peril and fatigues than I am myself and even less. Above all it is necessary that he be ready soon, because I am leaving Genoa on the first of this July. The English brig *Hercules* of John Scott which is going to Leghorn to unload some merchandise will return here at the end of June to take me on board. At that time the surgeon could come aboard the brig at Leghorn.

Address to Mr. Dunn, an English merchant well known in that place, who will be directed by him in everything. Excuse the inconvenience I put you to; please avail yourself freely of any of my works, if I can help you at all, and believe me

Your devoted servant
Noel Byron, *Peer of England*

[TO CHARLES F. BARRY] *June 4th, 1823*

Dear Sir,—If you think yt. [that] Lord B[lessington] was quite serious—I have no objection to part with the Schooner for the proposed sum of four hundred guineas.—There are one or two things—which would only be an incumbrance to him—which I could wish to retain—1stly the 2 Cannon—which *strain* her in sailing—and are obliged to be put down below—2dly.—some American and superfluous flags—giving him all those necessary and proper—and 3dly. two chairs which have my coronet upon them—and are therefore less suitable to his use.—

With regard to the Snuff-boxes—as soon as we can get an estimate I will compare it with the one previously made—and give an answer;

---

[2] In the end Byron employed as his personal physician the young Italian Francesco Bruno, recommended by Dr. Alexander in Genoa.

194

—if you will have the goodness to let me know—when you have settled any thing on the subject—I can deliver up the Schooner to your charge —or to those commissioned to receive her.

Ever and truly yrs.

N B

P.S.—The smaller Green Snuff-box is I believe of Jasper—at least it is so stated in the list.

[TO CHARLES F. BARRY] *June 6, 1823*

Dear Sir,—I am very glad to hear that I shall see you at *five* tomorrow (if it suits you). *Don't dress.* It is merely a "bachelor's dinner", and there will be only Lord Kinnaird and your acquaintance, Count Pietro G[amb]a. Don't put yourself out of the way, but come as to a bad inn—except that you will not be charged for indifferent entertainment.

Yours ever,

N B

[TO DOUGLAS KINNAIRD] *June 8th. 1823*

My dear Douglas/—Enclosed is a true copy of Capt. B[laquiere]'s letter to me from Zante—this day received. Of course if the next communication from the *Greek* seat of Government—at all resembles the present—I shall proceed to join the cause forthwith.—You can communicate as much of this letter of C[aptai]n B[laquiere]'s—as you think may be proper—to the Committee.——"Hospital Supplies"—I have already ordered for the [word torn out with seal] of a thousand men for two years—at least [as] Dr. Alexander states them—in a *letter* which I forwarded to you some time ago.—They did not cost above seventy or eighty pounds sterling.—The Artillery will be thought of—but it may be difficult to purchase it in time, to take up with me.—But I will convey them what I can—and put my resources at the disposal of the Cause—when there—and this is all an individual can do.—I shall proceed to avail myself of your handsome credits in my favour—according to circumstances.—

Ever yrs.

N B

P.S.—Address to me at Genoa—my letters will be forwarded—in case I should have sailed before their arrival.—You will of course

195

continue the insurances of Ly. B[yron]'s life—as being quite requisite
—in other respects you must retain all incoming monies to face the
credits with which you have furnished me.——I have to thank Hobhouse for his kind and somewhat daring quotation from me to his
Electors the other day.—He must be a bold man to venture during my
unpopularity amongst the English.—Your brother is here—looking
well—dines with me to-day—when we shall drink your health and
prosperity.—Pray make some arrangement with Hobhouse to include
him in, or devolve on him the Power of Attorney in case of anything
occurring—but I hope you will take care of yourself and do well.—

[TO DOUGLAS KINNAIRD]   *June 9th. 1823*

My dear Douglas/—By Saturday's post I sent you a letter from
Capt. Blaquiere to me—and if his *next* confirms it—I shall go up to
join the Greeks forthwith.—We cannot exactly make out—*what
stores* they *chiefly* want—but I suppose that money will be the most
useful—as they then can apply it as occasion dictates.—I would suggest
to the Committee's consideration—to send some *Congreve rockets*
speedily—and engineers to instruct the G[ree]ks in their application.—
Depend upon it they would have an effect—also if Wilson[1] quits Spain
—send him up—he would do wonders probably.—It is rather strange
that I hear nothing further either from Hobhouse or the Committee.

                                                        yrs. ever
                                                          N B

P.S.—Your brother dined with me lately—and went this morning;
—tomorrow I dine with Mr. Hill—to meet—(I believe] the Marquis
of Hastings.[2]—If you write—address as usual to Genoa—as the letters
can be forwarded—if I should precede them.—

[TO DR. JAMES ALEXANDER]   *June 9th. 1823*

Dear Doctor—You need not trouble yourself to send to me for
approbation—but merely have the goodness to order what *you approve*
—and my consent will not be wanting.—I hope that the quantity will
be sufficient—but if not—I could wish to encrease it—and as I think

---

[1] See March 1, 1823, to Kinnaird, note 2.
[2] Francis Rawdon, first Marquis of Hastings (1754–1826), Governor of Malta
(1824–1826), soldier and statesman, had distinguished himself in the American
and Napoleonic wars and held various administrative posts in India.

of going sooner than was at first expected I should like to have all ready—and the Professional Gentleman provided to accompany the stores in question.

ever yr. obliged & obedt. Servt.
N B

[TO LADY HARDY]   *June 10th. 1823*

"Very right—" my dear Cousin (or Cozen) but you see there was no danger—for I have an aweful dread both of new love and learning—and—besides to say truth—thought that I was as well off *at home.*—I suspect that it is only over a very young man that these *mature* enchantments are permanent—and indeed I know—in one instance at least of my own experience—that at entering into life—those full blown beauties *have* the power you describe.—But at present besides my long foreign liaison of *five* years—and my being exceedingly governed and kept tight in hand—I do not know how it is—but it would be difficult for me—to fall in love again with an Englishwoman of any description. —Besides I have laid down a rule never to have a feeling of that kind (that is a *new* one) after thirty—my present attachment began before I had turned that awkward corner of existence—so that it was but just in time.—Having begun it will probably continue to the end of the Chapter—unless something out of the way stops it—as it does many things of the kind.—To return to our Irish Aspasia—I did not know that she had been *Post*-mistress of Cahir—but I had heard that she had been a mistress of some kind or other before she espoused the Earl of Bl[essingto]n.—Her slight acquaintance with me was of the most decorous description—the poor woman seemed devoured with Ennui —extremely bored with her lord—and a little sick of her Parisian Paladin also—though *why*—I could not perceive—for he is not only remarkably handsome—but certainly clever—and apparently amiable. ——But it was hinted—that his temper was not good—and that he was exigeant—though I saw few signs of either.—I saw very little of them especially latterly—and now they are gone.——

Lord Kinnaird is just gone—with Lady Kin[nair]d to England—he dined with me the day before yesterday.——Tomorrow I dine with our Excellence—(the only one of the diplomatists I ever knew who really is *excellent*) Mr. Hill—to meet (I believe) the Marquess of Hastings who has arrived here Heaven knows how—from India.—

My latest news from Greece gives me reason to suppose that I shall be required to go up there—and probably soon.——In that case

Madame G[uicciol]i retires into a convent—(it is her own fancy—since I positively refused her request to accompany me *there*—as you may readily suppose) or to her father's—but there is a difficulty about the *Roman States*—as her lawful Lord—might have her shut up for life —it seems——till we can find our way back again—or till Greece is quiet enough for me to send for her.——I am glad that you like her picture.—Mr. West is not in fault about mine—for I was *then*—what it appears—but since that time—and indeed since you saw me——I am very much reduced—partly by uncertain health in the winter and partly by the rigorous abstinence necessary to preserve it.——But it is so far better—that it makes me more like what I used to be ten years ago—in part at least.—Kinnaird—who had not seen me for two years and a half—was as much struck with the *re-alteration* at present—as he had been with the *former* alteration in the fourth or fifth year since I left England.—It is now the *eighth*—that is the *seventh* is completed— and three months of the eighth.—As to *yr.* Chevalier W[ebster] W[edderbur]ne my Coz—to be sure I learnt from *himself* all about his [Seckoran?] surprise—but there is some little doubt of his accuracy.— At least it is very strange that he could never *prove* so *public* a voyage of discovery.———She—poor thing—has made a sad affair of it alto-gether.—I had the melancholy task of prophesying as much many years ago—in some lines—of which the three or four first stanzas only were printed—and of course without names—or allusions —and with a *false* date—I send you the concluding stanza—which never was printed with the others.—

Then—fare thee well—Fanny—
    Now doubly undone—
To prove false unto many—
    As faithless to *One*—
Thou art past all recalling
    Even *would* I recall—
For the woman once *falling*
    Forever must *fall*.—

There's morality and *sintiment*—for you in a [breath?]—but I was very tender hearted in those days.——If you want to know *where* the lines to which this stanza belongs—*are*—they are in I know not what volume —but somewhere (for I have no copy) but they begin with

"When we two parted
    In silence and tears["]
        &c. &c. &c.—

198

So here is a treasure for you in honour of our relationship—rhymes un-published—and a secret into the bargain—which you won't keep.————I have not seen your Sir Peter Teazle—I heard that he acted very well—and that you *looked* very well—but that the part was too good natured for you.—this last is an addition of my own.——

I assure you that there is no coldness between me and Mr. T[relawny?]—that I know of—but I never write letters—and that perhaps has displeased him;———I write to *you*—because besides our *relationship*—(though I never could make out the pedigree) you are an especial favourite.———

ever and affectly yrs.
N B

[TO EDWARD JOHN TRELAWNY]   *June 15, 1823*

My dear T.—You must have heard that I am going to Greece. Why do you not come to me? I want your aid, and am exceedingly anxious to see you. Pray come, for I am at last determined to go to Greece; it is the only place I was ever contented in. I am serious, and did not write before, as I might have given you a journey for nothing; they all say I can be of use in Greece. I do not know how, nor do they; but at all events let us go.

Yours, etc., truly,
N BYRON

[TO DOUGLAS KINNAIRD]   *June 16th. 1823*

My dear Douglas/—Yrs. of the third arrived this day. Pray take care of yr. health—I do not like the "torpor" you mention.—Perhaps before I can receive yr. answer to this—I shall be on my voyage to the Levant.—I am bargaining for my passage in an English Vessel.—You can address to Genoa.—Mr. Barry will forward all letters.———I sent a copy last week—of Blaquiere's very pressing [word torn off with seal] for me to go up to Greece without delay.—As to my affairs—my anxiety is as much on your account as my own——as I should not like to overdraw—and yet may have occasion for all the means that I can muster—as I should not like to give the Greeks but a *half helping* hand —but rather aid them as much as I can.—As to the M.S.S.—you really *must* publish them whenever I have sailed—my distance will diminish the hatred of my enemies—and the object on which I am employed will do us no dishonour—at least it ought not.——Mr. Murray ought to give something for "Werner"—as I before said.——You are aware—how seldom I can hear from you for some time;——I received yr. letter of credit—but shall also be obliged to use the former *one* (for two thousand) as the four thousand alone—will hardly be sufficient.—I have also some circulars—and shall take up what I have in Mr. Webb's bank—and sell my furniture books &c. &c. &c. and the Schooner and Snuff-boxes—that I may do my best in supplying "the sinews of war".—I recommend my affairs to you and am

yrs. ever
N B

[TO JOHN CAM HOBHOUSE]   *June 19th. 1823*

Dear H[obhous]e—You will see by the enclosed that I have engaged a vessel.—Your Committee have printed my letter—with what view or advantage is more than I can conjecture—as I hear nothing *from*—and little *of* them.—D[ouglas] K[innaird] says nothing on the subject.—I expect to sail early in July.—Accounts are contradictory—the Greeks at Leghorn say first one thing and then another.—From Blaquiere I have not heard since the letter from Zante—which I sent to D. K. a fortnight ago.——I expect soon a letter from him from the seat of the Government.——I shall go up —and see what is to be done —if good—well—if otherwise—I can console myself with the motive.

yrs. ever
N B

[TO DOUGLAS KINNAIRD]   *June 19th. 1823*

Dear Douglas/—I have engaged a vessel and expect to sail (if nothing particular occurs to prevent it) about the beginning of July.—You can address to the care of Messrs Webb—& Barry—bankers here —who will forward any letters or packages.—You can let H[un]t have any M.S.S., as they come to hand—I suppose that you have delivered to him the new Canto (i.e. the 16th.) which he must print carefully from the M.S.S. as I shall hardly receive the proof in time.—I recommend my affairs to your care as it will be months before we can communicate—

yrs. ever
N B

Dear Sir—I have made out partly your correspondent's epistle—but as I should prefer to have it's *exact* sense—I could wish (if there be any Greek here capable) to have a translation in Italian—which by the way—all the educated Greeks that ever I met with spoke or wrote fluently.—When I left Greece in 1811—I could gabble Romaic pretty fluently—but have been long out of the habit—and would rather not trust to what I may recollect of it in a matter of this kind—when it is requisite to make as few mistakes as possible.———I therefore return the letter for the present.———You do not mention if we have settled anything with the medical man proposed by your young man Monsieur G. I think of converting the letter of Credit into Cash or credit here—about Monday—as I could wish to hear once more—or have a chance of hearing at least from England—as it is possible—(in consequence of the note which I enclosed of yours) that Mr. D[ouglas] K[innaird] may send other letters which may render this one superfluous.—I have only to request that Capt. J[ohn] S[cott] may bring back a few things from Mr. Dunn of Leghorn—and Mr. Trelawny as a passenger—if Mr. T prefers this way of coming to Genoa.—If Capt. J[ohn] S[cott] can form (as he said)—a second Cabin—I should probably prefer that for my own—but I am not particular on this point.—Could I get three or four swivels here think you?—Believe me

yrs. ever truly
N B

Sir—I have to acknowledge yrs. of ye. 6th. Inst. I sent Mr. D[ouglas] K[innaird] the 16th. of D[on] J[uan] which has arrived—but you do not mention it's having been delivered to you.—Unless a proof is sent immediately—I shall have sailed—as I expect to embark about the beginning of July.—In that case—you must print as carefully as you can from the MS.——[Did] you get the note to the Island—also enclosed to Mr. D. K.?——I hope that you will succeed—but I still think your proposed arrangement too moderate to yourself—15 per Cent (and 30 too) can hardly be a fair proportion for your risk and trouble.—I will deliver yr. message to your brother and am

yrs. ever truly
N B

P.S.—I doubt any thing like fair play from a Jury so constituted as "the Gang's" but you will at least expose them.——

Dear Doctor/—Once more—will you have the goodness to order *whatever* is requisite—and I will stand by your ordination.—All that is necessary is that the things should be ready in time—and as to the expence—I have already said that I will meet it—

ever yrs, faithfully
N B

Sir—I have the honour to acknowledge yr. letter of the 12th. June—and have taken the liberty—(I hope without offence) to send a copy to Mr. Hobhouse M.P. for Westminster—who is an active and able member of Parliament as well as of the Greek Committee.——It will be for the Committee to decide on your proposition—to which I see but the objection of ignorance of the Greeks in the Management of Steam Vessels—and perhaps the expence—because I am not aware to what ⟨extent⟩ the Subscriptions amount up to the present time.—I have also informed Mr. Hobhouse that you may probably write to him by my request—his address is—J[ohn] H[obhouse] Esqre. M.P.—Whitton Park—Hounslow—London.—I have done this—because I shall probably sail before I could receive yr. reply.—

The accounts are so extraordinary as to *what* mode will be best for supplying the Greeks—that I have deemed it better to take up (with the exception of a few supplies) what cash and Credits I can muster—rather than lay them out on articles which might be deemed superfluous or unnecessary.——*Here*—we can learn nothing but from some of the refugees who appear chiefly interested for *themselves*.——My accounts from an Agent of the Committee—(an English Gentleman lately gone up to Greece) are hitherto favourable—but he had not yet reached the seat of the provisional Government—and I am anxiously expecting further advice—before I sail.—If you will write to my friend Mr. Hobhouse—I am confident that your proposal will receive every attention—and this method will save you both time and trouble.—No apology was necessary for addressing yourself to me—especially on such a subject—an American has a better right than any other to suggest to other nations—the mode of obtaining that Liberty which is the Glory of his own.—I have the honour to be

yr. very obedt. humble Servt.
NOEL BYRON

[1] Church was the United States Consul at Geneva.

My dear Hobhouse/—On the other half sheet is the copy of a letter from the American Consul at Geneva—on the subject of a steam boat for the Greeks.—You can judge whether it will be likely to attract the notice of the Committee—and act accordingly—I have referred Mr. Church to *you*—as it is probable I may sail early in July. I have no further news—except that the Greeks of Tuscany—have in *two* instances applied for *themselves*—and one had the kindness to propose that a committee of six or eight Greeks at Leghorn—should direct me *how* to lay out the money—and (abusing the Greeks of Morea) strongly advised that I should remain in Italy—and let this said Committee manage for me &c. &c. &c. the first proposal being to ransom his (the writer's) own family—and so forth.——I have not heard from Blaquiere since the letter of the 28th. April—a copy of which I sent to Douglas K[innair]d—From you I have hitherto heard nothing further——a sign that you had not much to communicate.—

yrs. ever

N B

[TO EDWARD JOHN TRELAWNY]¹   *Genoa. June 21st. 1823*

Dear T.—I have engaged a vessel (now on her way to Leghorn to unload—) and on her return to Genoa—we embark.—She is called the Hercules.——you can come back in her—if you like—it will save you a land journey.—I need not say that I shall like your company of all things.—I want a Surgeon—native or foreign—to take charge of stores and be in personal attendance—salary—a hundred pounds a year—all expences paid—and his treatment at our table and as a companion and a Gentleman. He must have recommendations of course—could you look out for me? perhaps—you could consult Vaccà to whom I have written on the same subject.—We are however pressed for time a little.—I expect you with impatience and am

ever yrs.

N B

[TO AUGUSTA LEIGH]   *June 23d. 1823*

Tell Lady B[yron] that she did quite right¹——and I am glad that

¹ Addressed to Trelawny at Leghorn, in care of Henry Dunn, the merchant.
¹ The church living at Kirkby Mallory, the Noel estate, became vacant in 1823, and Lady Byron, as Byron had requested, presented it to the Rev. Thomas Noel, illegitimate son of Lord Wentworth.

she did so without hesitation.———I do not know where the *law lies* (it *lies* always I believe) but I never would have promised the living to any one without her approbation—but have rather left the nomination to herself.—I sail for Greece in about a fortnight—address to Genoa—as usual—letters will be forwarded

yrs. ever
N B

[TO J. W. LAKE][1] *Genoa. June 25th. 1823*

Sir—I have to thank you for yr. obliging letter of ye. 11th. inst. it is true that I had some intention of publishing such an edition 1stly. because both Galignani's and even the London editions are extremely incorrect owing probably to my long absence abroad and distance from the press and 2dly. because I thought that Mr. Galignani had treated me with incivility and neglect in not replying to some letters accompanied with an order for books; so as to render any peculiar deference to his feelings an object unnecessary on my part.——However he has since explained his apparent negligence—and were it otherwise—I must have given up the notion of superintending the publication personally—because in a week or two I sail for Greece.——An edition similar to the very neat one published by you of the British Prose writers would have answered *my* purpose (i.e. a *correct* edition) extremely well—but I doubt upon the whole that it would have succeeded—as the Paris re-publications have been already sufficient to exhaust the demand.—I am extremely obliged to you personally for your kind offer of which I may one day (if I ever return) avail myself. ——I have the honour to be

yr. obliged and very obedt. Servt.
NOEL BYRON

[TO CHARLES F. BARRY] *June 27th. 1823*

Dear Sir—It will do very well.—There is some good English Gunpowder of Mr. Dunn's[,] Leghorn[,] which I could wish to have shipped there.—Mr. D[unn] is already apprized.—Also—if Mr. Trelawny is

---

[1] Lake did publish in 1825, after Byron's death, a seven-volume *Complete Works of Lord Byron*, with a biographical and critical notice by himself. It was printed in Paris by Baudry. He later published a one-volume edition which had a wide sale in England and America.

at Leghorn—as he is *my* passenger—he had better (if he likes) return here with Capt. Jonny S[cott].——The Engagement I presume commences—when he is *here (at Genoa) ready* for sailing as I am not responsible for his own delays up to that period.——If he is civil and obliging—he will perhaps find his account in it. Believe me

ever yrs obliged & faithly.

N B

[TO LEIGH HUNT] *June 28th. 1823*

Dear H.—I have received a note from Mrs. S[helley] with a fifth or sixth change of plans—viz.—not to make her journey at all—at least through my assistance on account of what she is pleased to call "estrangement &c."—On this I have little to say. The readiest mode now may be this—which can be settled between you and me without her knowing anything of the matter.——I will advance the money to *you*—(I desired Mr. B[arry] to say what would enable her to travel *"handsomely* and *conveniently* in all respects" these were the words of my note this afternoon to him) on Monday—you can then say that you have raised it as a loan on your own account—no matter with whom or how—and that *you* advance it to *her*—which may easily be made the fact if you feel scrupulous—by giving me a scrap of paper as your note of hand;—thus she will be spared any fancied humiliation;—and I am not aware of anything in the transaction which can render it obnoxious to yourself—at least I am sure that there is no such intention on my part—nor ever was in any thing which has passed between us—although there are circumstances so plausible—and scoundrels so ready in every corner of the earth to give a colour of their own to every thing.—The last observation is dictated by what you told me to-day to my utter astonishment—it will however teach me to know my company better or not at all. And Now pray—do not apply or misapply directly or indirectly to *yourself* any of these observations;—*I* knew you long before Mr. S[helley] knew either you or me—and you and *two* more of his friends are the only ones whom I can at all reflect upon as men whose acquaintance was honourable and agreeable. I have a thing more to state—which is that from this moment—I must decline the office of acting as his executor in any respect, and also all further connection with his family in any of it's branches,—now or hereafter.——There was something about a legacy of two thousand pounds—which he had left me—this of course I decline—and the more so that I hear—that his will is admitted valid; and I state this distinctly that in case of any-thing happening to me—my heirs may be instructed not to claim it.—

yrs. ever and truly
N B

P.S.—I enclose you Mr. B[arry]'s answer just received to my note of this afternoon.——

[TO DR. J. W. MACCARTHY, M.D.]   *Genoa. June 30th. 1823*

Sir—Nothing would have suited me better—but having heard nothing from Mr. Trelawny—I had in the mean time owing to the pressure of time concluded with an Italian recommended by Dr. Alex-ander.—I regret this extremely as I would have preferred a country-man on this occasion.—As I have put you to the expence of a journey to Leghorn I hope that you will not be offended at my request to be permitted to reimburse you for the amount.—This will be done by either Mr. Trelawny (whom I will immediately repay) or by Mr. Dunn of Leghorn—which I will settle with his account.—I have the honour to be

yr. very obedt. humble Sert.
NOEL BYRON

[TO JOHN HUNT]   *Genoa. June 30th. 1823*

[Fragment of letter quoted in catalogue]

... Yrs. has been duly received with a copy of the "Island". There are some mistakes such as "flower of Mankind" and "Proclaims their cause" for "proscribes their cause" which you can correct at leisure. I am sorry that you have had a dispute with Blackwood and are going to prosecute, being an enemy to all prosecutions when they can be avoided .... As I shall have sailed probably long before you can answer this letter, you must print the 16th canto as correctly as you can from the M.S.S. without forwarding the proofs. As to making up the volume, I have not the 17th. ready but you can manage to include the 15th. and 16th. in the same volume with the others by a proper distribution—there are eleven in all at present. I wish you very sincerely good luck and happiness and so God speed you.

Sir,—I shall be very happy to make your acquaintance, but I am very sorry to tell you, that, being unaccustomed either to speak or to write French, I shall be unable to derive all the benefit I could wish from your conversation. If, however, what I have said does not deter you, I shall be delighted to see you to-morrow at 2 o'clock.

    With profound respect, I have the honour to be

your most obedient, humble servant,

NOEL BYRON, Peer of England²

[TO J. J. COULMANN]   *Genoa, July* [7?], *1823*

    My dear Sir,—Your letter, and what accompanied it, have given me the greatest pleasure. The glory and the works of the writers who have deigned to give me these volumes, bearing their names, were not unknown to me, but still it is more flattering to receive them from the authors themselves. I beg you to present my thanks to each of them in particular; and to add, how proud I am of their good opinion, and how charmed I shall be to cultivate their acquaintance, if ever the occasion should occur. The productions of M. Jouy¹ have long been familiar to me. Who has not read and applauded *The Hermit* and *Scylla?* But I cannot accept what it has pleased your friends to call their *homage,* because there is no sovereign in the republic of letters; and even if there were, I have never had the pretension or the power to become a usurper.

    I have also to return you thanks for having honoured me with your compositions; I thought you too young, and probably too amiable, to be an author. As to the Essay, etc., I am obliged to you for the present, although I had already seen it joined to the last edition of the translation.² I have nothing to object to it, with regard to what concerns

---

¹ Nothing is known of Coulmann except what can be derived from Byron's letters.

² Coulmann published this and the following letter in French in *Mercure du Dixneuvième Siecle*, tome xii, année 1826. They were published in translation in *Paul Pry*, April 1, 1826. Prothero has followed the Paul Pry translation. The original manuscripts have not come to light. Presumably Byron wrote the letters in English.

¹ Victor Joseph Etienne de Jouy (1764–1846) wrote *L'Hermite de la Chaussé d'Antin; ou, Observations sur les Moeurs et les Usages Parisiens au commencement du XIXe. Siècle,* and a tragedy called *Sylla* (a fifth edition appeared in 1823).

² In a French translation of Byron's complete works, begun in Paris in 1821, appeared an "Essai sur le Génie et le Caractère de Lord Byron par A P....t [Amédée Pichot]" preceded by a preliminary notice by Charles Nodier. Speaking of Byron's father and Lady Carmarthen, Pichot wrote "Les vices du capitaine et sa brutalité la firent mourir de douleur".

myself personally, though naturally there are some of the facts in it discoloured, and several errors into which the author has been led by the accounts of others. I allude to facts, and not criticisms. But the same author has cruelly calumniated my father and my grand-uncle, but more especially the former. So far from being "brutal," he was, according to the testimony of all those who knew him, of an extremely amiable and (*enjoué*) joyous character, but careless (*insouciant*) and dissipated. He had, consequently, the reputation of a good officer, and showed himself such in the Guards, in America. The facts themselves refute the assertion. It is not by "brutality" that a young Officer in the Guards seduces and carries off a Marchioness, and marries two heiresses. It is true that he was a very handsome man, which goes a great way. His first wife (Lady Conyers and Marchioness of Carmarthen) did not die of grief, but of a malady which she caught by having imprudently insisted upon accompanying my father to a hunt, before she was completely recovered from the accouchement which gave birth to my sister Augusta.

His second wife, my respected mother, had, I assure you, too proud a spirit to bear the ill-usage of any man, no matter who he might be; and this she would have soon proved. I should add, that he lived a long time in Paris, and was in habits of intimacy with the old Marshal Biron, Commandant of the French Guards; who, from the similitude of names, and Norman origin of our family, supposed that there was some distant relationship between us. He died some years before the age of forty, and whatever may have been his faults, they were certainly not those of harshness and grossness (*dureté et grossièreté*). If the notice should reach England, I am certain that the passage relative to my father will give much more pain to my sister (the wife of Colonel Leigh, attached to the Court of the late Queen, *not* Caroline, but Charlotte, wife of George III.), even than to me; and this she does not deserve, for there is not a more angelic being upon earth. Augusta and I have always loved the memory of our father as much as we loved each other, and this at least forms a presumption that the stain of harshness was not applicable to it. If he dissipated his fortune, that concerns us alone, for we are his heirs; and till we reproach him with it, I know no one else who has a right to do so. As to Lord Byron, who killed Mr. Chaworth in a duel[3], so far from retiring from the world, he made the

---

[3] The fifth Lord Byron, from whom the poet inherited the title, killed his cousin William Chaworth in a duel in 1765. When his son married his impecunious cousin Juliana Elizabeth Byron, he tried to waste and destroy the inheritance, which on the early death of his son, came to the poet as sixth Baron.

tour of Europe, and was appointed Master of the Stag-hounds after that event, and did not give up society until his son had offended him by marrying in a manner contrary to his duty. So far from feeling any remorse for having killed Mr. Chaworth, who was a fire-eater (*spadassin*), and celebrated for his quarrelsome disposition, he always kept the sword which he used upon that occasion in his bed-chamber, where it still was *when he died*. It is singular enough, that when very young, I formed a strong attachment for the grand-niece and heiress of Mr. Chaworth, who stood in the same degree of relationship as myself to Lord Byron;[4] and at one time it was thought that the two families would have been united in us. She was two years older than me, and we were very much together in our youth. She married a man of an ancient and respectable family; but her marriage was not a happier one than my own. Her conduct, however, was irreproachable, but there was no sympathy between their characters, and a separation took place. I had not seen her for many years. When an occasion offered, I was upon the point, with her consent, of paying her a visit, when my sister, who has always had more influence over me than anyone else, persuaded me not to do it. "For," said she, "if you go, you will fall in love again, and then there will be a scene; one step will lead to another, *et cela fera un éclat*," etc. I was guided by these reasons, and shortly after I married; with what success it is useless to say. Mrs. C. some time after, being separated from her husband, became insane; but she has since recovered her reason, and is, I believe, reconciled to her husband. This is a long letter, and principally about my family, but it is the fault of M. Pichot, my benevolent biographer. He may say of me whatever of good or evil pleases him, but I desire that he should speak of my relations only as they deserve. If you could find an occasion of making him, as well as M. Nodier, rectify the facts relative to my father, and publish them, you would do me a great service, for I cannot bear to have him unjustly spoken of. I must conclude abruptly, for I have occupied you too long. Believe me to be very much honoured by your esteem, and always your obliged and obedient servant,

NOEL BYRON

P.S.—the tenth or twelfth of this month I shall embark for Greece. Should I return, I shall pass through Paris, and shall be much flattered in meeting you and your friends. Should I not return, give me as affectionate a place in your memory as possible.

4 Byron and Mary Chaworth were cousins by a fifth remove, through the marriage of William, third Lord Byron, and Elizabeth Chaworth, daughter of Viscount Chaworth.

Dear Sir—We sail on the 12th. for Greece.[1]—I have had a letter from Mr. Blaquiere too long for present transcription but very satisfactory.—The G[ree]k Government expects me without delay.——In conformity to the desire of Mr. B. and other correspondents in Greece —I have to suggest with all deference to the Committee—that a remittance of even *"ten thousand pounds only"* (Mr. B's expression) would be of the greatest service to the G[ree]k Government at present. —I have also to recommend strongly the attempt at a loan—for which there will be offered a sufficient security by deputies now on their way to England.——In the mean time I hope that the Committee will be able to do something effectual.——For my own part—I mean to carry up in cash or credits—above eight and nearly nine thousand pounds sterling—which I am enabled to do by funds which I have in Italy— and Credits from England.—Of this sum I must necessarily reserve a portion for the subsistence of my-self and Suite.—The rest I am willing to apply in the manner which seems most likely to be useful to the cause—having of course some guarantee or assurance that it will not be misapplied to any individual speculation.

If I remain in Greece—which will mainly depend upon the presumed probable utility of my presence there—and the opinion of the Greeks themselves as to it's propriety—in short—if I am welcome to them—I shall continue during my residence at least to apply such portions of my income present and future as may forward the object—that is to say— what I can spare for that purpose.—Privations—I can—or at least could once bear—abstinence I am accustomed to—and as to fatigue—I was once a tolerable traveller—what I may be now—I cannot tell— but I will try.——I await the commands of the Committee—address to Genoa—the letters will be forwarded to me—wherever I may be— by my bankers Messrs Webb and Barry.—It would have given me pleasure to have had some more defined instructions before I went— but these of course rest at the option of the Committee.—I have the honour to be

yr. obedt. and faithl. Sert.

N B

[1] Byron and his party went on board the *Hercules* on July 13 and were ready to sail on the 14th, but were becalmed and went ashore again. When they sailed on the 15th, they were at first becalmed and then ran into a storm that sent them back to port. Finally on the evening of the 16th they had a fair wind and reached Leghorn in five days. The party consisted of Byron, Trelawny, Count Pietro Gamba, Dr. Bruno, and Constantine Skilitzy who had asked for a passage to Greece. They carried five horses, Byron's bulldog Moretto and his Newfoundland Lyon, and a considerable quantity of arms and ammunition and medical supplies for the Greeks.

P.S.—Great anxiety is expressed for the printing press and types, &c. I have not the time to provide them, but recommend this to the notice of the Committee. I presume the types must, partly at least, be *Greek*: they wish to publish papers, and perhaps a Journal, probably in Romaic, with Italian translations.[2]

[TO CAPTAIN DANIEL ROBERTS]   *July 9th. 1823*

My dear R.—We have already engaged a medical man—otherwise your friend would have been very welcome.—Trelawny is here—we sail on the 12th.—I regret very much that you can't accompany us— but I hope that we shall all meet merrily some day or other either here or there.—I write in haste, not to keep your messenger—

ever yrs. obliged & truly
N B

[TO DOUGLAS KINNAIRD]   *July 10th. 1823*

Dear Douglas—We expected to sail on the 12th., but it may be a day or two longer before we can put to sea—as the wind is at present contrary—and the places for the reception of the horses have some need of alteration.—But by the 13th. or 14th. or even before if possible we expect to get under way.

I have to enclose you at the request of Colonel Stietz[1]—a plan of his for a foreign brigade in the Greek Service.—Of its practicability I can say nothing—but it is my duty to lay it before you—as requested—for your perusal, being addressed to the various Committees English as well as foreign. *The funds which he requires are too considerable I doubt. He himself is well recommended at least his papers seem to show it.*

I wrote to you last week enclosing a letter for Mr. Bowring. Blaquiere writes that even ten thousand pounds[2] would be of incalculable service to their cause at present.—I have other letters from Greece—urging the attempt at a loan.—I leave you to state and support these facts (i.e. the loan and the money for them from the Committee) as much as you can.

ever yrs.
N B

P.S.—Address to Genoa—letters will be forwarded.——

[2] This postscript is now missing from the manuscript and is supplied from *LJ.* VI, 229.
[1] See July 12, 1823, to Bowring.
[2] Words here printed in italics were written in another hand.

211

[TO JOHN BOWRING]   *Genoa. July 12th. 1823*

Sir—Colonel Stietz of the States of Hesse Cassel—but at present or recently in the Greek Service has requested a letter of introduction to the Greek Committee.—I have accordingly furnished him with these few lines—in the hope that you will have the goodness to permit him to submit his plan for consideration to the acting members.—As I cannot pretend to decide upon it's practicability—I must leave him to give his explanation.—I sent a sketch of it to Mr. D. Kinnaird a few days ago—in French—but in very *German* French—as you will perceive by a perusal.—I have the honour to be your

[Signature cut out]

P.S.—We were to sail today—but the winds are very light—and hardly favourable enough.—But tomorrow or next day—we expect to be under way, or weigh, for some say one and some the other.—It is at present a regular Calm.

[TO JOHN HUNT]   *July 14th. 1823*

Sir—I return the proofs.—The second will not arrive in time.—You must therefore correct it carefully from the M.S.S. Also the same with the 16th. Canto of D[on] J[uan].—You can publish the whole of the new eleven in *three* volumes—i.e.—three cantos in one vol.—and four in the 2d.—and four in the third—so that there will be three good sized—instead of four *thin* vols—as I have not had leisure to complete the 17th. Canto.—

yrs in haste but truly & [scrawl]
N B

P.S.—We sail tonight if the Gods are willing and the wind serves.

[TO COUNTESS TERESA GUICCIOLI]   *Livorno July 22d. 1823*

[Note added to Pietro's letter to Teresa]

My dearest Teresa—I have but a few moments to say that we are all well—and thus far on our way to the Levant—believe that I always *love* you —and that a thousand words could only express the same idea.

ever dearest yrs.
N B

Illustrious Sir—I cannot thank you as you ought to be thanked for the lines which my young friend Mr. Sterling[1] sent me of yours,—and it would but ill become me to pretend to exchange verses with him who for fifty years has been the undisputed Sovereign of European literature.—You must therefore accept my most sincere acknowledgements in prose—and in hasty prose too—for I am at present on my voyage to Greece once more—and surrounded by hurry and bustle which hardly allow a moment even to Gratitude and Admiration to express themselves.——I sailed from Genoa some days ago—was driven back by a Gale of Wind—and have since sailed again—and arrived here (Leghorn) this morning to receive on board some Greek passengers for their struggling Country.——*Here* also I found your lines and Mr. Sterling's letter—and I could not have had a more favourable Omen or more agreeable surprise than a word from Goethe written by his own hand.——I am returning to Greece to see if I can be of any little use there;—if ever I come back I will pay a visit to Weimar to offer the sincere homage of one of the many Millions of your admirers.—I have the honour to be ever & most respectfully

yr. obliged adm[irer] & Se[rvant]

NOEL BYRON

Aux Soins de Monsieur Sterling.

Sir—I received yrs. of the 20th. June on anchoring here Saturday. We were driven back to Genoa by a Gale of wind but put to sea the next day again and arrived here about 24 hours ago.

I find the Greeks here somewhat divided amongst themselves.—I have spoken to them about the delay of intelligence for the Committee's regulation—and they have promised to be more punctual. The Archbishop is at Pisa—but has sent me several letters etc. for Greece.— What they most seem to want or desire is—Money—Money— Money. I have carried with me some specie—and considerable credits (for an *individual* that is to say) to dispose of according to circumstances wherever the cause may appear to require them.—As the Committee has not favoured me with any specific instructions as to any line of conduct they might think it well for me to pursue—I of course

---

[1] Charles Sterling, son of the British Consul at Genoa, when he left for Germany carried a note from Byron expressing homage to the great German writer. Goethe's lines sent by young Sterling are printed in Moore, II, 676.

have to suppose that I am left to my own discretion. If at any future period—I can be useful—I am as willing to be so as heretofore.—From Mr. Blaquiere I have heard—and so will the Committee ere this—the substance of his information is much the same as the details before received.— —

We expect to sail again to-day. I called here for letters and two gentlemen who requested a passage. I have the honour to remain

Your very obedt. faithfl Sert.

N B

[TO CHARLES F. BARRY] *Leghorn Roads, Ship Hercules. July 24th.*
1823

Dear Sir—I have very little time to thank you for yr. very kind letter.—After our first rough experiment—we have had calms or contrary winds—but finally a light breeze brought us in here—about four and twenty hours ago.— —Though I perceive that I have dated from shore—I write on board—we expect to sail again to-day.—I have found the Greeks here—as expected—a little divided among themselves—but—we must make the best of it.—As I have bought several more necessary articles of Dunn—my order will exceed considerably the hundred and twenty crowns which I had set apart for his account.—Our Captain has conducted himself extremely well—and has all the appearance of continuing to do so.—Several vessels now here—were tost about and suffered damage in the Squall that sent us back for a day to Genoa— —I got what I believe to be the insured packet (from Goethe dated Weimar in Germany) and have signed an order for the Post office in future—and left it with your partners of the Leghorn House. You may be sure that I am very sensible of your obliging expressions—and ashamed of the various troubles which I have occasioned by the preparation for my voyage.—

Ever and truly yrs.

N B

P.S.—You had perhaps better sell the horse if any opportunity offers—as for the other things—you had better wait till you hear from me further. I particularly recommend to your Care my own travelling Chariot—which I would not part with for any consideration. I have heard from *the Earl*[1]—but not a word hitherto of the Schooner.—On the other side is a draft in favour of Mr. Dunn—as I mentioned it would be in the former part of my letter.

[1] The Earl of Blessington had agreed to buy the *Bolivar*, but was slow in making the payment.

Appendix I

LIST OF LETTERS AND SOURCES

Date	*Recipient*	*Source of Text*	*Page*
		1822	
Oct. 4	Mary Shelley	MS. Lord Abinger	11
Oct. 8	James Sterling	MS. Carl H. Pforzheimer Library	11
Oct. 8	Edward John Trelawny	MS. Henry E. Huntington Library	11
Oct. 9	John Murray	MS. Murray	12
Oct. 12	Augusta Leigh	MS. The Earl of Lytton	14
Oct. 20	Augusta Leigh	MS. The Earl of Lytton	15
Oct. 22	John Murray	MS. Murray	16
Oct. 23	John Hanson (*a*)	MS. Murray	16
Oct. 23	John Hanson (*b*)	Text: Maggs Cat. 753, 1946	16
Oct. 24	John Murray	MS. Murray	17
Oct. 26	James Wedderburn Webster	Text: *LJ*, VI, 131	18
Oct. 27	Douglas Kinnaird	MS. Murray	19
Oct. 28	Count Leopoldo Cicognara	MS. Murray	20
Oct. 29	Leigh Hunt	MS. Robert H. Taylor Coll., Princeton University Library	21
Oct. 31	John Murray (*a*)	Text: Copy, Murray MSS.	21
Oct. 31	John Murray (*b*)	MS. Murray	22
Oct. 31	John Hunt	MS. Carl H. Pforzheimer Library	23
Oct. 31	Douglas Kinnaird	MS. Murray	24
[Nov.]	Henry Hunt	MS. Henry E. Huntington Library	24
[Nov.]	Edward John Trelawny	MS. Henry E. Huntington Library	25
[Nov.?]	[Leigh Hunt]	Text: Park-Bernet, Cat. 110, April 26, 1939	25
Nov. 2	Douglas Kinnaird	MS. Murray	26

Date	Recipient	Source of Text	Page
		1823	
March 8	Douglas Kinnaird	MS. Murray	117
March 9	James Wedderburn Webster	MS. Murray	119
March 10	John Hunt	MS. Robert H. Taylor Coll., Princeton University Library	120
March 10	Douglas Kinnaird	MS. Lord Kinnaird	121
March 12	John Cam Hobhouse	MS. Houghton Library, Harvard University	121
March 12	Lord Holland	MS. British Library (Add. 51639)	122
March 12	I. Ingram	Text: Copy, Keats–Shelley Memorial, Rome	122
March 17	John Hunt	Text: *LJ*, VI, 172–174	122
March 19	John Cam Hobhouse	MS. Murray	124
March 20	Douglas Kinnaird	MS. Murray	126
March 24	R. B. Hoppner	Text: Albert Cohn in Berlin, 20–25 März, 1893	128
March 28	Lady Hardy	MS. Lord Hindlip	128
March 29	Joshua Henslow Hayward	MS. Houghton Library, Harvard University	131
March 30	Henry Fox	MS. Carl H. Pforzheimer Library	131
March 31	Douglas Kinnaird	MS. Murray	132
[April?]	John Hunt	MS. Facsimile, British Library (Add. 38108)	133
[April?]	Capt. Daniel Roberts	Text: Sotheby Cat., May 12, 1905	133
[April?]	Douglas Kinnaird	MS. Murray	134
April 2	Douglas Kinnaird	MS. Murray	135
April 2	Thomas Moore	Text: Moore, II, 632–634	136
April 2	Earl of Blessington	Text: Blessington (ed. Lovell), p. 14	138
April 5	Edward Blaquiere	MS. Stark Library, University of Texas	139
April 5	Earl of Blessington	MS. Carl H. Pforzheimer Library	139
April 6	Earl of Blessington	Text: Moore, II, 638–639	141

Date	Recipient	Source of Text	Page
		1823	
April 6	Lord Sydney Osborne	Text: Anderson Cat. 1025, April 16–27, 1914	142
April 7	John Cam Hobhouse	MS. Murray	142
April 7	Douglas Kinnaird	MS. Murray	144
April 9	John Hunt	MS. Robert H. Taylor Coll., Princeton University Library	145
April 9	Earl of Blessington	Text: Moore, II, 639	146
April 9	Douglas Kinnaird	MS. Murray	146
April 12	Dr. James Alexander	MS. Commander P.G.A. King	147
April 14	Earl of Blessington (*a*)	Text: Moore, II, 639	148
April 14	Earl of Blessington (*b*)	Text: Blessington (ed. Lovell), p. 15	148
April 14	John Cam Hobhouse	MS. Murray	149
April 14	Douglas Kinnaird	MS. Murray	150
April 14	John Hunt	MS. Carl H. Pforzheimer Library	150
April 17	John Cam Hobhouse	MS. Murray	151
April 19	[J. Webb]	Text: *Notes and Queries*, 4th. ser., V. 4, 291, Oct. 9, 1869	152
April 19	Douglas Kinnaird	MS. Murray	152
April 21	Douglas Kinnaird	MS. Murray	154
April 22	Count Alfred D'Orsay	MS. Bibliothèque Nationale, Paris	156
April 22	Earl of Blessington	MS. Facsimile (first page) Anderson Cat., Dec. 8, 1925 Text: *LJ*, VI, 195	156
April 23	Earl of Blessington	MS. Stark Library, University of Texas	157
April 24	John Hunt	Text: Maggs, Cat. 269, Summer 1911	158
April 24	Douglas Kinnaird	MS. Murray	158
April 25	Charles F. Barry	MS. Murray	159
April 29	John Hunt	MS. Carl H. Pforzheimer Library	160
April 30	Charles F. Barry	MS. Stark Library, University of Texas	161

Date	Recipient	Source of Text	Page
		1823	
May 21	John Bowring	MS. National Library, Athens	179
May 21	John Hunt	MS. Pierpont Morgan Library	181
May 21	Capt. Daniel Roberts	Text: Copy, Public Library at Forli	182
May 23	Earl of Blessington	MS. Stark Library, University of Texas	183
May 24	John Cam Hobhouse	MS. Murray	184
May 24	Douglas Kinnaird	MS. Murray	184
May 25	Charles F. Barry	MS. Murray	185
May 26	Douglas Kinnaird	MS. Murray	186
May 27	Dr. James Alexander	Text: Sotheby Cat., July 2, 1917	186
May 28	Douglas Kinnaird	MS. Murray	187
May 28	Charles F. Barry	MS. Stark Library, University of Texas	187
May 28	John Cam Hobhouse	MS. Murray	188
May 29	Henri Beyle	Text: Medwin (Paris, 1824), Appendix II, 169–171	189
[June]	Contessa d'Ysone	Text: Copy, Carl H. Pforzheimer Library	190
June 1	Earl of Blessington	Text: Anderson Cat. 2007, Dec. 8, 1925	192
June 2	Countess of Blessington	MS. Carl H. Pforzheimer Library	192
[June 2–4?]	Andrea Vaccà	Text: Tribolatti, *Saggi*, 199–200, note 2	193
June 4	Charles F. Barry	MS. Österreichischen Nationalbibliothek, Vienna	194
June 6	Charles F. Barry	Text: O. Intze, *Byroniana* (pamphlet) Bremen, 1914	195
June 8	Douglas Kinnaird	MS. Murray	195
June 9	Douglas Kinnaird	MS. Murray	196
June 9	Dr. James Alexander	MS. Carl H. Pforzheimer Library	196
June 10	Lady Hardy	MS. Lord Hindlip	197
June 15	Edward John Trelawny	Text: Trelawny, *Records*, p. 159	199
June 16	Douglas Kinnaird	MS. Murray	199

FORGERIES OF BYRON'S LETTERS

Oct. 5, 1822: To Capt. Hay. Text: Anderson Gallery, 2126, Jan. 17, 1927.

Nov. 11, 1822: To Major Sterling. Text: Schultess-Young, XLVI, 230–231.

Nov. 28, 1822: To Sir Godfrey Webster. Text: Bixby.

Dec. 8, 1822: To Douglas Kinnaird. Text: Schultess-Young, XXV 195–197.

Dec. 25, 1822: To Lord Holland. MS. Houghton Library, Harvard University.

Feb. 9, 1823: To Douglas Kinnaird. Schultess-Young, XXVI, 197–99.

April 5, 1823: To W. J. Banks, Schultess-Young, XXXIV, 211–13.

April 19, 1823: To John Hanson. MS. British Library.

BIBLIOGRAPHY FOR VOLUME 10
(*Principal short title and abbreviated references*)

Blaquiere, Edward: *Narrative of a Second Visit to Greece, Including Facts Connected with the Last Days of Lord Byron*....London, 1825.

Blessington—Lady Blessington's Conversations of Lord Byron, ed. Ernest J. Lovell, Jr., Princeton, N.J., 1969.

Broughton, Lord (John Cam Hobhouse): *Recollections of a Long Life*, ed. by his daughter, Lady Dorchester, 6 vols., London, 1909–1911.

Dictionary of National Biography.

Gamba, Count Peter (Pietro): *A Narrative of Lord Byron's Last Journey to Greece*, London, 1825.

Hunt, Leigh: *Correspondence*, ed. by his Eldest Son, 2 vols., London, 1862.

———*Lord Byron and Some of His Contemporaries*, 2 vols., 2d. ed., London, 1828.

[Iley, Matthew]: *The Life, Writings, Opinions, and Times of the Right Hon. George Gordon Noel Byron, Lord Byron*....3 vols., London, 1825.

Ingpen, Roger: *Shelley in England*, London, 1917.

Keats–Shelley Journal, Vol. II, 1953.

LBC—Lord Byron's Correspondence, ed. John Murray, 2 vols., London, 1922.

LJ—The Works of Lord Byron. A New, Revised and Enlarged Edition. Letters and Journals, ed. Rowland E. Prothero, 6 vols., London, 1898–1901.

Marchand, Leslie A.: *Byron, A Biography*, 3 vols., New York, 1957; London, 1958.

Medwin, Thomas: *Journal of the Conversations of Lord Byron*..... 2 vols., Paris, 1824.

Medwin's "Conversations of Lord Byron", ed. Ernest J. Lovell, Jr., Princeton, N.J., 1966.

Moore, Doris Langley: *The Late Lord Byron*, London, 1961.

———*Lord Byron: Accounts Rendered*, London, 1974.

Moore—Letters and Journals of Lord Byron, with Notices of His Life, by Thomas Moore, 2 vols., London, 1830.

Moore, Memoirs—Memoirs, Journals, and Correspondence of Thomas Moore, ed. Lord John Russell, 8 vols., London, 1853–1856.

Notes and Queries, 4th. series, vol. 4, p. 291, Oct. 9, 1869.

Origo, Iris: *The Last Attachment*, London, 1949.

Poetry—The Works of Lord Byron. A New, Revised and Enlarged Edition. Poetry, ed. Ernest Hartley Coleridge, 7 vols. London, 1898–1904.

Procter, Bryan Waller: *Autobiographical Fragment and Biographical Notes*, Boston, 1877.

Shelley, Mary W.: *The Letters of Mary W. Shelley*, ed. Frederick L. Jones, 2 vols., Norman, Oklahoma, 1944.

St. Clair, William: *Trelawny, The Incurable Romancer*, London, 1977.

Trelawny, Edward John: *Recollections of the Last Days of Shelley and Byron*, London, 1858.

——*The Letters of Edward John Trelawny*, ed. H. Buxton Forman, London, 1910.

Tribolatti, Felice: *Saggi, Critici e Biografici*, Pisa, 1891.

BIOGRAPHICAL SKETCHES

of Principal Correspondents and Persons
Frequently Mentioned
(*See also Sketches in earlier volumes*)

Charles F. Barry

Byron seemed to have a special friendly relationship with his bankers, whose probity and business sense he trusted, and who generally performed many services for him beyond simple financial transactions. This was true of his London banker friend, Douglas Kinnaird, who was also his business agent with Power of Attorney, his trustee and literary agent, as well as eager recipient of his facetious comments on men, women, and events. In Geneva Charles Hentsch was another banker friend who helped him find a house, took care of his mail, and introduced him to as much of Genevan society as he wanted. Charles F. Barry was the Genoa partner of Webb & Co., who had been Byron's bankers in Leghorn. Soon after his arrival in Genoa Byron was on the most familiar terms with Barry, and the intimacy increased to the point that he became not only business agent but friend and confidant. It was Barry who searched for a ship to take Byron to Greece and found the *Hercules*. And he took care of all the details of getting supplies and outfitting the vessel. Before he left Byron consigned to him his books, letters and papers, his travelling carriage, and his furniture. And he gave him a number of his poetry manuscripts. On his side Barry was inconsolable at losing a friend who had treated him with the greatest kindness and no condescension. From Greece Byron wrote him the fullest and most confidential news of his own and of Greek affairs. Barry handled all financial matters for him, even acting as agent for the London bankers, and was prompt in replying. In fact Byron found him the most satisfying of his correspondents. His last letter from Greece was addressed to Barry.

The Countess of Blessington

The "Blessington Circus", as it was called because of the elaborate trappings of the travelling caravan, had left England for an extensive

Continental tour on August 25, 1822, and arrived in Genoa on March 31, 1823. The party consisted of the Earl of Blessington, whom Byron had known slightly in London, his wife, the "Gorgeous Lady Blessington", painted by Lawrence as a famous beauty, her sister Mary Ann Power, and the handsome young friend and travelling companion, Count Alfred D'Orsay. Lady Blessington, (1789–1849), who because of her past history had a difficult time in establishing a place in society as the second wife of Lord Blessington, enjoyed the greater freedom of the Continent. She had been "sold" at an early age by her father to the brutal Captain Farmer, then rescued by an easy-going Captain Jenkins, who in 1816 relinquished her to Lord Blessington for a sum of £10,000. Lord Blessington married her after her husband died in 1818, and by sheer beauty, grace, and intellectual charm, she made her house in St. James's Square a rival of Holland House in drawing men of intellect and wit. She was already an admirer of Byron through his poetry and reputation before she met him. For two months Byron was closely associated with the Blessingtons, dining with them frequently and joining them in their daily rides. He came to value Lord Blessington for his taste and tact and sensibility.

Lady Blessington, just 33, a year younger than Byron, was at the prime of her life when she met him. She was exactly suited to draw his closest interest and near attachment. Despite her humble origins, she had developed, aided by the wealth and indulgence of Lord Blessington, an aristocratic bearing less self-conscious than his own. She combined beauty, womanly warmth and intellectual acuteness, and she made no demands on him. It was a long time since he had had such an opportunity to converse with English people on his own social and intellectual level and he opened his mind to Lady Blessington in a way that surprised, titillated, and pleased her. She duly recorded his frank conversation in her diary, which later furnished the basis for her *Journal of the Conversations of Lord Byron* (1834), with what colouring of her own personality and prejudices it is difficult to determine.

John Bowring

A man of many talents, John Bowring (1792–1872) when Byron first corresponded with him had just been elected Honorary Secretary of the London Greek Committee, established by a variety of Philhellenes to assist the Greeks in their war for independence from the Turks. Bowring and Edward Blaquiere were the chief organizers of the Committee, of which Byron's friend Hobhouse was a member. Bowring was already a master of many languages and a voluminous writer. He was a disciple and later an editor and biographer of Jeremy Bentham, and he became the first editor of the Benthamite *Westminster Review*. His knowledge of languages made his services valuable to an exporting company and gave him an opportunity as a young man to travel extensively and to form friendships with liberals throughout Europe. His later career was distinguished and might have been more so had not his interests been so widely scattered. He was one of the founders of the Anti-Corn Law League, was active and influential in politics, being instrumental in bringing down Lord Palmerston's government. He served in diplomatic posts in China, Japan, and Siam.

He was energetic in managing the affairs of the London Greek Committee, though sometimes, like Col. Stanhope, a little too doctrinaire in his expectations of the Greeks. In a number of letters Byron tried to give him a more realistic picture of the situation in the country and of the character of the Greeks. The Committee itself was torn by conflicting views. Bowring tried to keep it on an even keel though he got disparate reports from Byron and Stanhope.

INDEX OF PROPER NAMES

Page numbers in italics indicate main references and Biographical Sketches in the Appendix. Such main biographical references in earlier volumes are included in this index and are in square brackets.

Aglietti, Dr. Francesco, memorial to Canova, 76 and n
Albrizzi, Countess Isabella, 130
Alder, William, lover of Mary Anne Hanson, 119n, 129 and n
Alexander, Dr. James, 106, 128, 195; recommends Dr. Bruno to B., 7, 194n, 206; B. has a facial wart, 147, 148; stores for Greek expedition, 196–7, 202
Ali Pasha, at Jannina, 180 and n
Allegra, [*Vol. 5, 294*], 55, 162; burial in Harrow Church, 54, 64; lack of memorial inscription, 65
Alvanley, Lord, "Dandy", 141
Anstey, Christopher, *New Bath Guide*, 98 and n
Argostoli, Cephalonia, 8
Ariosto, Ludovico, 68, 132
Aristides the Just, 59
Arta, 179n, 180
Aucher, Padre Pasquale, 128; Armenian grammar, 112; and B.'s snuff boxes, 112

Barry, Charles F., *228*; B.'s Greek expedition, 151, 185, 186, 199; Genoa partner of Webb and Co., 159n, 228; recommends B. an advocate, 161; B.'s snuff boxes, 185 and n, 194–5; sale of *Bolivar* to Blessington, 194; to dine with B., 195; friend and confidant, 228
Bartolini, Lorenzo, bust of B., 18
Baxter, coachbuilder, B.'s outstanding debt, 91, 110 and n, 111, 113, 118, 153
Bees, Mr., in *Bolivar*, 43; B. and his clothes, 36, 37, 39–40, 40n, 45; incivility, 40 and n, 44, 75
Bellamy, Mr and Mrs., B. denies any legal claims, 16–17, 65, 74
Benzoni, Countess Marina, 130
Berkeley, Admiral Sir George, 30n, 130n

Berlinghieri, André Vaccà, head of Pisa school of surgery, 193n; B. asks for a personal physician, 194 and n
The Bible, *St Luke*, 52 and n
Blaquiere, Edward, founder member London Greek Committee, *139n*, 171, 229; visits B., 7, 126, 139, 142, 150; B.'s proposed Greek expedition, 144–5, 147, 149, 152–3; leaves for Greece, 151, 169, 179, 184; letters to B., 176, 179, 184, 195, 200, 211
Blessington, Earl of, in Genoa, 7, 135 and n, 229; buys *Bolivar* from B., 7, 182n, 214 and n; death of his only son, 141 and n; B. postpones a riding appointment, 148–9; quizzes B. on his "learned Thebans", 157; member reading Association, 171; second marriage, 229
Blessington, Marguerite, Countess of, 7, *228–9*; meetings with B. in Genoa, 135 and n; praises Kinnaird, 135–6; B. on, 137, 197; B. requests a miniature of Lady Byron, 163; sends her *Adolphe*, 167 and n; painted by Lawrence, 174–5; Teresa's jealousy, 177; sells her horse Mameluke to B., 183 and n; B. sends her a cameo of Napoleon, 197; bored with her husband, 197; early life and character, 229; *Journal of the Conversations of Lord Byron*, 229
Bowles, William Lisle, B.'s letter on his *Pope*, 134
Bowring, John, *229–30*; secretary London Greek Committee, 168 and n, 179 and n, 184; B.'s recommendation, 210; Benthamite, 230
Brougham, Henry (later Baron Brougham and Vaux), [*Vol. 7, 250n*], B. plans a duel, 89n, 126

Brummell, George B. (Beau), "Dandy" balls, 141

Bruno, Dr., 7; B.'s personal physician, 194 and n; accompanies him on board *Hercules*, 210n

Burdett, Sir Francis, [*Vol. 1, 186 and n*], 73, 75

Byron, Ada, *aet.* 7, 52; to be cared for as Lady Byron wishes, 163

Byron, Lady (neé Annabella Milbanke), [*Vol. 2, 284*], sends game to Augusta, 14; Kirkby Mallory living, 14, 34, 203 and n; her life insurance to be increased, 20, 35, 38, 49, 196; familiar with Harrow Church, 64; B. asks for a miniature, 163; her wishes for Ada to be carried out, 163; B.'s suppressed letter, 167 and n

Byron, Mrs. Catherine Gordon, [*Vol. 1, 273–4*], B. on, 208

Byron, George Gordon, sixth Baron (later Noel Byron)

Works:

The Age of Bronze, 7, 90; title page motto, 81; sent to Kinnaird with alterations, 94 and n, 121, 127; satirises Verona Congress, 94n; to be published on its own, 110, 111, 114, 115, 118; printers' blunders, 117, 128, 133; published by Hunt without B.'s name, 150 and n, 151; sales, 154; division of profits, 155, 158

The Blues, 108; published in *The Liberal*, 122 and n, 151

Cain, 12; reviewed by the *Quarterly*, 18, 68n

Childe Harold, treatment by "the trade", 62; B. to write no more, 108, 126, 127; "The Apostrophe to the Ocean", 93n

Collected Works, proposal for, 182

The Corsair, 90; sales, 161

The Deformed Transformed, 33 and n, 80 and n, 182 and n

Don Juan, eventual publication by Hunt, 23 and n; inspires a love letter from Pimlico, 29; prices to be paid, 53; piracies, 58; B. on publishing procedure, 62; defended by B. against Heber,

68; against indecency, 98; its object, 116; B. to continue publication, 132; popularity in Paris, 134, 145; satirises English high society, 146 and n; unpublished cantos, 149, 151, 154; copyright, 165; Canto IV, "Arcades Ambo", 67 and n; Cantos VI and VII, 69, 99, 121, 166n; Canto VIII, 104, 121, 166n; Cantos VIII–XII, 92, 98; Canto X, 12, 18; Canto XI, 12, 18, 19, 26; Canto XII, 7, 42, 51, 52, 53, 58, 59; Murray on, 60; Canto XIII, 104, 127; English Ennui, 139n; Canto XIV, quoted, 50 and n; 119, 121, 127, 135; Canto XV, 127, 132, 135, 206; Canto XVI, completion 7, 159, 182, 200, 201; Hunt to correct the proofs, 206, 212

English Bards and Scotch Reviewers, treatment by "the trade", 62

Heaven and Earth, 12, 73, 109; published in *The Liberal*, 7, 23, 24, 39n, 66; praised by Kinnaird, 134, 136; reviewed by *Edinburgh Review*, 166

Hebrew Melodies, 134

Hints from Horace, 25, 39

The Island, 7, 89n, 117–18, 121, 133, 153, 154, 158, 168; mutiny on the *Bounty*, 89 and n, 90, 182; sent to Kinnaird, 134, 135, 182

Manfred, 134

Memoirs, 22, 146; sold by Moore, 33

Morgante Maggiore (Pulci), 24–5, 39, 66, 81; to go into *The Liberal* if Hunt wishes, 110, 115, 118, 122n

Occasional Poems:
   "When we two parted' (last stanza), 198
   "When youthful Keppel's name was lost", 88 and n

Ode to Napoleon, 134

Prophecy of Dante, American edition, 93 and n

Sardanapalus, 64; reviewed in the *Quarterly*, 68 and n

The Two Foscari, reviewed in the *Quarterly*, 68n

Dunn, Henry, 11, 31, 194, 201
Dupuy, Francesco, B.'s lost lawsuit, 152 and n
D'Ussières, Henrietta, 29 and n
d'Ysone, Contessa Borgarelli, 83 and n, 108 and n; B. seeks her protection for Teresa, 191 and n, 192

Farquhar, George, *The Beaux' Stratagem*, 136
Fearman (Fairman), publisher, and *Don Juan*, 53
Fellowes, Hon. Newton, brother of Portsmouth, 119n
Fielding, Henry, 68; *Joseph Andrews*, 98 and n; *Tom Jones*, 62 and n, 98 and n
Finlay, George, on Negris, 169n
Fitzgibbon, Dick, brother of Lord Clare, 57
Fletcher, William, B.'s valet, 97
Ford, John, 113, 114 and n, 119
Fox, Henry Edward, to call on B., 7, 131 and n, 135; B. on his amiability, 135, 136, 174; lameness, 136
Frost, boatman, 12 and n, 37; B. and his clothes, 40 and n, 75; dishonesty, 40 and n, 43, 45
Fust (Faust), Johann, printer, 117 and n

Gaetano, groom, 12 and n, 43, 75
Galignani, Jean Antoine, copyright of B.'s poems, 95, 134; popularity of *Don Juan* in Paris, 134, 145, 146; incivility to B., 204
Galignani's Messenger, 40, 67, 105
Gamba Ghiselli, Count Pietro, [*Vol. 7, 275*], 7; with B. in Genoa, 19, 30, 69, 195; eager to go to Spain or Greece, 143, 176; to engage a boat for B., 161–2; recalled from exile, 191; on board *Hercules*, 210n
Gamba, Ghiselli, Count Ruggero, [*Vol. 7, 272*], 56; in Genoa with B., 30, 69; recalled from exile, 176, 191; to bring his daughter with him, 178, 191
Garrick, David, *A Miss in her Teens*, 56 and n
Gell, Sir William, *Journey in the Morea*, 171 and n

Genoa, 11-212; Casa Saluzzo, 7, 11 ff.
Gifford, William, 42
Giuliani, Signor, possible buyer of B.'s snuff boxes, 103, 107 and n
Godwin, William, 18; Shelley's will, 16
Goethe, Johann Wolfgang von, 8, 60, 99; subject of *Werner* dedication, 60; B.'s admiration, 73; his letter of homage, 213 and n
Goldsmith, Oliver, *The Traveller*, 92 and n
Grant, Sir William, 75
Greece (the Levant), B.'s proposed expedition, 86, 133, 143–4, 147, 149, 151–2, 154, 177–8; his knowledge of the language, 168; material needs, 169, 170, 172–3, 181, 213; conditions there, 170; area of speculation, 170–1; German survivors of General Norman's band, 180–1; will B. be welcome?, 184–5; plans to leave Genoa on 1 July, 194, 201; "Hospital supplies", 195; expected arrival of *Hercules*, 203; B. and party on board, 210 and n; reaches Leghorn, 210n, 212
Guiccioli, Count Allessandro, [*Vol. 6, 276–7*], wishes Teresa to return to him, 176, 178
Guiccioli (née Gamba Ghiselli), Countess Teresa, [*Vol. 6, 277–8*], 165n; Murray to have her picture and bust, 18; at Casa Saluzzo, 30, 52, 69; refuses a bequest from B., 55, 162; death of her sister, 100; wishes B. to stay in Genoa, 143, 176, 191; jealous of Lady Blessington, 175, 177; should return to Ravenna, 176; wishes to accompany B. to Greece, 178, 198; returns to the Romagna with her father, 191n; B. on his "foreign liaison", 197; to retire into a convent, 198; B.'s last note, 212

Halidon Hill, sent to B. by Scott, 40 and n
Hamilton, Anthony, *Vie du Comte de Grammont*, 156 and n
Hamlet, Mr., B.'s goods to be sent to Florence, 162 and n
Hanson, Charles (s. of John), B.'s finances, 6–8; a purchaser of

bonds, 48, 49; proposed mortgages, 72, 75; Scotch discharge, 90–1; B. to end correspondence, 96

Hanson, John, [*Vol. 1, 275*], Rochdale, 35n, 84–5, 99, 110; B.'s finances, 38, 110, 155; sale of Newstead, 46; B. to end correspondence, 96; has Webster's bond, 99; guardian and trustee of the Earl of Portsmouth, 119 and n; marries his daughter to him, 119n

Hanson, Laura, cruel treatment of Portsmouth, 124 and n

Hanson, Mary Anne, marriage to Portsmouth, 119n; cruel treatment of him, 119n

Hardy, Lady (neé Anne Louisa Emily Berkeley), 30n, 130n; visits B. in Genoa, 7; 30, 57; relationship to him, 30n, 31; to visit Leghorn, 31–2; gossiped about by Wedderburn Webster, 49, 130–1; defends B., 173–4

Hardy, Sir Thomas Masterman, with Nelson in *Victory*, 30

Harvey, Isabel ("Zorina Stanley"), asks B. for his picture, 175 and n

Hastings, Francis Rawdon, first Marquis, *196n*; to meet B., 196, 197

Hayward, Joshua Henslow, *131n*; calls on B., 131

Heber, Reginald, Bishop of Calcutta, reviews B. in the *Quarterly*, 68 and n

Hentsch, Charles, Geneva banker, 228

Herodotus, the Arimaspians, 116n

Hill, William Noel, Minister at Genoa, 69, 108, 156–7, 174; B.'s illness after dining with him, 126, 127, 128, 137; B. on his "Excellence", 197

Hobhouse, John Cam (later first Baron Broughton de Gyfford), [*Vol. 1, 275–6*], 14; his brother sends a visitor to B., 63; and Portsmouth trial, 124n, 127; member Greek Committee, 142–4, 170, 171; to have B.'s power of attorney, 154, 168; Stendhal's "tissue of fictions", 189n; quotes B. to his electors, 196

Holland, Lord and Lady, B. recommends Rasponi, 122

Holmes, James, painter, 175, 176

Homer, 63 and n

Hoppner, R.B., [*Vol. 5, 294–5*], to dispose of some of B.'s Turkish objects, 76, 82–3, 112, 122n

Hunt, Henry, s. of John, 24 and n; and *Don Juan* accounts, 66

Hunt, Henry ("Orator"), released from prison, 57 and n

Hunt, James Henry Leigh, [*Vol. 2, 281–2*], 21; B. on his children, 11, 32; assisted by B., 13, 60, 66, 105, 138; relationship with Murray, 21; B.'s opinion of him and his brother, 25 and n; B. and his poverty, 34; Murray showed B.'s letter on Hunt, 36, 57, 68; said to be living in B.'s house, 52, 55; B. on his own feelings towards, 69, 138; his brother's prosecution, 81; possible cause of B.'s unpopularity, 138; and the *Examiner*, 162; B.'s friendship with, 205; *The Dogs*, 39 and n; extract from *The Soldier's Journal*, published in *The Liberal*, 133 and n

Hunt, John, [*Vol. 9, 234*], ed. *The Liberal*, 13nn, 34, 72–3, 80, 110, 123–4; B.'s connection, 13nn, 34, 66, 72–3, 80, 87, 114, 116–17, 123; B.'s *Vision of Judgment*, 13n, 16, 18 and n, 21, 66; prosecution, 39n, 53, 57, 66, 67n, 98 and n, 136; in financial straits, 13, 70; as eventual publisher of B.'s works, 23 and n, 24, 53, 66, 69, 80 and n, 88, 89n, 90n, 122 and n, 133, 181–2; B. to pay for defence Counsel, 66, 72, 79–80, 97–8; to submit proper accounts, 66; B. blames two Murrays for his prosecution, 68; B.'s opinion of, 69–70, 138; alters B.'s text of *Don Juan*, 158; to receive 15% of profits, 182 and n, 201; dispute with Blackwood, 206

Ingram, Mr. and Mrs., 76 and n, 82, 83, 122

Irving, Washington, *Bracebridge Hall*, 83

Jersey, Lady, 31, 103

Johnson, Samuel, *Rasselas*, 22, 102; "Vanity of Human Wishes", 180 and n

Missolonghi, 179n, 180
Montaigne, Michel Eyquem de, Essays, 150
Moore, Thomas, [*Vol. 2, 284–5*], 174; B.'s feeling for, 34; warns B. against Hunt and *The Liberal*, 105 and n; trns. of Horace, Ode XI., 29 and n; *Loves of the Angels*, 105 and n; Moore makes concessions to the pious, 105 and n, 116, 137–8; publication, 137n
Morgan, Lady, 55–6; book seized by customs officers, 56n, 61n; *The Mohawks*, sent to B., 61 and n
Mountjoy, Viscount, s. of Lord Blessington, 137; death *aet* 10, 141 and n
Mountnorris, Arthur, eighth Viscount Valentia and first Earl of, f. of Lady Webster, litigant and bad debtor, 113 and n
Murray, Charles, attorney for Constitutional Association, 67 and n
Murray, John, [*Vol. 2, 285–6*], publisher of *Werner*, 7, 18 and n, 42, 96, 99, 110, 134, 159; B. complains of his dilatoriness and lack of attention to his poems, 12, 16, 17, 21–2, 27, 53, 58, 63–5, 96, 116, 135; bad relations with John Hunt, 13, 21, 32, 33, 41, 42; to have Teresa's picture and bust, 18; payment for B.'s poems, 19, 20; to relinquish all of B.'s compositions, 22, 23–4, 28; financial losses, 24; shows B.'s letter to Hunt, 36, 57; French copyright of *Don Juan*, 134; and *Quarterly Review*, 40, 67; publisher to the Admiralty, 67n

Negris, Theodore, *169n*; Greek revolution, 169
Newstead, sale, 46
Nodier, Charles, 207n, 209
Noel (formerly Milbanke), Lady, confusion over personal bequests, 47, 85, 113, 119, 126, 149, 153, 155
Noel (formery Milbanke), Sir Ralph ("Sir Jacob"), 19, 91
Noel, Rev. Thomas, 14n; asks B. for living of Kirkby Mallory, 14–15, 54 and n; presentation by Lady Byron, 203 and n, 204

Norman - Ehrenfels, Charles Frederick Lebrecht, Count of; in Greece with German troops, 179 and n, 180–1; death at Missolonghi, 179n

Odysseus, 169n
O'Meara, Barry E., *Memoirs of Napoleon*, 82 and n
Osborne, Lord Sydney, 143n; B. recommends Blaquiere, 142, 143, 171
Otto of Bavaria, 56n
Ovid, 176 and n

Parr, Dr Samuel, Harrow master, 142 and n
Peacock, Thomas Love, executor of Shelley's will, 16
Pellico, Silvio, 189 and n; *Francesca da Rimini*, 189n
Petersham, Viscount; *See* Stanhope, Charles
Petta, battle of, 179n, 180
Piat, General, anti-government plot, 140 and n
Pichot, Amedée, and B.'s father and Lady Carmarthen, 207 and n; B. defends his father 208–9; asked to rectify his allegations, 209
Pierrepoint, "Dandy", 141
Pisa, B.'s lawsuit, 152, 160, 161
Pius VI, Pope, 56
Pius VII, Pope, 56; wishes Teresa to return to Ravenna, 176; disapproves her liaison with B., 177
Pope, Alexander, 28 and n; B. to write another *Dunciad*, 28 and n; *Essay on Man*, 56 and n; *Moral Essays*, 12 and n; "But, Friend, take heed whom you attack", 137 and n
Portsmouth, Earl of, alleged insanity, 119n, 124n; B.'s presence at his marriage to Hanson's daughter, 119 and n, 120, 124–5, 129; trial of Mary Anne Hanson, 119n, 124n; his treatment by Laura Hanson, 124n; B.'s knowledge of the affair, 124–126, 129
Power, Mary Ann, sister of Lady Blessington, 135n, 157, 229
Proctor, Bryan Waller (Barry Cornwall), B.'s advice to, 115–16; The *Flood of Thessaly*, 116

Quantana, Mme, 101

Rasponi, Count Giulio, 121 and n; recommended to the Hollands, 122
Rawdon, Bessy, 129
Regny (Regnier), Mme, 56 and n
Reynolds, John Hamilton, "Peter Bell", 130 and n
Ridgway, James, publishers, *Don Juan*, 42, 62
Roberts, Capt. Daniel, RN, and the *Bolivar*, 11, 25, 36, 43–5, 133–4, 165–6, 182
Rochdale, coalpit lease, 35 and n; purchased by Dearden, 35n, 73, 99; Appeal before the Lords, 46, 98–9, 136; unlitigated part, 49 and n, 84, 86; toll business, 51, 60, 74, 86, 91; law suit, 53; subject to Arbitration, 73, 75–6, 77, 84, 113; settlement with creditors, 96; 4% mortgage, 112
Rochefoucauld, François duc de, 128
Rogers, Samuel, 18
Rousseau, Jean Jacques, 68, 109

Sagrati, Marchesa, 56 and n, 81
Saluzzo, Mme, B. and her poems, 83
Sandt, Charles, assassinates Kotzebue, 180 and n
Scott, John, owner of brig *Hercules*, 194, 201, 203, 205
Scott, Sir Walter, sends B. *Halidon Hill*, 40 and n; B. corrects Stendhal's opinion, 189–90; *The Antiquary*, 125n, 143 and n; *Bold Dragon*, 137 and n; *Guy Mannering*, 149 and n; *Heart of Midlothian*, 146 and n; *Legend of Montrose*, 181 and n; *Peveril of the Peak*, 123
Sebastiani and Flahault, General, 41
Sergent-Marceau, Mme, *165n*; gives B. *Notices Historiques sur le Général Marceau*, 165 and n
Shakespeare, William, *Coriolanus*, 17 and n; *Hamlet*, 118 and n, *Henry IV* pt. I, 67 and n, 180 and n; *Henry VI* pt. III; *King Lear*, 157 and n; *Macbeth*, 167 and nn, 176 and n; *Merchant of Venice*, 169 and n; *Merry Wives of Windsor*, 65 and n; *Much Ado about Nothing* 52 and n; *Othello*, 67 and n, 81 and n; *Richard III*, 49 and n

Shelley, Mary, B. to be her banker, 11; Shelley's will, 16; copies B.'s poems for him, 33 and n, 81, 90; said to be living in B.'s house, 52; with the Hunts, 69, 76–7; B. to assist her passage home, 203
Shelley, Percy Bysshe, effect of his death on the Hunts, 13, 25–6; B. his executor, 16, 77, 79, 205–6; B.'s feeling for him, 34, 69; Roberts brings his boat ashore, 44 and n; assists the Hunts, 138; location of his will, 158; B. rejects executorship and legacy, 205–6
Shelley, Sir Timothy, 16, 77, 108; B. asks his help for Mary and family, 78–9
Sheridan, Richard Brinsley, at Harrow, 142n; *The Critic*, 141 and n; *The Rivals*, 140 and n, 176
Skilitzy, Constantine, on board *Hercules*, 210n
Smollett, Tobias, *Roderick Random*, 68 and n, 98 and n
Southerne, Thomas, *The Fatal Marriage*, 176 and n
Southey, Robert, 17; B. satirises his apotheosis of George III, 13n; B. plans a duel, 89n; *Vision of Judgment*, 80, 81; *Wat Tyler*, 81
Sparrow, Lady Olivia, 65
Staël-Holstein, Mme de, [*Vol. 3, 272–273*], 68, 130, 140; supposed heroine of *Adolphe*, 167 and n
Stanhope, Charles, third Earl of Harrington, styled Viscount Petersham, 48 and n
Stanhope, Hon. Leicester (later fifth Earl of Harrington), with B. in Greece, 48n, 230
Stendhal (Henri Beyle), mentions B. favourably, 189 and nn
Sterling, Charles, 212 and n
Sterne, Laurence, *Tristram Shandy*, 150
Stietz, Col., suggest a foreign brigade in Greek service, 211; recommended by B. to London Greek Committee, 212
Stuart, Sir Charles, 174

Taaffe, John, jr, [*Vol. 9, 236*], 56n; and Masi affray, 102–3
Tierney, Hon. George, 140 and n

Trelawny, Edward John, [*Vol. 9, 236–237*], 7, 103; brings *Bolivar* to Genoa, 11–12, 12n 25 and n; robbed by Frost, 43, 75; hoisting a pendant on *Bolivar*, 165–6; B. invites him to come to Greece with him, 199, 201; expected arrival in Genoa, 203; on board *Hercules*, 210n, 211

Ugolini, Paoli, 107 and n

Vaccà, *see* Berlinghieri
Valerius Maximus, *Facta et Dicta Memorabilia*, 90 and n
Virgil, 67; *Aeneid*, 81 and n; *Eclogue*, 68 and n
Voltaire, François Marie Arouet de, 109

Warton, Joseph, 83
Webb, J., sale of B.'s boxes and watches, 152, 200
Webster, Sir James Wedderburn, 18–19, 108, 198; visits B., 7, 48, 49; knighthood, 48, 57, 100 and n; finds B. thinner, 48; B. and his ten-year old Bond, 48–9, 60–1; Webster v. Baldwin libel suit, 48n; talks of Lady Hardy, 49–50; wants a reconciliation with his wife, 95n, 101–2, 106–7. 109, 129, 174; sends B. a miniature of Lady Frances, 95 and n; asks for volumes of B.'s poems, 95 and n; B. and an endorsement of his Bill, 97–8, 99, 130, 153, 155, 174; behaviour in Genoa, 101 and n; B. on his Bills and debts, 101–2; behaviour in Paris, 174
Webster, Lady Frances, charged with adultery with Wellington, 48 and n; abortive affair with B. 48n, 95n, 102; her husband wants a reconciliation, 95n, 101–2, 106–7, 129; B. on her miniature, 95 and n; accuses her husband, 129; B.'s stanzas, 198
Wellington, Arthur Wellesley, first Duke of, 133n, 141; charged with adultery, 48 and n
Wentworth, Lord, 14n, 54n, 203n
West, Benjamin, painting of B., 18 and n; compared with present appearance, 198
Wharton, G.B., 114n
Whitton, Mr., solicitor to Sir Timothy Shelley, 16, 61, 78
Wilson, Dr., of Leghorn, Napoleon snuff box, 185n
Wilson John, *Blackwood's Edinburgh Magazine*, 81n
Wilson, Sir Robert Thomas, *114 and n,* 196

Yosy, Mme A. de, *Switzerland*, 22 and n; B. pleads with Murray on her behalf, 22–3, 64, 70

Zambelli, Lega, B.'s secretary, 161